Core List of Books and Journals in Education

By Nancy Patricia O'Brien and
Emily Fabiano

ORYX PRESS
1991

The rare Arabian Oryx is believed to have inspired the myth of the unicorn. This desert antelope became virtually extinct in the early 1960s. At that time several groups of international conservationists arranged to have 9 animals sent to the Phoenix Zoo to be the nucleus of a captive breeding herd. Today the Oryx population is nearly 800, and over 400 have been returned to reserves in the Middle East.

Library of Congress Cataloging-in-Publication Data

Core list of books and journals in education / edited by Nancy O'Brien
  and Emily S. Fabiano.
    p. cm.
  Includes index.
  ISBN 0-89774-559-0 (alk. paper)
  1. Education—Bibliography. 2. Education—United States-
-Bibliography. 3. Bibliography—Best books—Education.
I. O'Brien, Nancy P. II. Fabiano, Emily.
Z5811.C798 1991
[LB14.6]
016.37—dc20   90-42404
                                                    CIP

Contents

Introduction

PURPOSE

Core List of Books and Journals in Education (hereafter referred to as the *List*) assembles a selected group of approximately 1000 books and journals currently available in the field of education from the thousands of titles published in recent years. As the term "core" suggests, the *List* identifies a basic collection of books and journals in education within a predetermined scope. Library practitioners will find the *List* extremely useful in making acquisition decisions for collection development; checking collections against the *List* will allow librarians to update certain areas or to select missing titles. The *List* will also prove useful to teachers, students, and researchers in identifying resources critical to undertaking research or locating information relevant to education.

SCOPE

Coverage of titles in the *List* is current; most were published in the late 1980s. Some exceptions were made in certain categories to include a limited number of important or classic works that are still useful to educators and still in print.

All works are in the English language; almost all are American, with a few published in Canada and Great Britain. American government documents and monographs published by UNESCO, excellent sources of educational materials, have also been included.

Although the majority of entries are individual monographs and journal titles, some multi-volume standard sources have been included, as have been such traditional reference works as directories, encyclopedias, and bibliographies. For certain subject areas, specific types of resources were included; for example, collections of conference papers are peculiar to **Comparative Education** because the international scope of the discipline results in the sharing of information in conference settings. In **Special Education**, handbook-type materials are important;

in **Educational Research/Statistics**, textbooks are a natural format; and in **Educational Reform**, commissioned reports and publications from professional organizations are prevalent. A balance of perspectives was attempted whenever suitable materials were available. Educational materials with radical, conservative, and moderate viewpoints were annotated if they fell within the criteria for inclusion. In general, materials pertaining to children's literature were excluded since this subject is well-covered in other resources.

SELECTION GUIDELINES

In the case of books, selections were identified through database searches, reviews of recent publications, other published directories, and the education collections of the authors' respective institutions. The final decision on whether or not to include a title was made on the basis of its value and availability, and on some consideration of price. For instance, a monograph of a few pages costing over $100 would not have been included unless it was judged to be extremely valuable. Journal titles were identified in much the same way; inclusion rested on whether the journal title was covered by the major indexing and abstracting services in education and, again, on some consideration of price. A twice-yearly publication with a limited audience costing over $200 was not desirable for inclusion.

A very few important titles, no longer in *Books in Print*, have been included. Publishers must be contacted to determine availability of these books.

All books were examined personally by the authors.

ORGANIZATION

The *List* is organized around 18 categories representing these broad areas of education: **Comparative Education; Content Areas; Educational Administration and Law; Educational Psychology/**

Guidance/Counseling; Educational Reform; Educational Research/Statistics; Educational Technology/Media; Elementary/Secondary Education; General Sources; Health/Physical Education; Higher and Continuing Education; History and Philosophy of Education; Measurement; Multicultural Education; Resources for Teaching; Special Education; Teacher Education; and Vocational Education. A brief introductory paragraph precedes each category.

An overriding theme that can be found throughout the annotations in this work is the deep concern for professional ethics. Although there were insufficient numbers to justify a separate ethics section, at least 15 items dealing with ethics are scattered throughout such categories as Educational Administration and Law and Higher and Continuing Education. The emphasis on ethical considerations in education may be viewed as a phenomenon of the time period covered.

Within each category, entries are separated into sections labeled "Books" and "Journals," with the publications arranged alphabetically by title within these sections. Consecutive item numbers are assigned to each individual title. The Content Areas category is further divided into the subcategories of "Humanities," "Mathematics," "Reading," "Science," and "Social Studies."

For "Books" the bibliographic citation includes title; author/editor; series information; publisher; date of publication; number of pages; Library of Congress (LCCN) number; ISBN number; price; and any special information, such as ISSN number, number of volumes, or special production notes. Selected serial publications such as *Review of Research in Education* and the *Educational Media and Technology Yearbook* were included in book sections rather than journal categories.

For government publications, each record includes information similar to book entries with the exception of LCCN numbers or ISBN numbers, which may not be available for some government publications. Stock numbers are provided for ordering information.

Descriptive annotations are provided for books to further clarify and describe the content, note revisions, and highlight certain important aspects. Evaluative or critical opinions are not intentionally expressed, except in some instances where subjective terms such as "valuable," "important," or "useful" may have been used for exceptional titles.

Journal entries indicate title; publisher; publisher address; frequency of publication; cost; ISSN number; date of first publication; and any unusual information, such as title changes, which are not uncommon for journals. Annotations are not included for journal entries.

Elements of a Journal Entry

Title: Anthropology & Education Quarterly
Publisher: American Anthropological Association, Council on Anthropology and Education
Address: 1703 New Hampshire Ave., Washington, D.C. 20009
Frequency: Quarterly
Price: $30.00
ISSN: 0161-7761
Beginning Date: 1970
Former Titles: Council on Anthropology and Education Quarterly and CAE Newsletter

Cross-references to former titles of journals and journals known by acronyms will appear in the broad subject categories. These references may provide a useful finding aid for locating journals with a history of changing titles. For books that could fit into more than one broad subject category, the full entry has been placed in the most important category and cross-references to the item number of that entry have been placed in the other applicable subject categories.

INDEXES

In addition to the broad subject category arrangement, author/editor, title, and subject indexes are provided. Arrangement for each index is alphabetical and referral is made to the item number of the entry indexed.

The Subject Index is derived primarily from book entries, with only selected journals. A limit of six subject index assignments per entry was imposed; most entries appear under one or two subject terms.

SPECIAL NOTES

Price information has been based on *Books in Print* and publisher contacts. Some problems are unavoidable in providing price information: prices may have changed by the time the *List* appears; not all recent titles were listed with prices before the *List* went to press; or some titles may no longer be in print following publication of the *List*. If a publisher indicated "write for information" in *Books in Print*, this is noted in the *List* as "contact publisher for price information."

LCCN and ISBN numbers were not available for all titles and are therefore omitted in some entries.

Some serials have undergone frequent title changes; generally a limit of two former titles is provided. In such cases, the beginning date is given for the current title of the journal.

Core List of
Books and
Journals
in Education

Comparative Education

This section includes works written about comparative education as a field of study and as a methodology for exploring a wide variety of other subject areas, such as early childhood education or literacy. Some titles focus on a single geographic region and can be used for comparisons with other areas; in most cases the United States is one of the areas studied comparatively. A few comparative titles were annotated within other categories in this volume based on editorial decision. Not many reasonably priced journals related to comparative education are available; a select few are suggested.

Books

1. **Arab Education, 1956–1978: A Bibliography.** Pantelidis, Veronica S. H.W. Wilson, 1982. 552p. LC: 83-217147. ISBN: 0-7201-1588-4. $96.00.
   A comprehensive bibliography of mostly English-language sources of information on education in the Arab World from 1956 to 1978; the "Arab World" refers to the 21 member states of the Arab League, which are covered alphabetically. General sources, covering more than one country, are entered in the first category "The Arab World." Includes very brief annotations of books, journals, government reports, etc. Author, title, and subject indexes are extensive.

2. **Changing Patterns of Secondary Education: An International Comparison.** Edited by Lawson, Robert F. Univ. of Calgary Press, 1987. 312p. ISBN: 0-919813-40-2. $19.95.
   An international perspective on developments and innovations in Western secondary education presents a comparison and backdrop for Canada's internal review of public secondary education. Section one describes changing patterns of education in dominant industrialized countries, culturally similar to Canada; section two covers selected states in the United States. Section three is a comparative analysis of the country and state studies. A concluding chapter provides selected points related to educational decisions in Canada.

3. **China's Education and the Industrialized World: Studies in Cultural Transfer.** Edited by Hayhoe, Ruth and Bastid, Marianne. M.E. Sharpe, 1987. 369p. LC: 87-4744. ISBN: 0-87332-428-5. $17.95.
   The major theme examines China's historical educational relations and experience with Japan, the Soviet Union, and Western industrial powers. A minor theme is treated in two chapters—the impact of Chinese educational ideas and patterns on the industrialized world. Provides an extensive section of footnotes and a bibliography of materials in Western languages on Chinese education and its international relations.

4. **Comparative Early Childhood Education.** Edited by Lall, Geeta R. and Lall, Bernard M. Charles C. Thomas, 1983. 204p. LC: 82-16810. ISBN: 0-398-04777-4. $20.50.
   Essays on early childhood education in 11 countries for each of these general areas: philosophy, history, teacher training, administration, financing, and curriculum of early childhood education. A final chapter compares these 11 nations in each area. Has been designed for possible use as a textbook for early childhood education classes.

5. **Comparative Educational Systems.** Edited by Ignas, Edward and Corsisni, Raymond J. Peacock, 1981. 442p. LC: 80-52449. ISBN: 0-87581-260-0. $24.95.
   Following a critical examination of the traditional American educational system, the educational systems of eight "advanced" countries are covered including history, theory, curriculum roles, and a prospect for the future. Similar in format to a previous work *Alternative Educational Systems* although different countries' systems were examined.

6. **Comparative Studies and Educational Decision.** King, Edmund J. Bobbs-Merrill, 1968. 182p. LC: 68-15020. ISBN: 0-672-60627-5. $28.50.
   The major purpose here is to link the justification of comparative studies in education with what can be learned from other academic disciplines and fields of experience to better understand the problems of education itself. Discusses methodology of and a conceptual framework for comparative education; comparative education's historical development as a field of study and relationship to other disciplines; and need for comparative review as part of all decision-making processes affecting education.

7. **A Comparative Survey of Seven Adult Functional Literacy Programs in Sub-Saharan Africa.** Richmond, Edmun B. University Press of America, 1986. 107p. LC: 86-15826. ISBN: 0-8191-5520-9; 0-8191-5521-7 (pbk.). $20.25; $9.25 (pbk.).

Describes and examines the designs and implementation of functional literacy programs in seven Sub-Saharan African nations and analyzes the reasons for their success or failure. Comprehensive overviews are given for Gambia, Kenya, Liberia, Burundi, Rwanda, and Seychelles; a longitudinal study of Mali's literacy campaign is presented. Conclusions and implications for curriculum development are presented in the final chapter.

8. Comparing Adult Education Worldwide. Charters, Alexander N. et al. (AEA Handbook Series in Adult Education); (Jossey-Bass Series in Higher Education). Jossey-Bass, 1981. 272p. LC: 80-8911. ISBN: 0-87589-494-1. $28.95.

One of several volumes in the Adult Education Association Handbook Series in Adult Education; focuses on an emerging discipline "comparative international adult education", the consideration of one or more aspects of adult education in two or more countries. Chapters by distinguished adult educators cover cross-national comparisons of adult education for literacy, application of educational technology to adult education, laws governing adult education, and designing programs for literacy education. A "Postscript" section draws the preceding chapters together.

Conducting Interinstitutional Comparisons *See* **HIGHER AND CONTINUING EDUCATION (No. 531)**

9. Contemporary Issues in Comparative Education: A Festschrift in Honour of Professor Emeritus Vernon Mallinson. Edited by Watson, Keith and Wilson, Raymond. Croom Helm, 1985. 227p. LC: 84-21402. ISBN: 0-70993-607-9. $27.50.

Essays in this collection concern topics in comparative education as well as issues from a comparative perspective; some are based on themes which evolved in Mallinson's writings over the years—the concept of national character, comparative education and literature and educational reform. Closes with a bibliography of Mallinson's writings.

10. Education and Intergroup Relations: An International Perspective. Edited by Hawkins, John N. and LaBelle, Thomas J. (Praeger Special Studies Series in Comparative Education). Praeger, 1985. 411p. LC: 84-26353. ISBN: 0-275-90188-2. $42.95.

Based on a typology of intergroup relations developed in the first chapter. Authors of each of the 12 country case studies focus on the educational policies affecting intergroup relations in that country and place it in one of the four intergroup relations types described. The text concludes with a comparative review of the individual country analyses.

11. Education in Africa: A Comparative Survey. Edited by Fafunwa, A. Babs and Aisiku, J.U. G. Allen & Unwin, 1982. 270p. LC: 81-19129. ISBN: 0-04-370113-2. $12.50.

Following an opening chapter that covers traditional African education before the introduction of Islam and Christianity, education in 11 African countries is examined. Included for each country are a brief history, organization, administration, control, curriculum, and finance. A final chapter summarizes with "Progress and Prospect" of African education.

12. Education in East and West Germany: A Bibliography. Rust, Val D. (Reference Books in International Education, Vol. 1); (Garland Reference Library of Social Science, Vol. 202). Garland, 1984. 227p. LC: 83-48216. ISBN: 0-8240-9050-0. $35.00.

Part of a series focusing on English-language materials on education in a particular country—this volume covers the two Germanies. An opening essay covers the role of history of education followed by the major section, an annotated bibliography of English-language materials, most published after 1945 and most covering West Germany.

13. Education in Latin America. Edited by Brock, Colin and Lawlor, Hugh. Croom Helm, 1985. 196p. LC: 85-3750. ISBN: 0-7099-3273-1. $35.00.

Contributors concentrate on formal educational provision, national units, and critical analysis for each of the eight Latin American countries selected: Cuba, Mexico, Panama, Ecuador, Peru, Brazil, Chile, Argentina. In addition, some aspects of education of "distinctive contemporary significance" are presented for each region.

Education in Multicultural Societies *See* **MULTICULTURAL EDUCATION (No. 744)**

14. Education in Southeast Asia: A Select Bibliography of English Language Materials on Education in Indonesia, Malaysia, Philippines, Singapore and Thailand 1945–1983. Inglis, Christine et al. Gower, 1985. 554p. LC: 85-17731. ISBN: 0-566-03521-9. $74.95.

An extensive bibliography of English-language materials published since 1945 on education in the areas indicated. Main emphasis is on the social role and organization of education and the social processes involved in education and teaching. Content categories include Primary and Pre-Primary Education, Adult and Community Education, and Education for Special Groups. No index is available.

15. Education in the People's Republic of China: Past and Present: An Annotated Bibliography. Parker, Franklin and Parker, Betty June. (Reference Books in International Education, Vol. 2); (Garland Reference Library in International Education, Vol. 281). Garland, 1986. 845p. LC: 84-48394. ISBN: 0-8240-8797-6. $90.00.

Like other regional bibliographies in the Garland series an extensive essay on China's educational system precedes the bibliography. The 3,053 entries include books, pamphlets, serials, major newspaper accounts, etc. under some 70 headings such as English As a Second Language, Mathematics Education, and Confucianism and Anti-Confucianism.

16. Education, Industrialization, and Selection. Timmons, George. Routledge, Kegan & Paul, 1988. 242p. LC: 87-30789. ISBN: 0-415-00702-X. $57.50.

The theme of this work is how "selection" operates in industrialized societies and to what extent secondary education, especially, contributes to the process of selection. The education systems of four industrialized societies are examined—Great Britain, France, the United States, and the Soviet Union.

17. The Education of Minority Groups: An Enquiry into Problems and Practices of Fifteen Countries. Centre for Educational Research and Innovation, Organization for Economic Cooperation and Development. Gower, 1983. 376p. LC: 84-16242. ISBN: 0-566-00639-1. $65.00.

Reports on an extensive project that surveyed 15 countries' policies and practices by which special minority populations are designated and how treatment is governed, organized, and financed. Details, in particular, how the countries provide for linguistic and indigenous cultural minorities.

The Education of Nations: A Comparison in Historical Perspective *See* HISTORY AND PHILOSOPHY OF EDUCATION (No. 631)

18. Educational Policies in Crisis: Japanese and American Perspectives. Cummings, William K. et al. (Praeger Special Studies Series in Comparative Education). Praeger, 1986. 308p. LC: 86-78. ISBN: 0-275-52089-5. Contact publisher for price information.

Papers in this text were presented in August 1984 at a conference convened by the East-West Center to examine some of these issues: crises in education in the US/Japan; comparison of US/Japan curricula; overview of US/Japanese education; comparing youth cultures; transition from school to work; American images of Japanese education and vice versa. The final chapter proposes the usefulness of cross-national investigations to learn about each other.

Educational Reforms in the United States: A Report of the Japan-United States Cooperative Study on Education *See* EDUCATIONAL REFORM (No. 240)

19. The Encyclopedia of Comparative Education and National Systems of Education. Edited by Postlethwaite, T. Neville. (Advances in Education). Pergamon, 1988. 777p. LC: 86-9346. ISBN: 0-08-030853-8. $150.00.

Part 1 presents articles dealing with various aspects of comparative education (history, concepts, methods, major areas of study) by well-known authors in this field. Part 2 is devoted to articles describing the educational systems of 159 countries; a short descriptive overview is given of each system with a comprehensive bibliography for more detailed study.

20. Equality and Freedom in Education: A Comparative Study. Edited by Holmes, Brian. Allen & Unwin, 1985. 259p. LC: 84-6431. ISBN: 004-370153-1. $14.95.

Each of the contributors, members of the Department of Comparative Education, University of London, Institute of Education, approaches the theme of equality of educational opportunity in a particular country following these chapter headings: aims, administration, finance, organization, curriculum, teacher education, higher education, statistics. Covers England/Wales, France, the United States, the Soviet Union, Japan, and People's Republic of China.

21. Estranged Twins: Education and Society in the Two Germanys. Fishman, Sterling and Martin, Lothar. (Praeger Special Studies Series in Comparative Education). Praeger, 1987. 218p. LC: 86-21211. ISBN: 0-275-92460-2. $39.95.

A study of the effects of the politics and economics of the twin societies—East and West Germany—on the processes of education: curriculum development, instructional methods, school organization, values development, etc. The educational achievements and deficiencies of the two states are also revealed in comparisons.

22. Faith, Culture, and the Dual System: A Comparative Study of Church and County Schools. O'Keeffe, Bernadette. Falmer, 1986. 202p. LC: 86-13391. ISBN: 1-85000-110-3; 1-85000-111-1 (pbk.). $33.00; $17.00 (pbk.).

Four areas of research were identified for a comparative study of church and county schools in England: admissions policies, policies and practices in appointing teaching staff, school worship, assemblies and religious education, and multicultural education in the curriculum. The study sought to discover how schools respond to the presence of children from different cultures and faiths in each of the two school settings. Extensive research data supplied.

23. The Future of Literacy in a Changing World. Edited by Wagner, Daniel A. (Comparative and International Education Series, v. 1). Pergamon, 1987. 344p. LC: 87-10415. ISBN: 0-08-034264-7. $49.95.

An introductory chapter focuses on the common problems in discussions concerning literacy in any context. The remaining sections cover such topics as theoretical perspectives on comparative literacy, literacy acquisition in cultural context and literacy, and technology and economic development. Comparative analysis is used in some chapters.

Higher Education and Employment: An International Comparative Analysis *See* HIGHER AND CONTINUING EDUCATION (No. 552)

The Higher Education System: Academic Organization in Cross-National Perspective *See* HIGHER AND CONTINUING EDUCATION (No. 559)

24. Human Rights and Education. Edited by Tarrow, Norma Bernstein. (Comparative and International Education Series, v. e). Pergamon, 1987. 261p. LC: 87-10392. ISBN: 0-08-033887-9; 0-08-033415-6 (pbk.). $41.00; $19.90 (pbk.).

Each of the essays in Part I, "Education As a Human Right," focuses on a particular educational right, e.g., for employment, for literacy. Illustrates the rights implementation in selected societies in the world and in some cases compares the rights in two or more nations. The chapters in Part II, "Education About Human Rights," examine such issues as curriculum and teacher preparation for human rights education.

25. In the Nation's Image: Civic Education in Japan, the Soviet Union, the United States, France, and Britain. Edited by Gumbert, Edgar B. (Center for Cross-Cultural Education Lecture Series, v. 6). Center for Cross-Cultural Education, College of Education, Georgia State Univ., 1987. 120p. LC: 86-31683. ISBN: 0-8840-6203-1. Contact publisher for price information.

Each of the five chapters addresses the question "What and how do people in selected nations learn about their own nation and culture?" In other words, what are the attitudes and approaches to civic education of Japan, the Soviet Union, the United States, France, and Great Britain? No direct comparison of countries is made; to enhance comparability, however, the authors were asked to develop stated ideas about civic education in each of their countries.

26. The Incorporation of Education: An International Study in the Transformation of Educational Priorities. Hunt, Frederick J. (Routledge Education Books). Routledge, Kegan & Paul, 1987. 184p. LC: 87-4741. ISBN: 0-7102-1025-6. $39.95.

This report arises from the author's long-term research and study of national systems of education, their management and the exercise of influence and power on their operation, particularly as the result of economic circumstances. A series of case studies examines educational developments in recent years regarding these issues in Australia, the United States, England, Western Europe, Malaysia, and Singapore against a backdrop of events in the 1950s, 1960s, and 1970s.

27. International Handbook of Women's Education. Edited by Kelly, Gail P. Greenwood, 1989. 657p. LC: 88-34730. ISBN: 0-313-25638-1. $85.00.

Provides descriptive, comparable information about women's education across 23 countries focusing on the history and development of women's schooling; current status including enrollment trends, policies, etc.; and outcomes of education for women in the labor force, political system, and the family.

International Perspectives on Psychology in the Schools *See* EDUCATIONAL PSYCHOLOGY/GUIDANCE/COUNSELING (No. 202)

28. The Japanese School: Lessons for Industrial America. Duke, Benjamin. (Praeger Special Studies/Praeger Scientific). Praeger, 1986. 242p. LC: 86-5002. ISBN: 0-275-92053-4; 0-275-92003-8 (pbk.). $32.95; $12.95 (pbk.).

A description of how the Japanese school system really works that finds the main challenge to the industrial United States primarily in the Japanese classroom rather than in the factory; the Japanese school produces a loyal, literate, competent, and diligent worker. Strengths and weaknesses of Japanese education are highlighted and constant comparisons are made between the American and Japanese educational systems.

29. Key Issues in Education: Comparative Perspectives. Edited by Watson, Keith. Croom Helm, 1985. 127p. LC: 85-14961. ISBN: 0-70992-795-9. $23.00.

Seven contemporary issues are explored: examination reform, democratization, sex bias, post-compulsory education, multicultural provision, training for school leaders, and corporal punishment. Comparisons are made between the British school context and Western European schools.

30. The Learning Society Revisited: Essays. Husen, Torsten. Pergamon, 1986. 262p. LC: 85-29683. ISBN: 0-08-032660-9; 0-08-034037-7 (pbk.). $42.95; $19.95 (pbk.).

A collection of essays reflecting the author's 45 years of educational research and study in comparative education. Half of the papers have not been published elsewhere.

31. Literacy in Historical Perspective. Edited by Resnick, Daniel P. Library of Congress, 1983. 170p. LC: 82-600295. ISBN: 0-317-59979-8. $8.00.

A collection of papers presented at a conference sponsored by the Center for the Book in the Library of Congress, 1980. Covers the spread of literacy in the medieval and modern periods, focusing on the relationship between literacy demands and national environment in the United States, England, China, and Russia.

32. National Literacy Campaigns: Historical and Comparative Perspectives. Edited by Arnove, Robert F. and Graff, Harvey J. Plenum, 1987. 322p. LC: 87-10873. ISBN: 0-306-42458-4. $39.50.

Series of case studies representing major historical and significant recent examples of literacy campaigns in a variety of societies over the past 400 years: Cuba, Nicaragua, Tanzania, and major industrialized nations. Also examines adult literacy efforts in three Western industri-

alized countries—Great Britain, France, and the United States.

33. New Approaches to Comparative Education. Edited by Altbach, Philip G. and Kelly, Gail P. Univ. of Chicago Press, 1986. 336p. LC: 85-24523. ISBN: 0-226-01525-4; 0-226-01526-2 (pbk.). $30.00; $15.00 (pbk.).

Essays which were originally published in the *Comparative Education Review* have been collected to draw attention to the new and diverse directions comparative education research has taken since 1977 when a "state of the art" issue was published. The more recent research approach in comparative education reflects a broader scope concerned with intranational comparisons as well as transnational.

34. Politics and Education: Cases from Eleven Nations. Edited by Thomas, R. Murray. Pergamon, 1983. 330p. LC: 82-11296. ISBN: 0-08-028905-3; 0-08-028904-5 (pbk.). $52.00; $22.00 (pbk.).

The principal facets of the interaction of politics and education are presented in the first chapter; 11 country case studies follow to illustrate these facets and to compare each country with the model.

35. Professional Parents: Parent Participation in Four Western European Countries. Beattie, Nicholas. Falmer, 1985. 289p. LC: 85-16251. ISBN: 1-85000-098-6; 1-85000-077-8 (pbk.). $36.00; $20.00 (pbk.).

A comparison of parent participation in educational decision-making through case studies in four Western European countries—Italy, France, West Germany, and England/Wales. Special attention is given to the period since 1965 which saw the emergence and development of various structures or models to encourage parent involvement with schools and the development of the "professional parent."

36. Research on Foreign Students and International Study: An Overview and Bibliography. Altbach, Philip G., Kelly, David H. and Lulat, Y. G-M. (Praeger Special Studies Series in Comparative Education). Praeger, 1985. 403p. LC: 85-3372. ISBN: 0-03-071922-4. $38.95.

Following an opening essay and overview of the key issues and research related to foreign students, a selective and partially annotated bibliography of 2,811 listings forms the bulk of this text. Books, dissertations and theses, journals, reports, and documents are covered; most of the material is English-language since the largest number of the world's foreign students are studying in English-speaking countries, although references in French, Spanish, German, and Russian are included.

37. The Revival of Values Education in Asia and the West. Cummings, William K., Gopinathan, S. and Tomoda, Yasumasa. (Pergamon Comparative and International Education Series, v. 7). Pergamon, 1988. 183p. LC: 88-14037. ISBN: 0-08-035854-3; 0-08-035853-5 (pbk.). $39.95; $19.95 (pbk.).

Introductory chapters highlight the complexity of selecting content for values education, reliance on schools as the primary vehicle, and the historical development of values education. Case studies present the major distinctions in values education between Asia and the West.

38. The School and the University: An International Perspective. Edited by Clark, Burton R. Univ. of California Press, 1985. 337p. LC: 85-1158. ISBN: 0-520-05423-7. $37.50; $11.95.

Each of the papers in this collection examines the relationship between the secondary school system and the higher education system in a particular region. Chapters focus on parallel subjects to allow for cross-national comparisons: details of the country's secondary and higher education systems, how the secondary school shapes the university, and how the university shapes the school. The final chapter offers some cross-national observations.

Science Education in Global Perspective: Lessons from Five Countries *See* CONTENT AREAS (No. 111)

Soviet Education: The Gifted and the Handicapped *See* SPECIAL EDUCATION (No. 882)

39. **Studying Teaching and Learning: Trends in Soviet and American Research.** Edited by Tabachnick, Thomas S., Popkewitz, Thomas S. and Szekely, Beatrice Beach. (Praeger Special Studies Series in Comparative Education). Praeger, 1981. 251p. LC: 80-27528. ISBN: 0-030-56726-2. $38.95.
   As a result of the Soviet-American cultural exchange program this collection of papers was presented at a Moscow seminar reflecting the very different perspective on educational research of American versus Soviet scholars.

Vocationalizing Education: An International Perspective *See* VOCATIONAL EDUCATION (No. 964)

40. **Women's Education in Developing Countries: Opportunities and Outcome.** Smock, Audrey Chapman. (Praeger Special Studies Series in Comparative Education). Praeger, 1981. 293p. LC: 81-8560. ISBN: 0-275-90720-1. $38.95.
   This study offers considerable data on women's educational opportunities and the relationship between educational attainment and three life areas: marriage and family patterns, fertility behavior, and labor force participation. Comparative analysis focuses on five countries representing varying degrees of educational opportunities for women—Pakistan, Philippines, Ghana, Kenya, and Mexico—along with some data from other societies.

41. **The World Crisis in Education: The View from the Eighties.** Coombs, Philip H. Oxford Univ. Press, 1985. 353p. LC: 84-5713. ISBN: 0-19-503502-X; 0-19-503503-8 (pbk.). $22.50; $11.95 (pbk.).
   Explores the findings of a world-wide reassessment of trends and changes in education since the publication of Coombs' 1968 edition of *The World Educational Crisis*. Presents a comparative international perspective of the critical problems and issues comprising the crises likely to confront educational systems around the world in the late 1980s and 1990s: rapid growth of learning needs, growing financial squeeze, disparities and inequalities, etc.

42. **World Education Encyclopedia.** Edited by Kurian, George Thomas. Facts on File, 1988. 1720p. LC: 82-18188. ISBN: 0-87196-748-0. $175.00 set. 3 volumes.

A descriptive survey of some 180 national, working educational systems of the world. Reviews are grouped "A" to "Z" under three categories: Major Countries, Middle Countries, and Minor Countries; some are short, particularly for Third World nations, many of which are designated as minor countries. All follow a standardized but not rigid format providing basic data, history, legal foundations, needs, goals, administration, finance, and teaching profession. Includes valuable appendices.

43. **World Yearbook of Education, 1979-.** Nichols, 1989. 351p. ISBN: 0-89397-334-3. $47.50 (1989). 0084-2508.
   Each issue of this annual, since 1979, is devoted to a timely theme of international interest in the field of education. The yearbooks are addressed to "intelligent lay readers," and written by world scholars providing authoritative coverage with valuable references. Recent volumes include *Computers and Education* (1982), *Education for the New Technologies* (1988), and *Health Education* (1989). Many earlier volumes are still in print.

44. **1968: A Student Generation in Revolt.** Fraser, Ronald et al. Pantheon, 1988. 408p. LC: 87-46058. ISBN: 0-679-73953-X. $14.95.
   A study of the student rebellion of the 1960s in six of the West's industrialized countries: the United States, West Germany, France, Italy, Great Britain, and Northern Ireland. This oral history is based on interviews conducted between 1984 and 1985 of students who participated in the revolts, especially activists and well-known national student movement leaders. The United States edition includes 38 extra pages devoted specifically to American events.

Journals

45. **Comparative Education Review.** Univ. of Chicago Press, Journals Division, P.O. Box 37005, Chicago, IL 60637. Quarterly. $53.00. ISSN: 0010-4086. 1957. Official journal of the Comparative and International Education Society.

46. **International Education Magazine/Magazine De L'Education International.** Canadian Bureau for Intl. Education, 85 Albert St. Suite 1400, Ottawa, Ontario, KIP 6A4 Canada. 6/year. $20 Canadian. ISSN: 0827-0678. 1985. Text in English and French.

47. **International Review of Education.** UNESCO Institute for Education, UN, Kluwer Academic Publishing Co., 101 Philip Dr., Norwell, MA 02061. Quarterly. $80.50. ISSN: 0020-8566. 1955. Published by UNESCO, distributed in the U.S. by Kluwer.

48. **Prospects: Quarterly Review of Education.** Unipub, Box 433, Murray Hill Station, New York, NY 10016. Quarterly. Contact publisher for price information. ISSN: 0033-1538. 1969. Published by UNESCO, distributed in the US by Unipub.

Content Areas

Materials in this section are further subdivided into these categories: humanities, mathematics, reading, science, and social studies. Reading materials also include language arts. Humanities covers art, aesthetic education, and music. Book materials include textbooks, research materials and practical handbooks, and reference materials. Emphasis is on kindergarten through grade 12, although postsecondary education is also considered. Journals are balanced between postsecondary and elementary and secondary levels in all subject areas.

HUMANITIES

Books

49. Art and Adolescence: Teaching Art at the Secondary Level. Michael, John A. Teachers College Press, 1983. 224p. LC: 83-4147. ISBN: 0-8077-2743-1. $16.95 (pbk.).

Presents a framework for developing a secondary art program. Offers suggestions for evaluating, understanding, and assessing situations in the art teaching and learning environment. Presents philosophy, objectives, methodology, classroom management techniques, and an overview of art education. Appendixes, tables, and charts provide supplemental information about behavior, measurement instruments, curriculum design, and other pertinent data.

50. Art Education: Elementary. Greenberg, Pearl et al. Natl. Art Education Assn., 1980. 228p. Contact publisher for price information.

Written by a task force of specialists in elementary education, this report recognizes the national concern for the quality of life and the educational system. Outlines the goals of an excellent art program by focusing on the relationship between art and the individual, art in the community, and art within the culture. Discusses why art is important as well as specific strategies for bringing art into the elementary classroom.

51. A Cross-Section of Research in Music Education. Edited by Barnes, Stephen A. Univ. Press of America, 1982. 328p. LC: 81-43496. ISBN: 0-8191-2285-8. $33.75.

Supplementary text for research methods courses in music education consists of an anthology of 23 research studies taken from four music journals. Descriptive, historical, experimental, and philosophical research methods are reflected in the contents. No additional commentary is provided with the reprinted articles; however, an introductory chapter on evaluating research articles is complemented by an appendix on writing a critical review.

52. Educating for Art: Critical Response and Development. Taylor, Rod. Longman, 1986. 327p. ISBN: 0-582-36152-4. $21.95.

Report from the Critical Studies in Art Education Project in Great Britain focuses on secondary level art education. Parallels the U.S. concern about a lack of humanities courses in the classroom. Provides a theoretical justification for critical studies in art. Discusses strategies for developing critical appreciation skills as well as practical skills. Useful both to instructors and to educational staff in galleries and museums. Color illustrations and comments from students highlight various chapters.

53. Excellence in Art Education: Ideas and Initiatives. Smith, Ralph A. Natl. Art Education Assn., 1987. 138p. ISBN: 0-937652-34-2. $16.00. Updated version.

Reviews the educational reform literature as it pertains to art education. Interprets recommended improvements within the context of curriculum design and teaching at the secondary level for grades 7–12. Advocates the need to instill in students an appreciation of excellence in art as it affects human development. Discusses specific efforts toward excellence in art education and education in general.

54. Methods and Perspectives in Urban Music Education. Edited by Hicks, Charles E., Standifer, James A. and Carter, Warrick L. Univ. Press of America, 1983. 501p. LC: 82-16105. ISBN: 0-8191-2760-4. Contact publisher for price information.

Handbook for music educators that addresses the setting for classroom instruction, the problems faced by educators, and strategies for coping. Specifically addressed to urban music educators, although content is generally useful. Advocates teacher preparation for urban settings that sensitizes the educator to the special needs and problems of urban students. Strong emphasis on multicultural education.

55. Music Education: Tradition and Innovation. Walker, Robert. C.C. Thomas, 1984. 168p. LC: 83-4672. ISBN: 0-398-04861-4. $23.75.

Focuses on elementary music education, stating the position that music should be placed in context with other areas of the curriculum. Examines historical and current practices in music education in an attempt to recommend quality teaching strategies in the elementary classroom. Compares traditional and innovative methods of teaching music and addresses scientific, technological, and aesthetic issues as well.

Resources for Educating Artistically Talented Students *See* **SPECIAL EDUCATION (No. 878)**

56. Visual Arts. Brigham, Don L. (Focus on Fine Arts). Natl. Education Assn., 1989. 80p. LC: 89-3264. Contact publisher for price information. Stock no. 0304-7.

A joint publication of the NEA and the National Art Education Association, this report discusses the reform of art education, qualitative art education, and visual art education. Discusses programs appropriate at elementary, middle, and high schools as well as interdisciplinary art education programs. Assessment and evaluation of qualitative programs are explored in the final chapter. Utilizes research and the reform literature in making a case for the reform of art education.

Journals

57. American Music Teacher. Music Teachers Natl. Assn., 617 Vine St., Suite 1432, Cincinnati, OH 45202. 6/year. $7.50. ISSN: 0003-0112. 1936. Former title: *Music Teachers' National Association Bulletin.*

58. Art Education. Natl. Art Education Assn., 1916 Association Dr., Reston, VA 22091. 6/year. $50.00. ISSN: 0004-3125. 1947.

59. Bulletin of the Council for Research in Music Education. Univ. of Illinois at Urbana-Champaign, School of Music, 1205 W. California, Urbana, IL 61801. Quarterly. $22.50. ISSN: 0010-9894. 1963.

Design *See* **Design for Arts in Education CONTENT AREAS (No. 60)**

60. Design for Arts in Education. Heldref, 4000 Albemarle St., NW, Washington, DC 20016. 6/year. $37.00. ISSN: 0732-0973. 1974. Former title: *Design.*

61. Journal of Research in Music Education. Music Educators Natl. Conference, 1902 Association Drive, Reston, VA 22091. Quarterly. Membership. ISSN: 0022-4294. 1953.

62. Music Educators Journal. Music Educators Natl. Conference, 1902 Association Dr., Reston, VA 22091. 9/year. $37.00. ISSN: 0027-4321. 1914. Former title: *Music Supervisors Journal.*

Music Supervisors Journal *See* **Music Educators Journal CONTENT AREAS (No. 62)**

Music Teachers' National Association Bulletin *See* **American Music Teacher CONTENT AREAS (No. 57)**

63. School Arts: The Art Education Magazine for Teachers. Davis Publications, 50 Portland St., Printers Bldg., Worcester, MA 01608. Monthly (Sept.–May). $20.00. ISSN: 0036-6463. 1901.

64. Studies in Art Education: A Journal of Issues and Research in Art Education. Natl. Art Education Assn., 1916 Association Dr., Reston, VA 22091. Quarterly. $25.00. ISSN: 0039-3541. 1959.

MATHEMATICS

Books

65. . . . And Gladly Teach. Ford Foundation, 1987. 40p. LC: 87-11864. ISBN: 0-916584-27-5. Contact publisher for price information. A Ford Foundation Report on the Urban Mathematics Collaboratives.

Provides an overview of the problems confronting teachers of mathematics in metropolitan areas. Ford Foundation support of 11 collaboratives aimed towards improvement of mathematics education and general improvement in the teaching profession is described. Specific projects of each collaborative are described and general information about purpose, governance, and funding is provided.

66. Cognitive Processes in Mathematics. Edited by Sloboda, John A. and Rogers, Don. (Keele Cognition Seminars, no. 1). Clarendon Press, 1987. 208p. ISBN: 0-19-852163-4. $57.50.

Collection of edited papers from a 1985 conference on cognition held at the University of Keele. Topics include representation of mathematical information, associative interference in learning and retrieving arithmetic facts, students' acquisition of statistics, and understanding algebra. Papers address the current status of cognitive processes in mathematics as well as future directions research might take.

67. Cognitive Science and Mathematics Education. Edited by Schoenfeld, Alan H. L. Erlbaum, 1987. 291p. LC: 87-5362. ISBN: 0-89859-791-9. $39.95.

Explores the role of cognitive science in the learning process, particularly mathematics education. Addressed to teachers, cognitive scientists, mathematicians, and mathematics educators, this work discusses the foundations of cognitive theory, problem formulation, metacognition, and specific curricula, all within the context of mathematics education. Development of this book was a joint effort of mathematics educators, professional mathematicians, teachers, and cognitive scientists that provides a unique perspective.

68. Conceptual and Procedural Knowledge: The Case of Mathematics. Edited by Hiebert, James. L. Erlbaum, 1986. 309p. LC: 86-4599. ISBN: 0-89859-556-8. $36.00.

Focuses on the relationship between conceptual knowledge and procedural skill in mathematics learning. Theoretical stances and empirical data are presented in the separately authored chapters to illustrate this relationship. This relationship is theorized as being the key to understanding how children and adults do mathematics and how they think about their mathematical performance.

Everybody Counts: A Report to the Nation on the Future of Mathematics Education *See* **EDUCATIONAL REFORM (No. 241)**

Improving Indicators of the Quality of Science and Mathematics Education in Grades K-12 *See* **CONTENT AREAS (No. 105)**

69. Learning Mathematics: The Cognitive Science Approach to Mathematics Education. Davis, Robert B. Ablex, 1984. 392p. LC: 84-2853. ISBN: 0-89391-245-X. $39.50.

Based upon a seven-year study at the University of Illinois, this book addresses the controversy between memorization and a cognitive approach to teaching and learning mathematics. Explores the thought processes used by children in learning mathematics. Places the controversy in a broader social context and evaluates future directions of mathematics education.

70. Linguistic and Cultural Influences on Learning Mathematics. Edited by Cocking, Rodney R. and Mestre, Jose P. (Psychology of Education and Instruction Series). L. Erlbaum, 1988. 315p. LC: 87-22285. ISBN: 0-89859-876-1. $39.95.

Separately authored chapters address the complex issues surrounding mathematics performance and learning. Problems discussed include bilingualism, gender, culture, class, motivation, educational opportunities, learning style, and a host of similar problems. Learning mathematics (or other subjects) is greatly affected by the student's background and abilities as explored in these chapters.

Mathematics, Science and Technology Education: A Research Agenda *See* CONTENT AREAS (No. 109)

71. The Psychology of Learning Mathematics. Skemp, Richard R. L. Erlbaum, 1987. 218p. LC: 87-6767. ISBN: 0-89859-837-0. $36.00. Expanded American edition.

Presents Skemp's view that mathematics is a powerful and intense example of the functioning of human intelligence. Given this view, questions are raised about how intelligence functions so that relevant learning activities can be developed. The relationship between human intelligence and mathematics learning is the core of this expanded and revised edition of Skemp's 1971 classic.

72. A Review of Research in Mathematical Education. Bell, A.W. et al. NFER-Nelson, 1983. 3 vols. ISBN: 0-7005-0612-8(v.1); 0-7005-0613-6(v.2); 0-7005-0614-4(v.3). Contact publisher for price information.

A three-volume report for the Cockcroft Committee of Inquiry into the Teaching of Mathematics in Schools. The British report presents "Research on Learning and Teaching" in Part A, "Research on the Social Context of Mathematics Education" in part B, and "Curriculum Development and Curriculum Research" in Part C. Discusses the social and institutional constraints on the teaching of mathematics.

Science and Mathematics for the Year 2000 and Beyond *See* CONTENT AREAS (No. 110)

73. Speaking Mathematically: Communication in Mathematics Classrooms. Pimm, David. (Language, Education, and Society). Routledge & Kegan Paul, 1987. 217p. LC: 86-24849. ISBN: 0-7102-1133-3. $14.95 (pbk.).

Views mathematics as a language, and explores how this perception affects teaching. Examines spoken and written classroom language as used by students and teachers. The teacher's role as an intermediary and role model in the language of mathematics is discussed. Mathematical syntax, written mathematics, classroom communication, and meta-linguistics are covered as well.

74. Twice as Less: Black English and the Performance of Black Students in Mathematics and Science. Orr, Eleanor Wilson. Norton, 1987. 240p. LC: 87-5758. ISBN: 0-393-02392-3. $15.45.

Focuses on the language differences in Black English that may affect performance of Black students in mathematics and science. Advocates that teachers learn the structure and principles of Black English so that they can assist Black students in learning science and mathematics. Confusion in the use of language used to teach mathematics and science and student language is discussed and possible solutions are proposed.

75. The Underachieving Curriculum: Assessing U.S. School Mathematics from an International Perspective. McKnight, Curtis C. et al. Stipes, 1987. 127p. ISBN: 0-87563-298-X. Contact publisher for price information. International Association for the Evaluation of Education Achievement; A National Report on the Second International Mathematics Study.

Highlights the major findings of the Second International Mathematics Study. Advocates a renewed emphasis on mathematics education in the U.S. Compared to other countries, mathematics performance in the United States is quite poor. Research is used to substantiate this position, along with numerous charts and tables to illustrate the findings.

76. Young Children Continue to Reinvent Arithmetic—2nd Grade: Implications of Piaget's Theory. Kamii, Constance with Joseph, Linda Leslie. (Early Childhood Education Series). Teachers College Press, 1989. 203p. LC: 89-4451. ISBN: 0-8077-2958-2. $28.95.

Written with the intention of showing that traditional arithmetic instruction is taught contrary to the way children think and that there are better ways of teaching arithmetic, Kamii presents evidence supporting constructivism and social interaction in the classroom. Emphasizes the harmful effects of standardized achievement testing and "teaching to the test." Strongly focuses on Piaget's theory.

Journals

77. Arithmetic Teacher. National Council of Teachers of Mathematics, 1906 Association Dr., Reston, VA 22091. Monthly (Sept.–May). $45.00. ISSN: 0004-136X. 1954.

78. College Mathematics Journal. Mathematical Assn. of America, 1529 Eighteenth St., NW, Washington, DC 20036. 5/year. $60.00. ISSN: 0746-8342. 1970. Former title: *Two-Year College Mathematics Journal.*

79. Journal for Research in Mathematics Education. Natl. Council of Teachers of Mathematics, 1906 Association Drive, Reston, VA 22091. 5/year. $20.00. ISSN: 0021-8251. 1970.

Journal of Children's Mathematical Behavior *See* Journal of Mathematical Behavior CONTENT AREAS (No. 80)

80. Journal of Mathematical Behavior. Ablex, 355 Chestnut St., Norwood, NJ 07648. 3/year. $69.50. ISSN: 0732-3123. 1971. Former title: *Journal of Children's Mathematical Behavior.*

81. Mathematics and Computer Education. MATYC Journal, Box 158, Old Bethpage, NY 11804. 3/year. $44.00. ISSN: 0730-8639. 1967. Former title: *MATYC Journal.*

82. Mathematics Teacher. Natl. Council of Teachers of Mathematics, 1906 Assn. Dr., Reston, VA 22091. 9/year. $45.00. ISSN: 0025-5769. 1907.

MATYC Journal *See* **Mathematics and Computer Education CONTENT AREAS (No. 81)**

School Science and Mathematics *See* **CONTENT AREAS (No. 118)**

Two-Year College Mathematics Journal *See* **College Mathematics Journal CONTENT AREAS (No. 78)**

READING

Books

83. **The Administration and Supervision of Reading Programs.** Edited by Wepner, Shelley B., Feeley, Joan T. and Strickland, Dorothy S. Teachers College Press, 1989. 284p. LC: 88-25926. ISBN: 0-8077-2929-9. $37.95.
    Collection of papers provides a sourcebook of current research on the organization of a reading program. Offers a research-based, yet practical, approach to reading instruction programs for Pre-K through grade 12. Designed for administrators, supervisors, and pre-service and in-service reading specialists to aid in organizing reading programs.

84. **Chicorel Abstracts to Reading and Learning Disabilities.** Edited by Chicorel, Marietta. (Chicorel Index Series). American Library Publishing, 1983. 500p. LC: 78-58455. ISBN: 0-934598-85-1. $125.00.
    Published since 1974, this annual index provides abstracts of research related to reading and learning disabilities. Each entry provides a full citation to the source document, an abstract, and an indication of the type of document (e.g., nontechnical), the type of research (e.g., descriptive), the level of the audience, and whether a bibliography is included. A subject arrangement allows the reader to go directly to a topic such as hyperactivity. An author index is provided.

85. **A Dictionary of Reading and Related Terms.** Edited by Harris, Theodore L. and Hodges, Richard E. International Reading Assn., 1981. 382p. ISBN: 0-87207-944-9. $27.50.
    Fascinating compilation of vocabulary used in the field of reading. Defines, clarifies, and illustrates terminology in English. Word meaning equivalents in French, Spanish, German, Danish, and Swedish for selected dictionary entries are provided in an appendix.

86. **Dyslexia: An Annotated Bibliography.** Evans, Martha M. (Contemporary Problems of Childhood, no. 5). Greenwood Press, 1982. 644p. LC: 81-20319. ISBN: 0-313-21344-5. $50.95.
    Lengthy bibliography includes books, journal articles, reports, documents, dissertations, and chapters of books related to dyslexia. Excluded were materials dealing with hearing or vision impairments, brain damage or mental retardation, aphasia, acquired dyslexia, and textbooks for the dyslexic reader. Less attention is given to reading failure due to cultural deprivation, bilingualism, delinquency, lack of motivation, and nonstandard English usage. Resources are divided into the following categories: General Research, Causes, Diagnosis, Treatment, Historical Works, Case Studies, Bibliographies, and Reference Sources. Appendixes include a glossary and varying definitions of dyslexia.

87. **Group Assessment in Reading: Classroom Teacher's Handbook.** Warncke, Edna and Shipman, Dorothy. Prentice-Hall, 1984. 233p. LC: 83-4486. ISBN: 0-13-365742-6. Contact publisher for price information.
    Designed for classroom teachers and reading specialists, information about the use, interpretation, development, and validation of reading tests is included in this book. Five reproducible group reading diagnostic instruments are included as well.

88. **High/Low Handbook: Books, Materials, and Services for the Problem Reader.** Edited by LiBretto, Ellen V. (Serving Special Needs Series). Bowker, 1985. 264p. LC: 85-17514. ISBN: 0-8352-2133-4. $39.95. 2nd edition.
    Intended for teachers, librarians, and other practitioners, this guide offers a listing of easy reading material for the reluctant or disabled adolescent reader. Focuses on the selection, evaluation, and use of high/low materials. Chapters from publishers, authors, librarians, and teachers of high/low materials offer unique insights into the development, use, and distribution of these materials. A core collection of high/low materials is annotated with full publication and price information. Bibliographies and related reference sources are provided also.

89. **Measures for Research and Evaluation in the English Language Arts.** Edited by Fagan, William T. National Council of Teachers of English, v. 1, 1975; v. 2, 1985. 235p. (v.1); 245p. (v.2) LC: 74-31744. ISBN: v. 2, 0-8141-3101-8. $17.95 (pbk.). NCTE Stock no. 15343 (v.1).
    A project of NCTE, this compilation of measurement instruments is derived from journal articles and doctoral dissertations. Measurement instruments in the language arts that were in existence but not widely known are described in this work. The actual tests are reproduced or available in their entirety in journal articles or in the ERIC system. Evaluative information about each instrument is included.

The Politics of Reading: Power, Opportunity and Prospects for Change in America's Public Schools *See* **SPECIAL EDUCATION (No. 870)**

90. **Reading in the Language Classroom.** Williams, Eddie. (Essential Language Teaching Series). Macmillan, 1984. 137p. ISBN: 0-333-27179-3. Contact publisher for price information.
    Considers the role of reading in the language classroom and the teaching of reading skills to language learners. Particular attention is given to the nonnative speaker of English in the reading process. Explains the various activities within reading such as skimming and scanning, and recommends classroom activities to assist in the reading process.

Reading Instruction for the Gifted *See* **RESOURCES FOR TEACHING (No. 808)**

Reading/Learning Disability: An Ecological Approach *See* **SPECIAL EDUCATION (No. 875)**

91. **Reading: Tests and Assessment Techniques.** Pumfrey, Pete D. (UKRA Teaching of Reading Monographs). Hodder and Stoughton, 1985. 342p. ISBN: 0-340-3562-4. Contact publisher for price information. 2nd edition.
    Provides an overview of reading assessment and the instruments currently available for evaluation. Guidelines on selecting an appropriate test are provided to assist educators in determining the appropriate tool to diagnose reading difficulties. Additional sources of information and materials are presented and followed by an annotated bibliography.

92. Really Now, Why *Can't* Our Johnnies Read?. Eisenson, Jon. Pacific Books, 1989. 160p. LC: 88-23354. ISBN: 0-87015-258-0. $17.95.

Explores the reasons why so many U.S. school children, particularly males, have difficulty learning to read. Identifies students at high risk for failure to learn to read, presents alternatives to the current popular approaches to reading intervention, and discusses the special needs of dyslexics. Initial chapter defines reading and related terms with a statement of the author's personal stance on the definition. Subsequent chapters discuss reading failure, intervention strategies and models, dyslexia, and attaining even higher levels of reading ability.

Recommended English Language Arts Curriculum Guides, K-12 *See* RESOURCES FOR TEACHING (No. 809)

93. Report Card on Basal Readers. Goodman, Kenneth S., Shannon, Patrick, Freeman, Yvonne S. and Murphy, Sharon. Richard C. Owen Publishers, 1988. 167p. LC: 88-15130. ISBN: 0-913-46198-8. Contact publisher for price information.

Prepared for the Reading Commission of the National Council of Teachers of English, this work reviews the history and efficacy of basal readers. Contains critical evaluation of the content of and reliance on basal readers for instruction.

Secondary School Reading: What Research Reveals for Classroom Practice *See* RESOURCES FOR TEACHING (No. 811)

Teaching Thinking Skills: English/Language Arts *See* RESOURCES FOR TEACHING (No. 820)

Journals

94. Claremont Reading Conference. Yearbook. Claremont Reading Conference, Claremont Graduate School, Ctr. for Developmental Studies, Harper 200, 150 E. 10th St., Claremont, CA 91711-6160. Annual. $20.00. 1936.

95. College Composition and Communications. Natl. Council of Teachers of English, 1111 Kenyon Rd., Urbana, IL 61801. Quarterly. $12.00. ISSN: 0010-096X. 1950.

96. College English. Natl. Council of Teachers of English, 1111 Kenyon Road, Urbana, IL 61801. 8/year. $40.00. ISSN: 0010-0994. 1939.

97. Communication Education. Speech Communication Assn., 5105 Backlick Road, Building E, Annandale, VA 22003. Quarterly. $40.00. ISSN: 0363-4523. 1952. Former title: *Speech Teacher.*

98. English Journal. National Council of Teachers of English, 1111 Kenyon Rd., Urbana, IL 61801. 8/year. $40.00. ISSN: 0013-8274. 1912.

Journal of Developmental Reading *See* Journal of Reading CONTENT AREAS (No. 99)

99. Journal of Reading. International Reading Assn., Box 8139, Newark, DE 19714-8139. 8/year. Membership. ISSN: 0022-4103. 1957. Former title: *Journal of Developmental Readingei.*

100. Language Arts. National Council of Teachers of English, 1111 Kenyon Rd., Urbana, IL 61801. 8/year. $40.00. ISSN: 0360-9170. 1924.

101. Reading Horizons. Reading Horizons, College of Education, Western Michigan Univ., Kalamazoo, MI 49008. Quarterly. $16.00. ISSN: 0034-0502. 1960.

102. Reading Research Quarterly. Intl. Reading Assn., 800 Barksdale Road, Box 8139, Newark, DE 19714-8139. Quarterly. Membership. ISSN: 0034-0553. 1965.

103. Reading Teacher. Intl. Reading Assn., 800 Barksdale Rd., P.O. Box 8139, Newark, DE 19714-8139. 9/year. Membership. ISSN: 0034-0553. 1947.

Speech Teacher *See* **Communication Education CONTENT AREAS (No. 97)**

SCIENCE

Books

104. Development and Dilemmas in Science Education. Edited by Fensham, Peter. (Contemporary Analysis in Education Series, no. 23). Falmer, 1988. 318p. ISBN: 1-85000-350-5. $49.00.

Despite its British publication, this volume is international in scope. Each chapter has a theme such as gender and science and the role of language in science education. Case studies, bringing research into the science classroom, and the philosophical question of what counts as science education are all components of this work.

105. Improving Indicators of the Quality of Science and Mathematics Education in Grades K-12. Edited by Murnane, Richard J. and Raizan, Senta A. Natl. Academy Press, 1988. 220p. LC: 87-31230. ISBN: 0-309-03740-9. $17.50 (pbk.).

A second report of the Committee on Indicators of Precollege Science and Mathematics Education of The National Research Council addresses the need to develop an improved system of indicators to monitor the condition of science and mathematics education. In addition to reviewing the science content in nine selected achievement tests, student behavior, teaching quality, curriculum, financial support, and math and science learning are all evaluated in terms of key indicators with specific recommendations for improvement.

106. Improving Reading in Science. Thelen, Judith N. (IRA Reading Aids Series). International Reading Assn., 1984. 57p. LC: 84-4591. ISBN: 0-87207-217-7. $5.00 (pbk.). 2nd edition.

Argues that reading instruction in science means to teach simultaneously the science content and the reading and reasoning processes by which that content is learned. Covers diagnosing, prereading strategies, vocabulary reinforcement, and evaluation in the teaching of science. An informal skills inventory on a physical science textbook is included in an appendix.

107. Learning in Science: The Implications of Children's Science. Osborne, Roger and Freyberg, Peter. Heinemann, 1985. 198p. LC: 84-27915. ISBN: 0-86863-275-9. $15.00 (pbk.).

Addressed to teachers and curriculum developers, this work focuses on how children's perceptions of science and interpretation of terms used in science influence later ability to learn science in the classroom. Based on research undertaken in New Zealand, the findings have universal implications. Recommendations regarding reconciling student experiences with teacher intentions are provided. Also analyzes various science teaching models and provides a variation of these models.

108. Learning Science. White, Richard T. Basil Blackwell, 1988. 227p. LC: 87-18228-4. ISBN: 0-631-15698-4. $39.95.

Presents a psychology of learning science in formal instructional and everyday contexts. Explores the factors affecting learning, including memory, association, understanding, ability, aptitude, contextual perception, and instructional methods. Tables, figures, a lengthy list of references, and a comprehensive index enhance this overview of learning in science.

109. Mathematics, Science and Technology Education: A Research Agenda. Committee on Research in Mathematics, Science, and Technology Education Commission on Behavioral and Social Sciences and Education National Research Council. Natl. Academy Press, 1985. 92p. Contact publisher for price information.

Reviews current work and research in relevant fields to assess the state of mathematics, science, and technology education in the elementary and secondary classroom. Offers strategies for using research to improve classroom practice. Discusses the reasons for deficiencies in scientific education and presents recommendations to improve it. These include undertaking research on reasoning, better instruction, better educational environments, and development of new learning systems.

110. Science and Mathematics for the Year 2000 and Beyond. Edited by James, Robert K. and Kurtz, V. Ray. (Topics for Teachers Series, no. 4). School Science and Mathematics Assn., 1985. 114p. ISBN: 0-912047-05-4. Contact publisher for price information.

Presents a vision of the future in a technological society with particular emphasis on the mathematical and scientific knowledge needed to be prepared for such a future. The impact of future changes on education are explored and the goals, processes, and strategies that will be utilized in the year 2000 to teach students are discussed. Reactions of educators to these speculations and how they would affect their activities are presented for discussion. The final chapter proposes an integrated discipline of "sciematics" for the year 2000.

111. Science Education in Global Perspective: Lessons from Five Countries. Edited by Klein, Margrete Siebert and Rutherford, F. James. (AAAS Selected Symposia Series). Westview Press, 1985. 231p. LC: 85-51889. ISBN: 0-8133-7146-5. $26.50 (pbk.).

Based on a symposium held at the 1982 annual meeting of the American Association for the Advancement of Science, this study explores innovative approaches to science education in Japan, East and West Germany, the People's Republic of China, and the Soviet Union. The international cross-section of data is presented for the benefit of educators, lawmakers, and individuals concerned about the decline in the quality of American public schools, particularly in the areas of science and mathematics.

Teaching Science to Children: A Resourcebook *See* **RESOURCES FOR TEACHING (No. 818)**

112. What Research Says to the Science Teacher. National Science Teachers Assn., 1978–1982. 4 vols. ISBN: vol. 2, 0-87355-013-7; vol. 3, 0-87355-018-8; vol. 4, 0-87355-009-9. $7.00 per volume.

Transmits information about research and research projects to science teachers. Identifies unmet needs in the science classroom and recommends interventions and teaching strategies to address these concerns. Each volume focuses on a specific aspect of science education. Emphasis is placed on the implications of science research for classroom practice.

Journals

113. American Biology Teacher. Natl. Assn. of Biology Teachers, 11250 Roger Bacon Dr., Reston, VA 22090. 8/year. $38.00. ISSN: 0002-7685. 1938.

114. Journal of Chemical Education. American Chemical Society, 20th and Northampton St., Easton, PA 18042. Monthly. $46.00. ISSN: 0021-9584. 1924.

115. Journal of College Science Teaching. Natl. Science Teachers Assn., 1742 Connecticut Ave., NW, Washington, DC 20009. 6/year. $33.00. ISSN: 0047-231X. 1971.

116. Journal of Research in Science Teaching. John Wiley & Sons, 605 Third Ave., New York, NY 10158. 9/year. $119.00. ISSN: 0022-4308. 1963.

117. The Physics Teacher. American Assn. of Physics Teachers, 5112 Berwyn Rd., College Park, MD 20740. 9/year. $90.00. ISSN: 0031-921X. 1962.

118. School Science and Mathematics. School Science and Mathematics Assn., 126 Life Sciences Bldg., Bowling Green Univ., Bowling Green, OH 43403-0256. 9/year. $32.00. ISSN: 0036-6803. 1901.

119. Science and Children. National Science Teachers Assn., 1742 Connecticut Ave., NW, Washington, DC 20009. 8/year. $42.00. ISSN: 0036-8148. 1963.

120. Science Education. John Wiley & Sons, 605 Third Ave., New York, NY 10158. 5/year. $72.00. ISSN: 0036-8326. 1916.

121. Science Teacher. National Science Teachers Assn., 1742 Connecticut Ave., NW, Washington, DC 20009. 9/year. $42.00. ISSN: 0036-8555. 1934.

SOCIAL STUDIES

Books

122. Social Studies for Children: A Guide to Basic Instruction. Michaelis, John Udell. Prentice-Hall, 1988. 428p. ISBN: 0-13-818832. Contact publisher for price information. 9th edition.

Written for the student teacher or practitioner in the elementary or middle school. Provides examples of social studies instruction through lesson plans, charts, and learning activities. Chapters cover topics such as group work, lesson plans, incorporating current affairs into the curriculum, specific skills, and evaluation. Each chapter presents an overview and concludes with study questions.

Journals

Historical Outlook *See* **The Social Studies CONTENT AREAS (No. 127)**

123. The History Teacher. Society for History Education, CSU Long Beach, Long Beach, CA 90840. Quarterly. $28.00. ISSN: 0018-2745. 1967.

History Teacher Magazine *See* **The Social Studies CONTENT AREAS (No. 127)**

124. Journal of Geography. Natl. Council for Geographic Education, Central Ofc., Indiana Univ. of Pennsylvania, Indiana, PA 15705-3147. 6/year. $48.00. ISSN: 0022-1341. 1902.

125. Journal of Social Studies Research. Univ. of Georgia, Dept. of Social Science Education, 215 Tucker Hall, Athens, GA 30602. Semi-annual. $10.00. 1977.

126. Social Education. National Council for the Social Studies, 3501 Newark St., NW, Washington, DC 20016. 7/year. $35.00. ISSN: 0037-7724. 1937.

Social Studies for Secondary School Teachers *See* **The Social Studies CONTENT AREAS (No. 127)**

127. The Social Studies: For Teachers and Administrators. Heldref, 4000 Albemarle St., NW, Washington, DC 20016. 6/year. $37.00. ISSN: 0037-7996. 1918. Former titles: *History Teacher Magazine; Historical Outlook; Social Studies; Social Studies for Secondary School Teachers.*

Educational Administration and Law

Educational law materials are primarily reference materials and case studies. The area of administration emphasizes discipline and classroom management. A certain amount of overlap with **Teacher Education** and **Elementary/Secondary Education** occurs within such areas as leadership and supervision. Materials on effective schools may also be found in the **Educational Reform** section. The Subject Index should be consulted for comprehensive coverage of the topics mentioned above.

Books

Becoming an Effective Classroom Manager: A Resource for Teachers *See* RESOURCES FOR TEACHING (No. 775)

Building Classroom Discipline *See* RESOURCES FOR TEACHING (No. 778)

128. **The Central Office Supervisor of Curriculum and Instruction: Setting the Stage for Success.** Pajak, Edward. Allyn and Bacon, 1989. 243p. LC: 88-14575. ISBN: 0-205-11710-4. Contact publisher for price information.

Draws attention to the uniqueness of the position of central office instructional supervisor. Based upon original data, a basic model for understanding the role of the supervisor of instruction is developed. Describes and clarifies the activities of the instructional supervisor and how that affects teaching effectiveness. Special emphasis is placed on interactions with principals and superintendents.

129. **Child Care Administration.** Seaver, Judith W. and Cartwright, Carol A. Wadsworth, 1986. 438p. LC 85-17961. ISBN: 0-534-03681-3. Contact publisher for price information.

Provides an overview and history of child care with descriptions of different child care operations, such as infant day care, school age care, family day care, and Head Start. Discusses environment, equipment, staffing, funding, and legal regulations as well as theoretical issues in child care. Appendixes contain information about resources, professional associations, and state licensing offices.

130. **Choice in Public Education.** Elmore, Richard F. (CPRE Joint Note Series, JNE-01). Rand Corporation, 1986. 40p. Contact publisher for price information.

Sponsored by the Center for Policy Research in Education, this report explores the policy issues surrounding choice in public schools. Analyzes policy options and concludes that enhanced choice in public schooling is the optimum arrangement. Strictly private schooling or a monopoly of public schools would create greater problems than they resolve.

Classroom Discipline: Case Studies and Viewpoints *See* RESOURCES FOR TEACHING (No. 783)

Classroom Management for Elementary Teachers *See* RESOURCES FOR TEACHING (No. 785)

Complete Legal Guide to Special Education Services: A Handbook for Administrators, Counselors and Supervisors *See* SPECIAL EDUCATION (No. 831)

131. **Control Theory in the Classroom.** Glasser, William. Harper & Row, 1986. 144p. LC: 86-45106. ISBN: 0-06-055015-5. $14.95.

Recommends a major change in the structure of how to teach and in the role of the teacher within that structure. Advocates the use of learning teams to increase student motivation. These recommendations are based on the author's control theory, which focuses on satisfaction as the key motivating force. Expands on control theory within the classroom setting, provides a model and classroom examples of the learning team, and suggests ways to begin implementing control theory in the classroom.

132. **The Culture of the School and the Problem of Change.** Sarason, Seymour B. Allyn and Bacon, 1982. 311p. LC: 81-12806. ISBN: 0-205-07700-5. $26.00. 2nd edition.

Addresses the need to recognize the role and impact that the community context plays in the effort to create change in schools. In the debates over educational reform, the author poses questions about the school's constituency, limited resources, purpose, and effectiveness that need to be addressed from the basis of the culture of the school. Change mechanisms, change agents, and the consequences of change are explored.

133. **Deskbook Encyclopedia of American School Law.** Data Research, 1989. 556p. LC: 86-657590. ISBN: 0-939675-12-9. $68.50. Earlier editions published by the editors of *Legal Notes for Education* .

Published since 1981, this compilation regularly updates state and federal appellate court decisions that affect education. Provides educators and lawyers with access to the most current available cases in education. Includes pertinent excerpts from the U.S. Constitution, a brief summary of the U.S. judicial system, and updated appendixes of recently published law review articles and U.S. Supreme Court cases.

134. Diploma Mills: Degrees of Fraud. Stewart, David W. and Spille, Henry A. (The American Council on Education/Macmillan Series on Higher Education). American Council on Education/Macmillan, 1988. 253p. LC: 88-17462. ISBN: 0-02-930410-5. $19.95.

Explores the problems of fraudulent credentials, how to recognize an agency offering invalid degrees, and how to resolve these abuses. Includes lists of agencies to contact to verify legitimate educational institutions.

135. Discipline in Our Schools: An Annotated Bibliography. Karnes, Elizabeth Lueder, Black, Donald D. and Downs, John. Greenwood Press, 1983. 700p. LC: 83-12847. ISBN: 0-313-23521-X. $56.95.

Extensive bibliography of books, papers, dissertations, journal articles, school district publications, and nonprint materials related to school discipline. Includes psychological aspects as well as intervention strategies.

136. Discipline with Dignity. Curwin, Richard L. and Mendler, Allen N. Assn. for Supervision and Curriculum Development, 1988. 267p. LC: 88-39922. ISBN: 0-87120-154-2. $9.95 (pbk.). ASCD Stock no. 611-88166.

This revised edition of *Taking Charge in the Classroom* offers practical techniques that have been proven effective in the school and classroom. Advocates consistent manner of handling behavior problems by helping students to consider their own actions, examine the logical consequences, and decide which results they will choose. A behavior management inventory and school discipline survey are included in appendixes.

137. Education Law: Public and Private. Valente, William D. West Publishing, 1985. v.1, 570p.; v.2, 672p. LC: 85-17784. ISBN: 0-314-87700-2. Contact publisher for price information.

Compilation of state and federal education-related laws that govern the educational efforts of schools, parents, and society.

138. Education Laws: A Compilation of Statutes in Effect Today. Edited by Ratzlaff, Leslie A. Capitol, 1988. 489p. ISBN: 0-937925-45-4. Contact publisher for price information. 2nd edition.

Contains copies of federal legislation that applies to U.S. Department of Education programs. Three separate tables of contents list by public law number, by title of statute, and by program area. In the body of the text, laws are arranged by public law number. Includes a program guide describing all Department of Education programs and the applicable public laws.

139. Educational Administration Glossary. Dejnozka, Edward L. Greenwood Press, 1983. 247p. LC: 83-5719. ISBN: 0-313-23301-2. $50.95.

Defines terms used in educational administration and provides a number of useful appendixes. Appendixes include a statement of ethics for school administrators and several directories of educational administrative organizations and agencies.

140. Educational Administration: Theory, Research, and Practice. Hoy, Wayne K. and Miskel, Cecil G. Random House, 1987. 488p. LC: 86-10185. ISBN: 0-394-34089-2. Contact publisher for price information. 3rd edition.

Uses a social-systems perspective to explore educational organizations and their functions. Provides a theoretical and historical background followed by an examination of the school as a social system, external environments, the school bureaucracy, group dynamics, and organizational effectiveness.

141. Effective School Leadership: Policy and Process. Edited by Land, John J. and Walberg, Herbert J. (NSSE Series on Contemporary Educational Issues). McCutchan, 1987. 218p. LC: 86-63774. ISBN: 0-8211-1115-9. Contact publisher for price information.

Summarizes and discusses recent research relating effective school leadership to effective schools. Reviews the philosophy underlying the purposes of education, summarizes research on educational productivity and effective schools, and discusses the characteristics of effective principals. Argues that educational reform should focus on effective leadership.

142. Encyclopedia of School Administration and Supervision. Edited by Gorton, Richard A., Schneider, Gail T. and Fisher, James C. Oryx, 1988. 321p. LC: 87-34959. ISBN: 0-89774-232-X. $74.50.

Contains 250 individually authored articles on key terms and concepts in school administration. Useful for a quick survey of a topic related to supervision and school administration. Includes subject and corporate name indexes and a guide to related topics.

143. Ethics: A Course of Study for Educational Leaders. Kimbrough, Ralph B. American Assn. of School Administrators, 1985. 87p. LC: 85-70228. ISBN: 0-87652-078-6. $8.95. Stock no. 021-00139.

Discusses the meaning and dimensions of administrative ethics. Useful to pre-service and in-service education programs, this work uses case studies to explore the ethical implications involved in a variety of administrative issues. Discussion questions pose provocative considerations following each case study. Conflicting sources of ethics, whistle blowing, and legal obligations of administrators are just some of the many issues explored in this timely work.

144. Ethics, Education and Administrative Decisions: A Book of Readings. Edited by Sola, Peter Andre. (American University Studies: Series 14, Education, v. 8). Peter Lang, 1984. 358p. LC: 84-47867. ISBN: 0-8204-0148-X. $38.55.

Explores the use of ethics in decision making in education and is addressed to administrators, students at the graduate level, parents and teachers. The objective of sensitizing administrators to ethical considerations is addressed by a discussion of ethics in decision making with case studies to illustrate utilization of ethics. Case studies include the areas of race relations, fiscal issues, and professional development.

145. The Ethics of School Administration. Strike, Kenneth A., Haller, Emil J. and Soltis, Jonas F. (Professional Ethics in Education Series). Teachers College Press, 1988. 137p. LC: 87-26740. ISBN: 0-8077-2887-X (pbk.). $12.95 (pbk.).

The first in a series of educational ethics books uses case studies to teach ethical concepts important to educational administration. Explores the process of ethical reasoning through thought-provoking studies followed by questions for further discussion.

146. Evaluation-Based Leadership: School Administration in Contemporary Perspective. Glasman, Naftaly S. (SUNY Series in Educational Leadership). State Univ. of New York Press, 1986. 198p. LC: 85-31714. ISBN: 0-88706-303-9. $52.50.

Discusses the relationship between school leadership and change. Argues that evaluation facilitates change and that evaluation is a crucial component of leadership. Effective administration requires constant assessment and evaluation of the needs of the administrator's constituency. Emphasis is placed on the role of the principal in effective leadership through evaluation.

Good Teachers: An Unblinking Look at Supply and Preparedness *See* TEACHER EDUCATION (No. 915)

147. Handbook for Educational Fund Raising: A Guide to Successful Principles and Practices for Colleges, Universities and Schools. Edited by Pray, Francis C. (Jossey-Bass Series in Higher Education). Jossey-Bass, 1981. 442p. LC: 81-81964. ISBN: 0-87589-501-8. $42.95.

Contains 71 commissioned papers including case examples, techniques, and specific strategies related to fundraising. This practical guide to development programs in higher education and private schools includes a bibliography and index.

148. Handbook of Research on Educational Administration. Edited by Boyan, Norman J. Longman, 1988. 767p. LC: 87-3663. ISBN: 0-582-28517-8. $59.95. A Project of the American Educational Research Association.

Thirty-three separately authored chapters address research about administrators and administration for the community of research scholars in educational administration. Topics addressed include decision making, equity, and policy analysis.

149. A History of Thought and Practice in Educational Administration. Campbell, Roald F., Fleming, Thomas, Newell, L. Jackson and Bennion, John W. Teachers College Press, 1987. 241p. LC: 87-1871. ISBN: 0-8077-2844-6; 0-8077-2843-8 (pbk.). $17.95 (pbk.); $27.95.

Offers a historical perspective of educational administration in public schools, colleges, and universities. Covers twentieth-century philosophy of educational administration in the United States as well as its actual practice. Includes an extensive bibliography.

150. Improving School Performance: How New School Management Techniques Can Raise Learning, Confidence, and Morale. Genck, Frederick H. Praeger, 1983. 299p. LC: 82-18127. ISBN: 0-275-90986-7. $35.00.

Written by a management consultant, this work recommends new and improved management techniques for school administration. Describes management techniques, the urgent need for reform in school administration, and offers case studies of effective school management. Emphasizes the importance of human interaction in effective administration.

151. Improving the Preparation of School Administrators: An Agenda for Reform. National Policy Board for Educational Administration. Curry School of Education, Univ. of Virginia, 1989. 34p. $6.50.

Recommends a nine-item agenda for reform in the preparation of educational administrators. Describes the agenda, discusses each agenda item in some detail, and explores the difficulties involved in implementing the agenda. Formulated by the National Policy Board for Educational Administration, this report is addressed to the public, and to the state, local, and educational agencies concerned with improvement in educational administration.

152. Introduction to Educational Administration. Campbell, Roald F., Corbally, John E. and Nystrand, Raphael O. Allyn and Bacon, 1983. 269p. LC: 82-24475. ISBN: 0-205-07983-0. $41.00. 6th edition.

Provides an overview of educational administration and assists teachers in understanding the role of the administrator and participating effectively in administration. Discusses the organizational environment and characteristics, function of administrators, fiscal responsibilities, leadership, and evaluation issues. Useful introductory textbook to the field.

Leaders for America's Schools: The Report and Papers of the National Commission on Excellence in Educational Administration *See* EDUCATIONAL REFORM (No. 253)

153. Leadership: Examining the Elusive. Edited by Sheive, Linda T. and Schoenheit, Marian B. (Yearbook of the Assn. for Supervision and Curriculum Development, 1987). Assn. for Supervision and Curriculum Development, 1987. 141p. LC: 86-73014. ISBN: 0-87120-142-9. $13.00. ASCD stock no. 610-87003.

With a focus on symbolic leadership and culture, the 1987 ASCD yearbook states that leaders' abilities to communicate intent and meaning is oftentimes more important than their actions. Nine separately authored chapters focus on the different traits and abilities required for effective leadership, as well as some of the most pressing issues and obstacles facing leaders in schools.

Litigating Intelligence: IQ Tests, Special Education and Social Science in the Courtroom *See* SPECIAL EDUCATION (No. 861)

154. The Managerial Imperative and the Practice of Leadership in Schools. Cuban, Larry. (SUNY Series in Educational Leadership). State Univ. of New York Press, 1988. 293p. LC: 87-6512. ISBN: 0-88706-593-7. $57.50.

Asserts that teaching and administering are integral activities and should not be viewed as completely separate functions. Examines the organizational experiences that link teachers and administrators, and argues that a common purpose is crucial to school improvement. Utilizes empirical data, personal experience, and conceptual knowledge to support the argument for the similarity of teacher and administrator roles.

155. Managers of Virtue: Public School Leadership in America, 1820–1980. Tyack, David and Hansot, Elizabeth. Basic Books, 1982. 312p. LC: 81-22923. ISBN: 0-465-04376-3. $11.95 (pbk.).

Provides historical view of leadership in public education from 1820 to the present. Focus is on motivation for and philosophy of public education. From mobilizing support and developing an educational system in the mid-1800s to dealing with the current series of crises in schools, school leaders have based their actions on perceived needs that reflect social and political issues of the period. Extensive notes supplement this examination of the ideologies of school leaders within a historical framework.

156. Managing Productive Schools: Toward an Ecology. Snyder, Karolyn J. and Anderson, Robert H. Academic Press, 1986. 577p. LC: 85-70463. ISBN: 0-12-654030-6. $28.00.

Intended to serve as a guide to effective principalship. Useful to students, practitioners, and researchers, this volume incorporates terminology and strategies from the business and industry sectors. A companion volume, *Competency Training for Managing Productive Schools*, offers ten leadership-training modules. Promotes a systems approach to attain successful, effective leadership.

157. The New Encyclopedia Dictionary of School Law. Gatti, Richard D. and Gatti, Daniel J. Parker Publishing, 1983. 400p. LC: 83-3956. ISBN: 0-13-612580-8. $34.95.

Serves as a general guide on legal problems that affect school administrators, teachers, students, and board members. Provides a functional knowledge of school law relating to day-to-day activities as well as other situations, such as negligence, library censorship, and parental liability. Organized like a dictionary, each topic is covered in a brief summary, description, or definition.

158. Organizational Behavior in Education. Owens, Robert G. Prentice-Hall, 1987. 332p. LC: 86-587. ISBN: 0-13-641093-6. $24.75. 3rd edition.

Addresses the theory that the culture of the organization has a tremendous influence on the behavior and philosophy of those working within the organization. Provides an overview of the history of educational administration, its philosophy, general organization theory and systems theory, organizational culture, change, and conflict. Emphasis is placed on leadership and motivation in the organization.

159. Productive School Systems for a Nonrational World. Patterson, Jerry L., Purkey, Stewart C. and Parker, Jackson V. Assn. for Supervision and Curriculum Development, 1986. 125p. LC: 86-71233. ISBN: 0-87120-136-4. $7.50 (pbk.). ASCD stock no. 611-86022.

Draws from corporate studies, sociology, and effective school research to develop a foundation for understanding the operation of educational organizations in a nonrational world. Provides examples of utilizing this theory to create productive and effective organizations. Focuses on the school district, but also discusses applying theory and practice at the school level.

160. Professional Ethics in University Administration. Edited by Stein, Ronald H. and Baca, M. Carlota. (New Directions for Higher Education, no. 33). Jossey-Bass, 1981. 100p. LC: 80-84278. ISBN: 87589-831-9. Contact publisher for price information.

Excellent compilation of articles covering the ethical implications of topics such as higher education administration, sexual harassment, student recruitment, and governmental and self-regulation. Includes policy statements on professional ethics from the American Association of University Professors and the American Association of University Administrators. A brief bibliography and index complete the volume.

161. Public School Law: Teachers and Students' Rights. McCarthy, Martha M. and Cambron-McCabe, Nelda H. Allyn and Bacon, 538p. LC: 87-1110. ISBN: 0-205-10489-4. $36.95. Second edition.

Provides a comprehensive treatment of the history and current status of public school law. Oriented toward practicing educators and school personnel, this book may also interest concerned parents and policy makers. Covers comprehensively the rights of students and teachers.

162. School Law in Changing Times. Edited by McGhehey, M.A. Natl. Organization on Legal Problems of Education, 1982. 256p. Contact publisher for price information.

Selection of papers presented at a 1981 NOLPE conference on "The Law School of School Law." Topics include home schooling, creationism, discipline by grade reduction, copyright laws, and handicapped litigation. Useful to practicing attorneys needing case citations, education law professors, and the educational practitioner needing information on legal issues affecting school operation.

163. School Law: Theoretical and Case Perspectives. Menacker, Julius. Prentice-Hall, 1987. LC: 86-8889. ISBN: 0-13-793753-9. Contact publisher for price information.

Combines an explanation of school law based on major cases and a selection of appropriate, edited court decisions. Provides educators with a legal framework for education, and the theory and principles related to legal concepts. Each chapter focuses on a concept such as due process or student rights and is followed by edited cases and a summary review of policy implications.

164. The Self-Managing School. Caldwell, Brian and Spinks, Jim M. (Education Policy Perspectives). Falmer Press, 1988. 278p. LC: 87-33077. ISBN: 1-85000-330-0. $55.00.

Outlines how schools can manage themselves, with a detailed study of an Australian self-managing school to illustrate the concept and procedures. A survey of decentralization attempts in the United Kingdom, the United States and Australia serves as background to the movement to allow school staff to administer their own programs. Practical emphasis is enhanced by policy documents, checklists, and related materials of use to school staff.

Sports Law for Educational Institutions *See* **HEALTH/PHYSICAL EDUCATION (No. 503)**

165. Staff Development for School Improvement: A Focus on the Teacher. Edited by Wideen, Marvin F. and Andrews, Ian. Falmer, 1987. 233p. LC: 87-13410. ISBN: 1-85000-171-5. $38.00.

Presents several perspectives on staff development within the school setting and its importance to creating effective schools. Separately authored chapters place staff development within the school context, explore varying approaches, and present implementation and evaluation plans. Views the teacher as the key to school improvement and staff development as a crucial aid to the teacher.

Strategies for Classroom Discipline *See* **RESOURCES FOR TEACHING (No. 815)**

166. Supervision: Human Perspectives. Sergiovanni, Thomas J. and Starratt, Robert J. McGraw-Hill, 1988. 440p. LC: 87-26045. ISBN: 0-07-056313-6. $34.95. 4th edition.

Focuses on the supervisor's role as a link to organizational, educational, and instructional systems within the school. Utilizes theoretical foundations to connect research with practice in supervision. More of the authors' own theories are introduced in this edition, particularly as related to leadership and to moral action.

167. Supervision in Education: Problems and Practices. Tanner, Daniel and Tanner, Laurel. Macmillan, 1987. 565p. LC: 85-23932. ISBN: 0-02-418950-2. Contact publisher for price information.

Focuses on educational supervision as a problem-solving process. Addresses historical, theoretical, practical, organizational, and administrative issues related to supervision. Includes teachers principals and superintendents in the discussion of supervisory and administrative roles.

168. Teaching and Managing: Inseparable Activities in Schools. Wilkinson, Cyril and Cave, Ernie. (Croom Helm Educational Management Series). Croom Helm, 1987. 189p. LC: 87-20132. ISBN: 0-7099-3693-1. $49.95.
Addressed to the practitioner or teacher in training, this work focuses on school management utilizing both theory and practical applications. Uses fictional situations to analyze management issues and potential strategies. Argues that teaching and managing are inseparable, although identifiable activities in education.

169. Theories of Educational Management. Bush, Tony. Harper & Row, 1986. 143p. ISBN: 0-06-318347-1. $30.00.
Links examples of management practice in colleges and in elementary and secondary schools within a conceptual framework. Defines educational management, considers the relationship between theory and practice, and presents five major models of management. The final chapter compares the various forms of the models. Although British in its focus, the theories and applications are relevant to many educational settings.

170. Towards the Effective School: The Problems and Some Solutions. Reid, Ken, Hopkins, David and Holly, Peter. Basil Blackwell, 1987. 305p. ISBN: 0-631-14722-5. Contact publisher for price information.
Summarizes and synthesizes current research and knowledge on effective schools. The emphasis is on secondary schools, and a blend of research, theory, and practice is used to make recommendations regarding the effectiveness of those schools. Presents strategies and guidelines to improve secondary schooling.

171. Women in Educational Administration. Shakeshaft, Charol. Sage, 1989. 220p. LC: 89-6337. ISBN: 0-8039-3612-5. Contact publisher for price information. Updated edition.
First published in 1987, this volume collects and synthesizes the literature up through 1985 in an effort to document the experiences of women administrators. Focuses on theories of organizational behavior as related to women and emphasizes the difference in administrative styles of men and women, with suggestions for the most effective administrative strategies.

Journals

172. American School Board Journal. Natl. School Board Assn., 1680 Duke St., Alexandria, VA 22314. Monthly. $38.00. ISSN: 0003-0953. 1891.

173. Educational Administration Quarterly. Sage Publications, 2111 W. Hillcrest Dr., Newbury Park, CA 91320. Quarterly. $85.00. ISSN: 0013-161X. 1964.

174. Educational Leadership. Assn. for Supervision and Curriculum Development, 125 N. West St., Alexandria, VA 22314. Monthly. $32.00. ISSN: 0013-1784. 1943.

175. Journal of College and University Law. Natl. Assn. of College and Univ. Attorneys, One Dupont Circle, Suite 620, Washington, DC 20036. Quarterly. $38.00. ISSN: 0093-8688. 1973.

176. Journal of Educational Equity and Leadership. Sage, 275 S. Beverly Dr., Beverly Hills, CA 90212. Quarterly. $53.00. 1980.

177. Journal of Law and Education. Jefferson Law Book Co., Box 1936, Cincinnati, OH 45201. Quarterly. $35.00. ISSN: 0275-6072. 1972.

178. NASSP Bulletin. Natl. Assn. of Secondary School Principals, 1904 Association Dr., Reston, VA 22091. 9/year. $7.00. ISSN: 0192-6365. 1917. Former title: *National Association of Secondary School Principals Bulletin.*

National Association of Secondary School Principals Bulletin *See* **NASSP Bulletin EDUCATIONAL ADMINISTRATION AND LAW (No. 178)**

National Elementary Principal *See* **Principal EDUCATIONAL ADMINISTRATION AND LAW (No. 180)**

179. Planning and Changing. Illinois State Univ., Dept. of Educational Administration and Foundations, 331 DeGarma, Normal, IL 61761. Quarterly. $18.00. ISSN: 0032-0684. 1970.

180. Principal. National Assn. of Elementary School Principals, 1615 Duke St., Alexandria, VA 22314. 5/year. $110.00. ISSN: 0271-6062. 1921. Former title: *National Elementary Principal.*

181. The School Administrator. American Assn. of School Administrators, 1801 N. Moore St., Arlington, VA 22209. 11/year. Membership. ISSN: 0036-6439. 1943.

Educational Psychology/Guidance/ Counseling

School psychology materials are the primary focus of this section. Counseling covers both psychological and career counseling topics. Additional career counseling and guidance information may be located in the **Vocational Education** section. Some overlap with the **Special Education** and **Measurement** sections occurs because of the interrelated aspects of counseling and screening special populations. Materials in this section contain practical approaches as well as research-based handbooks and journals.

Books

Applying Educational Psychology in the Classroom See RESOURCES FOR TEACHING (No. 774)

Behavioral Assessment in School Psychology See MEASUREMENT (No. 690)

182. Case Studies in Clinical and School Psychology. Blanco, Ralph F. and Rosenfeld, Joseph G. C.C. Thomas, 1978. 243p. LC: 78-5914. ISBN: 0-398-03807-4. $31.50.
Useful to students and practitioners, this case study text provides a representative sampling of different problems. Advocates the need to closely interrelate diagnosis and treatment in clinical and school settings. Clinical data, interventions, and workbook-type exercises are provided for discussion and research. A variety of problems (mental and physical) and appropriate interventions are described.

183. Childhood and Adolescence: Counseling Theory and Technique. Edited by Walsh, William M. McCutchan, 1985. 329p. LC: 84-61506. ISBN: 0-8211-2262-2. $25.75. Rev. edition.
Surveys the major nonclassical models of counseling. Concentrates on short-term, nonanalytic counseling techniques to assist children and adolescents in coping with adjustment problems. Contributors discuss rational-emotive therapy, reality therapy, behavior counseling, eclectic, Adlerian, Gestalt, client centered counseling, play therapy, and existential counseling. Strategies and interventions of use in school, the home, and community are presented.

184. Cognitive Behavior Therapy with Children in Schools. Hughes, Jan N. (Pergamon General Psychology Series, v. 154). Pergamon, 1988. 267p. LC: 87-7274. ISBN: 0-08-034326-0. $32.50.
Provides an account of selected cognitive behavioral approaches within the school framework. Philosophical background of cognitive behaviorism is covered, influences on current theory are reviewed, and assessment strategies are discussed. Specific interventions for six different populations are addressed in separate chapters, such as hyperactive children and depression. Research on school-based prevention is addressed in the final chapter. Supported by extensive references.

185. Cognitive Structure and Conceptual Change. Edited by West, Leo T. and Pines, A. Leon. (Educational Psychology Series). Academic Press, 1985. 274p. LC: 84-20415. ISBN: 0-12-744590-0. $35.00.
Provides instructors and researchers with methodology for presenting cognitive structures and ways in which to encourage conceptual change among students. Although science learning is used as a model in most chapters, the information, methods, and theories are applicable to all areas of learning. Addresses the conflict and resolution between intuitive knowledge and formal instruction.

186. Controlling Stress in Children. Humphrey, James H. and Humphrey, Joy N. C.C. Thomas, 1985. 195p. LC: 84-8651. ISBN: 0-398-05050-3. $26.25.
Practical guide to reducing or controlling stress in children from two to twelve years. A variety of approaches are discussed with recommendations regarding successful implementation of these approaches. Often, stress reducing activities are described for both adults and children. Research related to children and stress is used in support of each chapter. Stress reduction activities include physical activity, meditation, and progressive relaxation.

187. Counseling: A Crucial Function for the 1980s. Edited by Thurston, Alice S. and Robbins, William A. (New Directions for Community Colleges, no. 43, September 1983). Jossey-Bass, 1983. 137p. LC: 82-84180. ISBN: 87589-941-2. $7.95. ISSN: 0194-3081.
Stresses the equal importance of classroom instruction and student support services in community colleges. Individually authored chapters address current status, roles of counselors, counselor preparation, special populations, future trends, and additional resources for counseling. Descriptions of specific community college counseling programs are included.

188. Counseling Children. Thompson, Charles Lowell and Rudolph, Linda B. Brooks/Cole, 1983. 400p. LC: 82-4415. ISBN: 0-534-01151-9. $23.75.
Textbook that relates theory and practice in the counseling of children. Presents research-based strategies for helping children cope with shyness, fighting, stealing, lying, and family problems such as divorce, alcoholism, and death. The proposed second edition of this book promises to be another excellent presentation of theory and practice, with practical approaches and interventions accompanied by case studies for discussion.

189. A Counselor's Guide to Vocational Guidance Instruments. Edited by Kapes, Jerome T. and Mastie, Marjorie Moran. National Vocational Guidance Assn. (NVGA), 1982. 254p. Contact publisher for price information.
Developed specifically for counselors in schools, colleges, and agencies. Describes over 110 tests with in-depth evaluations of 40 tests. Policy statements, bibliographies, publishers' addresses, and indexes are included.

190. Crisis Counseling: Intervention and Prevention in the Schools. Edited by Sandoval, Jonathon. (School Psychology Series). L. Erlbaum, 1988. 271p. LC: 87-17341. ISBN: 0-89859-823-0. $29.95.
Presents general principles and conceptions of crisis counseling, with individual chapters devoted to particular types of crises. These crises include peer conflicts, family disruptions, illness, death, abuse, suicide, moving, teenage parenthood, and sexual orientation. The prevalence of the types of crises, and intervention and prevention strategies are discussed. Written for the benefit of school psychologists and other mental health professionals, as well as administrators and teachers.

191. Dealing with Abnormal Behavior in the Classroom. Romney, David M. (Fastback Series, no. 245). Phi Delta Kappa Educational Foundation, 1986. 40p. LC: 86-61752. ISBN: 0-87367-245-3. $.90 (pbk.).
Phi Delta Kappa's *Fastback Series* is an excellent source of brief overviews, discussions, and strategies of current topics in education written by practitioners and researchers. This particular issue addresses abnormal behavior such as hyperactivity, depression, extreme shyness, and aggressive behavior in the classroom. Each behavior is explored for possible causes, assessment tools, and intervention strategies.

192. The Dictionary of Developmental and Educational Psychology. Edited by Harre, Rom and Lamb, Roger. MIT Press, 1986. 271p. LC: 86-10400. ISBN: 0-262-58077-2. $9.95.
Dictionary of psychological and educational terms provides lengthy definitions and bibliographical references.

Educating the Young Thinker: Classroom Strategies for Cognitive Growth *See* **RESOURCES FOR TEACHING (No. 795)**

193. Effective Classroom Learning: A Behavioral Interactionist Approach to Teaching. Wheldall, Kevin and Glynn, Ted. (Theory and Practice in Education). Basil Blackwell, 1989. 189p. LC: 88-34294. ISBN: 0-631-16825-7. $55.00.
Presents a behavioral interactionist perspective on teaching and classroom management. The behavior modification approach is recommended for all areas of education, not just special education. Despite its British background, this book has general application to classroom management.

194. Ethical and Legal Issues in School Counseling. Edited by Huey, Wayne C. and Remley, Theodore P., Jr. American School Counselor Assn./American Assn. for Counseling and Development, 1988. 341p. LC: 88-34273. ISBN: 1-55620-055-2. Contact publisher for price information. AACD Order no. 79659.
Invaluable aid to practicing school counselors in dealing with legal and ethical dilemmas. Provides guidelines and information to the practitioner to assist in the decision making process. Covers ethical, legal, and legislative issues about topics such as privacy, child abuse, and group work. Clearly presents the need to consult the most current legal and research information and reprints the ethical standards from relevant organizations.

195. Ethical Standards Casebook. Callis, Robert, Pope, Sharon K. and DePauw, Mary E. American Personnel and Guidance Assn., 1982. 180p. Contact publisher for price information. 3rd edition.
Provides specific examples to illustrate and clarify the meaning and intent of the APGA ethical standards. Specific to the membership of the APGA, each standard has meaning to any responsible member of the guidance and education professions. The APGA ethical standards are reprinted, illustrated with case studies and incidents to clarify meaning, and supported with a selected bibliography and several appendixes. Appendixes include the Family Educational Rights and Privacy Act, procedures for handling ethical violations, and several other professional organizations' ethical guidelines.

196. Handbook of Behavior Therapy in Education. Edited by Witt, Joseph C., Elliott, Stephen N. and Gresham, Frank M. Plenum, 1988. 834p. LC: 88-4191. ISBN: 0-306-42633-1. $85.00.
Addresses the benefits of behavior therapy to the field of education. Contributions by individual authors offer a synthesis of research and practice with an emphasis on practical applications of interest to school psychologists, researchers, special education teachers, and teachers-in-training.

197. Handbook of Counseling in Higher Education. Gallagher, Phillip J. and Demos, George D. Praeger, 1983. 331p. LC: 82-14484. ISBN: 0-03-063216-1. $46.95.
Addresses the role of the counseling center in colleges and universities. Chapters cover the historical development of centers, confidentiality and records management, psychological assessment, academic advising, career counseling, and minority needs. The Appendix includes standards, guidelines, and an ethics statement from the American Psychological Association.

198. Handbook of Cross-Cultural Counseling and Therapy. Edited by Pedersen, Paul. Greenwood, 1987. 377p. LC: 84-12832. ISBN: 0-275-92713-X. $19.95.

Provides access to the network of resources on cross-cultural therapy and counseling with additional references to the major publications in the area. This handbook provides brief topical chapters that generally include the history, present status, fundamental assumptions and theories, and future directions of cross-cultural counseling.

199. The Handbook of School Psychology. Edited by Reynolds, Cecil R. and Gutkin, Terry B. Wiley, 1982. 1284p. LC: 81-3375. ISBN: 0-471-05869-6. $95.95.

Descriptive guide to school psychology offers current scientific information and practical recommendations for the school psychologist. Seven sections cover current status, assessment, intervention, evaluation and training, medical issues, legal issues, and international perspectives. Separately authored chapters offer differing viewpoints, philosophies, and practices. Extensive references support this encyclopedic work.

200. Helping Children Cope with Grief. Wolfelt, Alan. Accelerated Development, 1983. 176p. LC: 83-70222. ISBN: 0-915202-39-5. $49.95.

Written for parents, teachers, and counselors trying to help a child confronting the death of a loved one. Includes a range of topics directed toward the adult to help in understanding children's efforts to cope with grief. Activities, resources such as children's books, and inventory and assessment instruments are presented in this practical handbook which blends research, practice, and theory in a useful text.

201. Improving Guidance Programs. Gysbers, Norman C. and Moore, Earl J. Prentice-Hall, 1981. 212p. LC: 80-21184. ISBN: 0-13-452656-2. Contact publisher for price information.

Advocates establishing guidance as a developmental program integrated into the educational structure with its own content base. Explains how to improve school guidance programs, how to evaluate the current program, how to select and implement a program model, and how to evaluate student performance and interests. Appendixes list student competencies by domains and goals and by grade level.

202. International Perspectives on Psychology in the Schools. Edited by Saigh, Philip A. and Oakland, Thomas. Erlbaum, 1989. 277p. LC: 88-3041. ISBN: 0-8058-0110-3. $39.95.

Promotes an international perspective on practicing psychology in the schools. Describes psychological services in schools in 25 countries, including the United States. Emphasizes that child psychology is generally provided by schools rather than other public or private sectors.

203. Lawrence Kohlberg's Approach to Moral Education. Power, F. Clark, Higgins, Ann and Kohlberg, Lawrence. (Critical Assessments of Contemporary Psychology). Columbia Univ. Press, 1989. 322p. LC: 88-18970. ISBN: 0-231-05976-0. Contact publisher for price information.

Describes the Just Community Approach, particularly as it relates to moral development and education. Three experimental alternative high schools that utilize this approach are discussed, and compared to their parent high schools with research data. Kohlberg's approach is also compared to R.L. Mosher's philosophy of the democratic community. Concludes with a discussion of

applications to other school settings to foster moral training.

204. Play Therapy: Dynamics of the Process of Counseling with Children. Edited by Landreth, Garry L. C.C. Thomas, 1982. 364p. LC: 82-5798. ISBN: 0-398-04716-2. $42.25.

Designed to assist the child therapist in communicating accurately and responsively with children. Addressed to student teachers and practitioners in counseling, this collection of previously published articles focuses on the practical and theoretical issues involved in play therapy. Topics range from confidentiality to special settings such as hospital play programs. Useful overview of the subject.

205. The Psychoeducational Assessment of Preschool Children. Edited by Paget, Kathleen and Bracken, Bruce. Grune & Stratton, 1983. 551p. LC: 82-15826. ISBN: 0-8089-1475-8. $39.50.

Provides detailed information on assessment of different preschool skills in 20 separately authored chapters. Included tests cover giftedness, creativity, adaptive behavior, and auditory functioning.

206. Psychoeducational Interventions in the Schools: Methods and Procedures for Enhancing Student Competence. Edited by Maher, Charles A. and Zins, Joseph E. (Pergamon General Psychology Series, no. 150). Pergamon, 1987. 208p. LC: 87-8268. ISBN: 0-08-033632-9. $30.00.

Sourcebook of various procedures oriented toward the practice of psychological evaluation and counseling in educational settings. Responds to the need for professional information related to practical interventions and strategies in the school setting. Addresses the areas of academic achievement, cognitive development, affective functioning, socialization, and vocational preparation as part of the psychoeducational evaluation process.

207. The Psychological Foundations of Education: A Guide to Information Sources. Baatz, Olga K. and Baatz, Charles Albert. (Education Information Guide Series, v. 10). Gale, 1981. 441p. LC: 81-2832. ISBN: 0-8103-1467-3. $68.00.

Lengthy, selectively annotated bibliography of books, reports, and journal articles focuses on several areas of educational psychology. These include intellectual education, moral education, affective education, poetic education, and the self. Extensive author, title, and subject indexes are provided to aid the user.

208. Psychotherapeutic Techniques in School Psychology. Cull, John G. and Golden, Larry B. C.C. Thomas, 1984. 247p. LC: 83-17943. ISBN: 0-398-04927-0. Contact publisher for price information.

Concerned that the increasingly negative aspects of society (war, pollution, etc.) are felt by children at younger ages, this volume offers some alternative interventions that school psychologists and counselors can use. Eighteen contributed chapters on different methods and aspects of psychotherapy are presented by proponents and practitioners of those methods. Case studies for each method offer additional strategies and approaches. Methods range from Adlerian to Transactional Analysis and offer the practitioner a variety of techniques to implement for different counseling situations.

209. The School Psychologist in Nontraditional Settings: Integrating Clients, Services and Settings. Edited by D'Amato, Rik Carl and Dean, Raymond S. (School Psychology). L. Erlbaum, 1989. 223p. LC: 88-30076. ISBN: 0-89859-996-2. $29.95.

Separately authored chapters explore the idea of school psychology regardless of the setting of service. Develops a model of school psychology services applied to medical facilities, residential treatment centers, community agencies, businesses, and private practices. Stresses the concept of school psychology as an approach to problem solving and not a "setting-specific" profession.

210. School Psychology: Essentials of Theory and Practice. Reynolds, Cecil R., Gutkin, Terry B., Elliott, Stephen N. and Witt, Joseph C. Wiley, 1984. 501p. LC: 83-21918. ISBN: 0-471-08327-5. $50.95.

Reflects the current status of school psychology and explores its future development. Reviews the development of school psychology as an area of professional specialization; discusses different models of service delivery; addresses assessment techniques and interventions; and explores legal, ethical, and research issues. Appendixes include standards and ethical statements from pertinent organizations. Offers a clear overview of school psychology.

Student Stress: A Classroom Management System *See* **RESOURCES FOR TEACHING (No. 816)**

Testers and Testing: The Sociology of School Psychology *See* **MEASUREMENT (No. 718)**

211. Testing in Counseling; Uses and Misuses. Christiansen, Harley D. P. Juul Press, 1981. 96p. LC: 81-3715. ISBN: 0-915456-03-6. $11.95.

Offers guidance to the counselor or psychologist in determining the usefulness of particular tests. Provides evaluation and uses and misuses of the SAT, ACT, GATB, SCII, KOIS, and MMPI.

212. The Transfer of Cognitive Skill. Singley, Mark K. and Anderson, John R. (Cognitive Science Series, v.9). Harvard Univ. Press, 1989. 300p. LC: 88-28404. ISBN: 0-674-90340-4. $30.00.

Applies cognitive psychology to the transfer of learning. Assesses the ACT* theory of skill acquisition and its transfer, or the study of how knowledge acquired in one situation applies to other situations. A rather technical presentation is supported by an extensive bibliography and adequate indexes.

Journals

213. Career Development Quarterly. American Assn. for Counseling and Development, 5999 Stevenson Ave., Alexandria, VA 22304. Quarterly. $20.00. ISSN: 0889-4019. 1952.

214. Cognition and Instruction. L. Erlbaum, 365 Broadway, Suite 102, Hillsdale, NJ 07642. Quarterly. $55.00. 1984.

215. Contemporary Educational Psychology. Academic Press, 1250 Sixth Ave., San Diego, CA 92101. Quarterly. $89.00. ISSN: 0361-476X. 1976.

216. Counselor Education and Supervision. Assn. for Counselor Education and Supervision, American Assn. for Counseling Development, 5999 Stevenson Ave., Alexandria, VA 22304. 4/year. $12.00. ISSN: 0011-0035. 1961.

CUPA Journal *See* **Journal of the College and University Personnel Association EDUCATIONAL PSYCHOLOGY/ GUIDANCE/COUNSELING (No. 223)**

CUPA News *See* **Journal of the College and University Personnel Association EDUCATIONAL PSYCHOLOGY/ GUIDANCE/COUNSELING (No. 223)**

217. Educational Psychologist. L. Erlbaum, 365 Broadway, Hillsdale, NJ 07642. 3/year. $80.00. ISSN: 0046-1520. 1963.

218. Elementary School Guidance & Counseling. American Assn. for Counseling Development, 5999 Stevenson Ave., Alexandria, VA 22304. 4/year. $20.00. ISSN: 0013-5976. 1967.

219. Journal of Counseling and Development. American Assn. for Counseling and Development, 5999 Stevenson Ave., Alexandria, VA 22304. 10/year. $40.00. ISSN: 0748-9833. 1922. Former title: *Personnel and Guidance Journal.*

220. Journal of Counseling Psychology. American Psychological Assn., 1200 17th St., NW, Washington, DC 20036. Quarterly. $80.00. ISSN: 0022-0167. 1954.

Journal of Cross-Cultural Psychology *See* **MULTICULTURAL EDUCATION (No. 767)**

221. Journal of Educational Psychology. American Psychological Assn., 1400 N. Uhle St., Arlington, VA 22201. Quarterly. $120.00. ISSN: 0022-0663. 1910.

Journal of Multicultural Counseling and Development *See* **MULTICULTURAL EDUCATION (No. 768)**

222. Journal of School Psychology. Pergamon, Maxwell House, Fairview Park, Elmsford, NY 10523. Quarterly. $90.00. ISSN: 0022-4405. 1963.

223. Journal of the College and University Personnel Association. College and Univ. Personnel Assn., Suite 210, 11 Dupont Circle, Washington, DC 20036. Quarterly. $30.00. ISSN: 0010-0935. 1949. Former titles: *CUPA News*; *CUPA Journal.*

224. Language Learning: A Journal of Applied Linguistics. Research Club in Language Learning, 178 Frieze Bldg., Univ. of Michigan, Ann Arbor, MI 48109-1285. Quarterly. $50.00. ISSN: 0023-8333. 1948.

NASPA *See* **NASPA Journal EDUCATIONAL PSYCHOLOGY/GUIDANCE/COUNSELING (No. 225)**

225. NASPA Journal. Natl. Assn. of Student Personnel Administrators, 1700 18th St., NW, Suite 301, Washington, DC 20009-2508. Quarterly. $25.00. ISSN: 0027-6014. 1963. Former Title: *NASPA.*

Personnel and Guidance Journal *See* **Journal of Counseling and Development EDUCATIONAL PSYCHOLOGY/ GUIDANCE/COUNSELING (No. 219)**

226. Psychology in the Schools. Clinical Psychology Publishing, 4 Conant Square, Brandon, VT 05733. Quarterly. $80.00. ISSN: 0033-3085. 1964.

227. The School Counselor. American Assn. for Counseling and Development, American School Counselors Assn., 5999 Stevenson Ave., Alexandria, VA 22304. 5/year. $25.00. ISSN: 0036-6536. 1954.

Educational Reform

The national emphasis on educational reform in the 1980s led to the publication of a number of books and reports. While this section is not an exhaustive listing of these materials, it does contain some of the most significant and frequently referred to reports. Many of the reports were commissioned by government bodies or professional organizations. Generally inexpensive, these reports should be in all library collections because they address some of the most difficult educational questions confronting American society in a particular decade. Reports that are no longer in print may also be available in microfiche as a part of the ERIC system. No journals were included in this section, although many journals address the national issue of educational reform in selected articles.

Books

228. Academic Preparation for College: What Students Need to Know and Be Able to Do. The College Board, 1983. 46p. Free.

A product of the College Board's Educational Equality Project, this report advocates improving academic or college preparatory education. Outlines the skills and knowledge needed by college entrants, and how high schools can achieve the needed outcomes.

Academic Work and Educational Excellence: Raising Student Productivity *See* HISTORY AND PHILOSOPHY OF EDUCATION (No. 606)

229. Achieving Excellence in Our Schools:...By Taking Lessons from America's Best-Run Companies. Lewis, James Jr. J.L. Wilkerson, 1986. 207p. LC: 85-51152. ISBN: 0-915253-03-8. $24.95.

Author presents his "success-emulation" theory of adopting successful practices and principles of other organizations as appropriate to improve a separate organization. Advocates studying the methods of successful businesses, particularly those that value their human resources, and applying those methods to schools. Numerous recommendations are included in this thought-provoking book.

230. Action for Excellence: A Comprehensive Plan to Improve Our Nation's Schools. Education Commission of the States, Task Force on Education for Economic Growth. Education Commission of the States, 1983. 50p. $5.00.

Calls for urgent action by states and local communities to improve public education. Outlines the problems and challenges faced by education and provides specific remedies. Promotes school-business partnerships.

231. Allies in Educational Reform: How Teachers, Unions, and Administrators Can Join Forces for Better Schools. Rosco, Jerome M., Zager, Robert with Casner-Lotto, Jill and associates. (Jossey-Bass Education Series). Jossey-Bass, 1989. 353p. LC: 88-46095. ISBN: 1-55542-158-X. $24.95. A Work in America Institute Publication.

Divided into two sections, this report examines how to develop alliances to improve urban public education, with specific recommendations. The main report is followed by 11 case studies of effective labor-management alliances in public schools.

232. Bad Times, Good Schools. Edited by Frymier, Jack. Kappa Delta Pi, West Lafayette, IN, 1983. 104p. LC: 82-21261. ISBN: 0-912099-01-1. $6.50.

Six essays from Kappa Delta Pi's Good Schools Project address the erosion of quality public schooling and the structure, characteristics, and development of good schools.

233. ". . .The Best of Educations:" Reforming America's Public Schools in the 1980's. Chance, William. John D. and Catherine T. MacArthur Foundation, 1986. 201p. LC: 86-83266. Contact publisher for price information.

Reviews the national educational reform movement of the 1980s with emphasis on California, Colorado, Florida, Illinois, South Carolina, Texas, and Washington. Supports the efforts already undertaken, but recommends further efforts toward reform. Includes a summary of the major national reports.

234. Blue Ribbon Commissions and Higher Education: Changing Academe from the Outside. Johnson, Janet Rogers-Clarke and Marcus, Laurence R. (ASHE-ERIC Higher Education Report, no. 2, 1986). Assn. for the Study of Higher Education, 1986. 99p. LC: 86-71526. ISBN: 0-913317-29-2. $10.00. ISSN: 0884-0040.

Reviews the activities of blue ribbon commissions and evaluates their effectiveness. Focuses on college level commissions, although some of the conclusions can be applied to other levels of educational commissions. In-depth evaluations of the Wessel and Rosenberg Commissions are used as models for assessment.

235. A Call for Change in Teacher Education. National Commission for Excellence in Teacher Education. American Assn. of Colleges for Teacher Education, 1985. 56p. LC: 85-60490. ISBN: 0-89333-035-3. $7.00.
Organized around five issues of concern toward the improvement of teacher education: supply and demand for quality teachers, content of teacher education programs, accountability for teacher education, resource requirements, and conditions required to support highest quality of teaching. Sixteen recommendations to address these concerns follow an analysis of the issues.

236. The Closing of the American Mind: Education and the Crisis of Reason. Bloom, Allan. Simon and Schuster, 1987. 392p. LC: 86-24768. ISBN: 0-671-47990-3. $18.45.
Bloom's controversial work discusses the state of intellectual life in the United States and the impact of higher education on the development of the individual.

College: The Undergraduate Experience in America *See* HIGHER AND CONTINUING EDUCATION (No. 529)

Colleges of Education: Perspectives on Their Future *See* TEACHER EDUCATION (No. 910)

237. A Conspiracy of Good Intentions: America's Textbook Fiasco. Tyson-Bernstein, Harriet. Council for Basic Education, 1988. 113p. Contact publisher for price information.
Critical examination of the process of textbook adoption and textbook publishing. Explores the relationship between school district demands and the development of textbooks. Discusses the content of quality textbooks and how many textbooks are watered down in the effort to sell to several diverse markets. Presents an ideal textbook adoption process and statistical tables with cost of textbooks per state per pupil as well as estimated industry sales by state. Provocative review of the textbook adoption process.

Culture Wars: School and Society in the Conservative Restoration, 1969–1984 *See* HISTORY AND PHILOSOPHY OF EDUCATION (No. 616)

Ed School: A Brief for Professional Education *See* HIGHER AND CONTINUING EDUCATION (No. 536)

238. Education by Choice: The Case for Family Control. Coons, John E. and Sugarman, Stephen D. Univ. of California Press, 1978. 249p. LC: 77-20318. ISBN: 0-520-03613-1. $27.50.
Timely discussion of the role of choice in the provision of schooling. Examines variations of the voucher system, methods of implementation, and philosophical issues.

239. Education on Trial: Strategies for the Future. Edited by Johnston, William J. Institute for Contemporary Studies, 1985. 352p. ISBN: 0-917616-72-3. $29.95.
Directed to policymakers, educators, parents, and administrators, this compilation of contributed papers addresses the issue of educating all students to the maximum potential. Recommendations to achieve excellence are offered by an array of educational experts. Discusses broad issues as well as specific problems, with a special emphasis on educational standards.

240. Educational Reforms in the United States: A Report of the Japan-United States Cooperative Study on Education. Japanese Study Group, Japan-United States Cooperative Study on Education. Japan-United States Cooperative Study on Education, 1987. 95p. Contact publisher for price information.
Provides unique perspective on the history and current status of educational reform in the United States by the Japanese Study Group of a cooperative Japan-U.S. enterprise. Addresses secondary and higher education, with emphasis on the need for both equality and diversity in American education.

241. Everybody Counts: A Report to the Nation on the Future of Mathematics Education. National Academy Press, 1989. 114p. LC: 88-37684. ISBN: 0-309-03977-0. $7.95.
Sponsored by the National Research Council, this report calls for reforms in mathematics education and outlines specific changes needed to meet student needs. Emphasizes the increased understanding of mathematics required for individual occupations and to maintain the nation's position globally in technological and economic advancement.

242. Excellence in Education. Edited by Mangieri, John N. Texas Christian Univ. Press, 1985. 247p. LC: 85-50539. ISBN: 0-87565-020-1. $25.00.
Contains nine essays on achieving excellence in education. Each essay addresses the obstacles blocking excellence in a particular area of education and provides recommendations and strategies for attaining excellence.

243. Experiences in School Improvement: The Story of 16 American Districts. Paulu, Nancy. (Programs for the Improvement of Practice, PIP 88-843). Office of Educational Research and Improvement, U.S. Dept. of Education, 1988. 79p. Contact publisher for price information.
Describes programs in 16 districts participating in Project Education Reform as viewed by school superintendents and principals. Includes background information on the project and individual programs as well as results and recommendations.

244. First Lessons: A Report on Elementary Education in America. Bennett, William J. U.S. Department of Education, 1986. 83p. ISBN: 0-318-21680-9. $4.25.
Discusses the condition and direction of elementary education in America. Offers Bennett's views and recommendations regarding the improvement of elementary education. Of interest to parents, legislators, school administrators, and teachers.

245. From the Campus: Perspectives on the School Reform Movement. Edited by Cohen, Sol and Solmon, Lewis C. Praeger, 1989. 239p. LC: 89-33960. ISBN: 0-275-93263-X. $42.95.
Directed to the general public, concerned parents, and educational policymakers, this collection of essays attempts to improve and enhance the overall public discourse about education. Contributors from UCLA's Graduate School of Education offer diverse viewpoints regarding school reform. While offering recommendations and courses of action, the contributors recognize the complexity of the school reform movement and intend that this volume serve as a catalyst for further debate among teacher educators.

Good Teachers: An Unblinking Look at Supply and Preparedness *See* TEACHER EDUCATION (No. 915)

246. The Great School Debate: Which Way for American Education?. Edited by Gross, Beatrice and Gross, Ronald. Simon & Schuster, 1985. 544p. LC: 84-27555. ISBN: 0-671-54136-6. $14.95 (pbk.).

The great school debate begins after the publication of the 1983 report *A Nation at Risk*. The text begins with a reproduction of that report and a comparative summary of it and other national reports on education. The remainder of the text presents the views of the contending voices and bodies in the great debate on educational reform with special emphasis on the concept of "excellence" that characterized *A Nation at Risk*.

247. High School: A Report on Secondary Education in America. Boyer, Ernest L. Harper & Row, 1985. 363p. LC: 83-47528. ISBN: 0-06-091224-3. $9.95.

Sponsored by the Carnegie Foundation for the Advancement of Teaching, this report examines the current condition of American public secondary education. Recommendations for improved secondary education are directed to students, teachers, administrators, policy-makers, and college faculty.

248. Horace's Compromise: The Dilemma of the American High School. Sizer, Theodore R. Houghton Mifflin, 1985. 256p. LC: 83-18500. ISBN: 0-395-37753-6. $8.95.

Urges renewed focus on the importance of teaching in high schools. Sponsored by an inquiry into adolescent education, A Study of High Schools, this book addresses both learning and teaching in secondary education.

249. Humanities in America: A Report to the President, the Congress, and the American People. Cheney, Lynne V. National Endowment for the Humanities, 1988. 47p. Contact publisher for price information.

The state of the teaching and learning of humanities is explored through the impact of colleges, universities, television, libraries, and museums that bring humanities education to the public. Includes recommendations for improvement in humanities education.

Inside Schools: A Collaborative View *See* ELEMENTARY/ SECONDARY EDUCATION (No. 395)

250. Insult to Intelligence: The Bureaucratic Invasion of Our Classrooms. Smith, Frank. Heinemann, 1988. 289p. LC: 88-8082. ISBN: 0-425-08478-X. $14.00 (pbk.). Revised edition.

Provocative discussion of the dangers of programmatic instruction. Argues that prescribed methods and curricula undermine the student's ability to learn and the teacher's ability to instruct. Focuses on the tyranny of testing and generalized expectations versus the importance of good teaching and individual development.

251. Investing in Our Children: Business and the Public Schools. Committee for Economic Development, Research and Policy Committee. Committee for Economic Development, 1985. 107p. LC: 85-15189. ISBN: 0-87186-780-X. $11.50.

Focuses on four educational reform issues: employability, educational investment, teachers and schools, and business/school collaboration. Research was based on papers, reform reports, and a commissioned national survey. Extensive recommendations include public schools, government, and private sector participation.

252. James Madison High School: A Curriculum for American Students. Bennett, William J. U.S. Dept. of Education, 1987. 49p. ISBN: 065-000-00350-3. $2.50 (pbk.).

Proposes former Secretary of Education Bennett's ideal curriculum for the secondary school. Focus is on core courses in math, science, English, and social studies with supplemental courses in foreign languages, physical education, art, and music. Course descriptions are provided and sample student schedules illustrate the possibilities for incorporating elective courses. Profiles of excellent secondary schools are offered as models and incentives.

253. Leaders for America's Schools: The Report and Papers of the National Commission on Excellence in Educational Administration. Edited by Griffiths, Daniel E., Stout, Robert T. and Forsyth, Patrick B. McCutchan, 1988. 470p. LC: 88-60449. ISBN: 0-8211-0616-3. Contact publisher for price information.

Addresses the need for capable, visionary leadership in education. Specific recommendations are followed by commissioned papers that serve as background information. Focuses on the roles of superintendents and principals. International review of these issues is included through the background papers.

254. Making the Grade: Report of the Twentieth Century Fund Task Force on Federal Elementary and Secondary Education Policy. Twentieth Century Fund, 1983. 174p. ISBN: 0-87078-151-0. $6.00.

A lengthy background paper on the federal role in education serves as a focus for an independent task force to respond to issues, statistics, and recommendations. Discusses historical trends in federal policy as well as what programs and policies should be.

255. Marva Collins' Way. Collins, Marva and Tamarkin, Civia. J.P. Tarcher, Distributed by Houghton Mifflin, 1982. 228p. LC: 82-10516. ISBN: 0-87477-235-4. $6.95.

Biographical portrait of Marva Collins, her teaching methods, and school reform. A provocative view of one teacher's well-publicized program of instruction.

256. A Nation at Risk: The Imperative for Educational Reform. National Commission on Excellence in Education. U.S. Dept. of Education, 1983. 65p. ISBN: 0-318-11805-X. $4.50. Also available as ERIC Document No. ED 226 006.

A core report on the need for educational reform that should be in every library collection. Examines the quality of American education and recommendations to improve it. The commissioned papers serving as the framework for this report are available through the ERIC System.

257. A Nation Prepared: Teachers for the 21st Century. Carnegie Forum on Education and the Economy, Task Force on Teaching as a Profession. Carnegie Forum on Education and the Economy, 1986. 135p. LC: 86-11743. ISBN: 0-9616685-0-4. $9.95.

The Task Force on Teaching as a Profession urges educational reform in order to improve America's ability to uphold and compete in industry, commerce, social justice and progress, and democracy. Specific reforms are proposed as are the benefits and costs of improved education.

258. The Nation Responds: Recent Efforts to Improve Education. U.S. Department of Education. 1984. 229p. ISBN: 0-318-18790-6. $7.50.

Reports reform efforts in each of the 50 states and the District of Columbia in both narrative and chart format. Selected programs by local schools, postsecondary institutions, the private sector, and associations are also highlighted. Published as a follow-up to *A Nation at Risk.*

259. The Nation's Report Card: Improving the Assessment of Student Achievement. National Academy of Education, Harvard Graduate School of Education, 1987. 76p. $9.00.

Report of the Study Group formed by the U.S. Secretary of Education in 1986 to examine the procedures used to update the nation's report card, issued by the National Assessment of Educational Progress (NAEP). Reviews the history of NAEP, its achievements, and recommendations for improvement. Includes a list of 46 commissioned papers, available through the ERIC system.

260. Neighborhood Organizing for Urban School Reform. Williams, Michael R. Teachers College Press, 1989. 182p. LC: 88-29439. ISBN: 0-8077-2931-0. $27.95.

Explores the reasons urban schools fail, as well as the conditions required for change. Emphasis is placed on the neighborhood organization as the change agent. Historical background, case studies, and extensive notes and references form part of this convincing argument for the attainable improvement of urban schools.

261. The New Servants of Power: A Critique of the 1980s School Reform Movement. Shea, Christine M., Kahane, Ernest and Sola, Peter. (Contributions to the Study of Education). Greenwood, 1989. 203p. LC: 88-15490. ISBN: 0-313-25475-3. $39.95.

A collection of critical essays that assesses the national educational reports, books, and related policy that have spurred the contemporary debate about school and educational reform. Some of the sociopolitical factors debated in the school reform literature and the claims of reconciliation proposed are the concept of work and education, equity and excellence, the new curriculum, discrimination, and continuing education.

262. Our Children and Our Country: Improving America's Schools and Affirming the Common Culture. Bennett, William J. Simon and Schuster, 1988. 238p. LC: 88-17498. ISBN: 0-671-67062-X. Contact publisher for price information.

Former U.S. Secretary of Education Bennett's controversial views on the state of American education are expressed in the edited versions of the 24 speeches delivered during his tenure in that office.

263. The Paideia Proposal: An Educational Manifesto. Adler, Mortimer J. Macmillan, 1982. 84p. LC: 82-7169. ISBN: 0-02-064100-1. $4.95.

Proposes educational reform through a grass roots movement designed to improve opportunities for American youth, economic prospects, and democracy. Affirms the importance of equal educational opportunity through public schools and provides specific recommendations for reform.

264. The Path to Excellence: Quality Assurance in Higher Education. Marcus, Laurence R., Leone, Anita O. and Goldberg, Edward D. (ASHE-ERIC/Higher Education Research Report, no. 1, 1983). Assn. for the Study of Higher Education, 1983. 68p. ISBN: 0-913317-00-4. $7.50. ISSN: 0737-1292.

Explores the issues surrounding educational quality and public policy, particularly the role of voluntary accreditation as a measure of institutional excellence.

265. A Place Called School: Prospects for the Future. Goodlad, John I. McGraw-Hill, 1984. 396p. LC: 83-9859. ISBN: 0-07-023627-5 (pbk.). $12.00.

Proposes an agenda for school improvement after extensive description and analysis of the critical issues currently confronting schools. Studies individual schools as models of good and poor educational institutions.

Politics of School Reform, 1870–1940 *See* HISTORY AND PHILOSOPHY OF EDUCATION (No. 659)

Power and the Promise of School Reform: Grassroots Movements During the Progressive Era *See* HISTORY AND PHILOSOPHY OF EDUCATION (No. 660)

266. Profiling Excellence in America's Schools. Roueche, John E. and Baker, George A. III, with Mullin, Patricia L. and Omaha Boy, Nancy Hess. American Assn. of School Administrators, 1986. 177p. LC: 86-70022. ISBN: 0-87652-106-5. $16.95.

Recommends improvements in teaching and educational leadership in secondary schools through an in-depth study of teachers, principals, and climate in exceptional schools. Introduces the Model of Excellent Schools.

267. Raising Academic Standards: A Guide to Learning Improvement. Keimig, Ruth Talbott. (ASHE-ERIC/Higher Education Research Report, no. 4, 1983). Assn. for the Study of Higher Education, 1983. 89p. LC: 84-117233. ISBN: 0-913317-03-9. $7.50. ISSN: 0737-1292.

Offers a guide for improvement in college programs with specific, pragmatic steps for implementation. Discusses the advantages and disadvantages of academic standards.

268. Reforming Education: The Opening of the American Mind. Adler, Mortimer J. Edited by Van Doren, Geraldine. Macmillan, 1988. 362p. LC: 88-8339. ISBN: 0-02-500551-0. $19.95.

Presents Adler's educational philosophy through essays written from 1939 to 1988. Emphasizes the importance of a "great books program" in education.

269. Reforming Schools: Problems in Program Implementation and Evaluation. Abt, Wendy Peter and Magidson, Jay. (Contemporary Evaluation Research, v. 4). Sage Publications, 1980. 230p. LC: 80-23339. ISBN: 0-8039-1459-8. Contact publisher for price information.

Describes the Experimental Schools Program and general program evaluation. Discusses methodologies for program evaluation with emphasis on the median polish and causal modeling techniques.

270. Reforming Teacher Education: The Impact of the Holmes Group Report. Edited by Soltis, Jonas F. Teachers College Press, 1987. 140p. LC: 87-6427. ISBN: 0-8077-2871-3. $11.95.

Includes invited papers from the first symposium to celebrate Teachers College's centennial. Reacts to the recommendations of the Holmes Group in *Tomorrow's Teachers.*

271. Schooling for Tomorrow: Directing Reforms to Issues that Count. Edited by Sergiovanni, Thomas J. and Moore, John H. Allyn and Bacon, 1989. 403p. LC: 88-14530. ISBN: 0-205-11690-6. $36.95.

Presents papers delivered at a 1987 conference on restructuring schooling. Focuses on moving reform efforts in new directions that will carry into the next century. Emphasizes daily practices in the classroom as the primary area for causing change and improvement.

272. Schools in Crisis: Training for Success or Failure?. Sommer, Carl. Cahill, 1984. 335p. LC: 83-71106. ISBN: 0-9610810-0-7(pbk.); 0-961-0810-1-5. $13.95.

This personal critique of American education provides balance with its conservative and controversial recommendations to reform education.

273. The Schools We Deserve: Reflections on the Educational Crises of Our Times. Ravitch, Diane. Basic Books, 1985. 337p. LC: 84-45303. ISBN: 0-465-07236-4. $19.95.

Collection of essays by Ravitch offers her views on the interrelationship between society and education. While pointing out the problems and issues confronting education, the Introduction provides an optimistic view of the current status and future of American schooling.

274. Selling Students Short: Classroom Bargains and Academic Reform in the American High School. Sedlak, Michael W., Wheeler, Christopher W., Pullin, Diana C. and Cusick, Philip A. Teachers College Press, 1986. 225p. LC: 86-14539. ISBN: 0-8077-2818-7. Contact publisher for price information.

Examines and summarizes reform efforts and explores the effect of interactions between students, teachers, and administrators on academic standards. Focuses on the role of disengaged students in the learning process as a major factor in academic decline.

Social Goals and Educational Reform: American Schools in the Twentieth Century *See* **HISTORY AND PHILOSOPHY OF EDUCATION (No. 662)**

275. Straight Shooting: What's Wrong with America and How to Fix It. Silber, John. Harper & Row, 1989. 336p. LC: 89-45065. ISBN: 0-06-016184-1. Contact publisher for price information.

Discusses the decline of modern American society and the need to reintroduce and reinforce values and moral education. Offers recommendations to reverse this decline by focusing on critical evaluation of the problems rather than rigid adherence to doctrines and ideologies. Suggests that a combination of traditional values and critical examination of beliefs will lead to a more productive educational system and society.

276. Time for Results: The Governors' 1991 Report on Education. National Governors' Association, 1986. 171p. $12.95. National Governors' Association Center for Policy Research and Analysis.

A summary of a 1985 meeting that addresses seven issues confronting education: salaries, administration, parent involvement, readiness, technology, school facilities, and college quality. Includes strategies for monitoring progress in addressing these seven issues. Full copies of the seven task force reports with bibliographies are also available.

277. To Secure the Blessings of Liberty: Report of the National Commission on the Role and Future of State Colleges and Universities. American Assn. of State Colleges and Universities, 1986. 53p. LC: 86-22338. ISBN: 0-88044-080-5. $14.50.

Identifies some of the social, political, economic, and educational conditions confronting public higher education. Proposes a series of policy recommendations for governmental and educational leaders to use in improving the quality of American life. Delineates the role state colleges and universities should take in the national effort of educational reform.

Tomorrow's Teachers: A Report of the Holmes Group *See* **TEACHER EDUCATION (No. 936)**

Visions of Reform: Implications for the Education Profession *See* **TEACHER EDUCATION (No. 939)**

278. What Next? More Leverage for Teachers. Edited by Green, Joslyn. (Teacher Renaissance Series, TR-86-3). Education Commission of the States, 1986. 49p. ISBN: 0-318-22546-8. $12.50.

Remarks from educational experts interviewed individually for this report are grouped according to topic. Recommendations to improve education and the teaching profession are offered in both general and pragmatic terms.

Educational Research/Statistics

In the area of research, included books cover the research process, conducting research start-to-finish, how to conduct classroom (action) research, and applying techniques such as case study and the qualitative method. Handbooks and encyclopedias are also included. Books in the field of statistics cover theoretical and methodological areas and also works that are compilations of statistics in education. Both fields are represented by a great number of textbooks rather than trade books. Also, the British publishing market is a strong influence in educational research; some important British publications are included.

Books

279. After the School Bell Rings. Grant, Carl A. and Sleeter, Christine E. Taylor & Francis, 1986. 294p. LC: 85-29404. ISBN: 1-85000-085-9; 1-85000-086-7 (pbk.). $36.00; $18.00 (pbk.).

Illuminating, in-depth research into the complexities of school life, in this case a midwestern junior high school, and what happens *After the School Bell Rings* from a number of vantage points. An ethnographic case study approach was used to collect the data during a three-year period of visits, observations and interviews, and examination of documents. The researchers examined race, class, gender, and handicap from the point of view of students, teachers, and administrators.

280. Applying Educational Research: A Practical Guide for Teachers. Borg, Walter R. Longman, 1987. 327p. LC: 86-15382. ISBN: 0-582-28673-5. $26.95. 2nd edition.

The goal of this textbook is to help the reader become an intelligent consumer of educational research literature by taking the reader through sequential steps in the research process: locating sources of information and evaluating research reports and the educational measures and statistics used in them. Concludes with examples of studies and application of principles learned.

281. Case Study Research in Education: A Qualitative Approach. Merriam, Sharon B. (Jossey-Bass Education Series); (Jossey-Bass Higher Education Series); (Jossey-Bass Social and Behavioral Science Series). Jossey-Bass, 1988. 226p. LC: 88-42795. ISBN: 1-55542-108-3. $21.95.

The two-fold purpose of this text is to delineate what a qualitative case study is and present the mechanics of conducting a case study—designing the study, collecting and analyzing data, and writing the case report (Part One). Chapters in Parts Two and Three can be followed in sequential steps to complete the research investigation of a topic using the qualitative case-study method.

282. Completing Dissertations in the Behavioral Sciences and Education. Long, Thomas J., Convey, John J. and Chwalek, Adele R. (Jossey-Bass Higher Education Series); (Jossey-Bass Social and Behavioral Science Series). Jossey-Bass, 1985. 210p. LC: 85-45063. ISBN: 0-87589-658-8. $21.95.

Presents a systematic approach to the steps in the dissertation writing process, beginning with the choice of a topic and concluding with the final oral defense. An interesting first chapter discusses overcoming obstacles to completing dissertations and a sample timeline for completing the dissertation is provided.

283. Condition of Education. National Center for Education Statistics. U.S. Government Printing Office, 1975–. LC: 75-643861. $5.50 Volumes 1, 2 (1989); $6.50 Volume 3 (1989). ISSN: 0098-4752; 3 Volumes; Stock no. 065-000-00377-5.

This annual series reports statistical information (indicators) on the most significant national measures of the condition and progress of and the important developments and trends in education. For the 1989 edition, the first two volumes address elementary and secondary education (Volume 1) and postsecondary education (Volume 2). Volume 3 contains the technical data, supplemental information, and data sources.

284. Conducting Educational Research. Tuckman, Bruce W. Harcourt Brace Jovanovich, 1988. 536p. LC: 87-80737. ISBN: 0-15-512982-1. $26.00. 3rd edition.

This third edition has been revised to include some new features—worksheets, a chapter on the case-study approach, new sets of examples and sample studies. The focus is still on the "variable" as the building block of a research study.

285. Decision-Oriented Educational Research. Cooley, William K. and Bickel, William. Kluwer-Nijhoff, 1986. 297p. LC: 85-14828. ISBN: 0-89838-201-7. $42.00.

Decision-oriented educational research (DOER) is applied research designed to help educators considering educational policy to improve an educational system or manage a system on a day-to-day basis. Following background information on and some basic generalizations about the DOER method, case histories, with details of specific areas of DOER activity with the Pittsburgh public schools, are detailed.

286. Digest of Education Statistics. National Center for Education Statistics. U.S. Government Printing Office, 1975–. LC: sc825029. $19.00 (1988). ISSN: 0502-4102; Stock no. 065-000-00293-1.

An annual abstract of statistical information on American education for all levels from nursery school through graduate school including federal programs. A wide range of subjects is covered and updated with each *Digest* : number of schools and colleges, teachers, enrollments, graduates, finances, libraries, etc. Data are drawn from government and private sources, especially the Center's surveys and activities.

287. Educational Research Methodology and Measurement: An International Handbook. Edited by Keeves, John P. (Advances in Education Series). Pergamon, 1988. 832p. LC: 88-18023. ISBN: 0-08-036510-8. $125.00.

The bulk of the 115 articles in this handbook were drawn from the *International Encyclopedia of Education*, with 24 additional articles prepared for this volume as an update of developments since the *Encyclopedia* was published. Four sections cover methods of educational inquiry; creation, diffusion, and utilization of knowledge; measurement for educational research; and research techniques and statistical analysis.

288. Effective Schools: A Summary of Research. Edited by Block, Alan W. Educational Research Service, 1983. 125p. LC: 84-119175. $15 subscribers; $30 non-subscribers.

A large body of research that was produced in the 1970s on instructionally effective schools, i.e., high levels of student achievement and performance. Effectiveness is analyzed against such interacting factors as instructional staff, leadership, and school/class size. These "Research Briefs" are produced periodically by Educational Research Service and made available to ERS subscribers and non-subscribers.

289. Encyclopedia of Educational Research. Edited by Mitzel, Harold E. Free Press, 1982. LC: 82-2332. ISBN: 0-02-900450-0 (set). $315.00. 5th edition; 4 volumes; Sponsored by the American Educational Research Association.

This fifth edition of the *Encyclopedia* continues to present "a critical synthesis and interpretation of reported educational research" with new information and developments that have occurred in educational research in the interval between the fourth and this edition. The four-volume set includes 256 articles with individual bibliographies and an extensive index in volume four.

290. The Enquiring Teacher: Supporting and Sustaining Teacher Research. Edited by Nias, Jennifer and Groundwater-Smith, Susan. Taylor & Francis, 1988. 273p. LC: 88-16376. ISBN: 1-85000-295-9; 1-85000-296-7 (pbk.). $38.00; $19.00 (pbk.).

A collection of essays by a cross-section of contributors focusing on the British movement to provide enquiry-based courses in teacher education, pre-service and in-service. Provides the rationale for such courses and describes programs and current developments.

291. Finances of Public School Systems in 1985–86. U.S. Bureau of the Census. (1986 Governmental Finances Series). U.S. Government Printing Office, April 1988. 62p. LC: 80-644330. $3.75. ISSN: 0270-8868; Stock no. 003-024-06839-7.

Provides statistics on the revenue, expenditure, debt, and financial assets of school systems nationally, by states and for individual school systems having 15,000 or more enrollment. Includes local government higher education systems as well as elementary and secondary systems.

292. Interviewing in Educational Research. Powney, Janet and Watts, Mike. (Routledge Education Books). Routledge, Kegan & Paul, 1987. 205p. ISBN: 0-710-20623-2. Contact publisher for price information.

A practical guide on the technique of interviewing in educational research using a mixture of discussion and advice. Covers style, issues of ethics, how to prepare and conduct interviews, and more. Six case studies of interviews conducted in a variety of educational research settings are included.

293. Issues in Educational Research: Qualitative Methods. Burgess, Robert G. Taylor & Francis, 1985. 289p. LC: 85-6754. ISBN: 1-85000-036-0; 1-85000-035-2 (pbk.). $36.00; $20.00 (pbk.).

Essays concerned with issues in educational research that arise out of using qualitative methods of investigation: the relationship between theory and method, problems teachers face, contributions to social policy. Covers educational settings from preschool through higher education.

294. Library Research Guide to Education: Illustrated Search Strategy and Sources. Kennedy, James. (Library Research Guide Series, no. 3). Pierian, 1979. LC: 79-88940. ISBN: 0-87650-115-3. $25.00.

Still a useful guide for undergraduate and graduate students in education describing how to locate library materials for research papers. Covers choosing a topic, finding the best part of a book, using government documents, and using other guides. Contains a self-graded test to determine where to begin in the research process.

295. Planning Small Scale Research: A Practical Guide for Teachers and Students. Evans, K.M. NFER-Nelson, 1984. 76p. ISBN: 0-70050-677-2. 3rd edition.

A "small scale" practical introduction to experimental research of the type likely to be conducted by teachers and pre-service education students in a school. The author stresses the need for some knowledge of statistics for any educational research project.

296. Projections of Education Statistics. National Center for Education Statistics. Edited by Frankel, Martin M. and Gerald, Debra E. U.S. Government Printing Office, 1966–. LC: 67-62767. $8.50 (1988). Stock no. 065-000-00356-2.

Provides detailed ten-year projections of statistics for elementary and secondary schools and institutions of higher education on enrollments, graduates, teachers, and expenditures. Also presents the assumptions and methods used to develop projections and examines the accuracy of past projections in a methodological report. The 1988 issue, published in two volumes, projects to 1997–98.

297. Prospects for Research and Development in Education. Edited by Tyler, Ralph W. (Series on Contemporary Educational Issues of the National Society for the Study of Education). McCutchan, 1976. 183p. LC: 75-36111. ISBN: 0-8211-1906-0. $19.00.

Identifies the problems and prospects for educational research and development through a collage of excerpts of articles and publications assembled with comments by the editor.

298. Qualitative Data Analysis: A Sourcebook of New Methods. Miles, Matthew and Huberman, A. Michael. Sage, 1984. 263p. LC: 84-2140. ISBN: 0-8039-2274-4. $35.00.

A practical sourcebook outlining and illustrating, in detail, 49 methods of data display with practical suggestions for the user. Emphasis is on graphs, charts, matrices, and networks derived directly from the authors' research projects.

299. Reclaiming the Classroom: Teacher Research As an Agency for Change. Goswami, Dixie and Stillman, Peter R. Boynton/Cook, 1987. 242p. LC: 86-21581. ISBN: 0-86709-065-0. $14.00.

The trend toward "action research," teachers conducting their own classroom research, is described here. Some of the essays were written by theorist-practitioners but most are by teacher-researchers documenting their classroom inquiries and results.

300. Research and Evaluation in Education and the Social Sciences. Smith, Mary Lee. Prentice-Hall, 1987. 322p. LC: 86-15163. ISBN: 0-13-774050-6. Contact publisher for price information.

Designed as a textbook for students and professionals who produce research or who read and evaluate research reports. Deals with all approaches to research—quantitative, theoretical, evaluation research and qualitative methods presenting concepts in a spiral method, i.e., a partial understanding introduced initially and elaborated upon in later chapters.

301. Research Design and Statistics for Physical Education. Rothstein, Anne L. Prentice-Hall, 1985. 353p. LC: 84-15014. ISBN: 0-13-774142-1. $31.67.

Intended as a generic "how to" text on research design and statistics while focusing on physical education and sport as examples in application. Major areas addressed are descriptive and inferential statistics, research design, and special topics such as using computers in research and meta-analysis.

302. Research in Education. Best, John W. and Kahn, James V. Prentice-Hall, 1989. 388p. LC: 88-22747. ISBN: 0-13-774290-8. Contact publisher for price information. 6th edition.

A basic, popular text for an introductory course in research methods in education or as a reference on educational research. Some revisions and new material added for this 6th edition.

303. The Research Process in Educational Settings. Burgess, Robert G. Taylor & Francis, 1984. 282p. LC: 83-20796. ISBN: 0-90527-392-3; 0-90527-391-5 (pbk.). $31.00; $18.00 (pbk.).

A collection of essays addressing major issues in the use of qualitative methods of research in educational settings focusing on the research process. The contributors, drawn also from disciplines other than education, provide first-hand accounts of how they handled problems associated with ethnographic or case-study research using a set of guidelines to direct their analyses.

304. Review of Research in Education. American Educational Research Association, 1973–. $18.00 (Volume 14, 1987). ISSN: 0091-732-X.

A continuous series intended as a review of research in education and "to survey disciplined inquiry in education through critical and synthesizing essays." Each volume focuses on current research in one or two related areas, covering an indefinite period of time. The most recent *Review*, Volume 14, 1987, concerns research in cognitive science and knowledge development and transfer.

305. Statistical Analysis in Psychology and Education. Ferguson, George A. McGraw-Hill, 1989. 587p. LC: 88-27126. ISBN: 0-07-020485-3. $38.95. 6th edition.

A standard, popular introductory textbook on the concepts and applications of statistics in education and psychology. Some changes made to the 6th edition but topical sections remain the same: basic statistics, design of experiments, nonparametric statistics, psychological testing, and multivariate statistics.

306. Statistics for Educators. Horvath, Michael John. Special Child Publications, 1985. 144p. LC: 86-102891. ISBN: 0-87562-084-1. $14.50.

Emphasizes conceptual understanding and practical application of descriptive statistics used in the diagnostic-prescriptive approach. Covers interpreting psychological reports, assessment data, constructing an IEP (Individualized Education Program), and explaining data to parents. Case studies used extensively to illustrate concepts.

307. Statistics for the Behavioral Sciences: A First Course for Students of Psychology and Education. Gravetter, Frederick J. and Wallnau, Larry B. West Publishing, 1988. 531p. LC: GB901884. ISBN: 0314-59996-7. $38.25. 2nd edition.

The purpose of this text is to teach statistical methods and how to apply them appropriately. This second edition has some changes and additions to the textual content and the special features and study techniques.

308. Strategies of Educational Research: Qualitative Methods. Edited by Burgess, Robert. (Social Research and Educational Studies Series: I). Falmer, 1985. 351p. LC: 85-4584. ISBN: 1-85000-033-6; 1-85000-034-4 (pbk.). $38.00; $22.00 (pbk.).

A set of essays describing how various qualitative methods have been used by the researchers-authors to conduct contemporary and historical educational research: interviewing, case study, ethnographic conversation, historical documentary research, and other methods. The discussion is devoted to strategies and tactics used to collect data and not the theoretical framework of the research.

Studying Teaching and Learning: Trends in Soviet and American Research *See* COMPARATIVE EDUCATION (No. 39)

309. A Teacher's Guide to Classroom Research. Hopkins, David. Taylor & Francis, 1985. 136p. LC: 84-27178. ISBN: 0-33515-028-4. $16.00.

Designed as a practical guide for teachers doing research in their classrooms, i.e., action research. Stresses the need for teacher research to provide critical reflection on individual teaching with the aim of improving and controlling the teaching environment. Basic information on planning, conducting, and reporting the research with case studies.

310. The Thesis Writer's Handbook: A Complete One-Source Guide for Writers of Research Papers. Miller, Joan I. and Taylor, Bruce J. Alcove, 1987. 322p. LC: 86-17290. ISBN: 0-937473-12-X. $10.95.

The major purpose of this handbook is to guide the user through the procedural steps required in writing a master's thesis. Additional sections detail organizational and typing directions and a clearly defined set of instructions for documentation styles in the thesis development but also applicable to writing college term papers.

311. Understanding Reading and Writing Research. Kamil, Michael, Langer, Judith and Shanahan, Timothy. Allyn & Bacon, 1985. 199p. LC: 84-20392. ISBN: 0-205-08423-0. $35.00.

Explains the techniques and perspectives of reading and writing research to help practitioners recognize and evaluate the validity of research they can apply to personal instructional situations or for program implementation. Examines the major research methods: ethnographic, descriptive, correlational, experimental, and multivariate as they apply to reading and writing research.

312. Writing Research Papers: A Complete Guide. Lester, James D. Scott, Foresman, 1987. 280p. LC: 86-24875. ISBN: 0-673-18533-8. Contact publisher for price information. 5th edition.

Extensive revisions were made to this fifth edition. It continues to present the most current guidelines of the MLA Style Sheet as comprehensibly as possible to students. In addition, the book offers increased coverage of the new APA style and format and includes a more detailed discussion of doing research and the rationale behind research writing.

313. Youth Indicators 1988: Trends in the Well-Being of American Youth. Office of Educational Research and Improvement, U.S. Department of Education. U.S. Government Printing Office, 1988–. 135p. $7.00. Stock no. 065-000-00347-3.

The initial volume of a new series intended to provide a comprehensive longitudinal perspective on the welfare of youth and the context of their schooling, beginning with the arbitrary date of 1950. Youth is defined as the age span of 14 to 24 years. The indicators are organized into five areas: demographics and family composition, family income, education, employment and finances, health, behavior and attitudes outside the school environs as well as within.

Journals

314. American Educational Research Journal. American Educational Research Assn., 1230 17th St., NW, Washington, DC 20036. Quarterly. $29.00. ISSN: 0002-8312. 1964.

California Journal of Educational Research *See* **Educational Research Quarterly EDUCATIONAL RESEARCH/STATISTICS (No. 315)**

315. Educational Research Quarterly. Univ. of Southern California, School of Education, University Park, WPH 703, Los Angeles, CA 90089-0031. Quarterly. $23.00. ISSN: 0008-1213. 1976. Formerly *California Journal of Educational Research* (1950–1976).

316. Grants Magazine: The Journal of Sponsored Research and Other Programs. Plenum, 233 Spring St., New York, NY 10013. Quarterly. $130.00. ISSN: 0160-9734. 1978.

317. Journal of Educational Research. Heldref, 4000 Albemarle St., NW, Washington, DC 20016. 6/year. $48.00. ISSN: 0022-0671. 1920.

318. Journal of Educational Statistics. American Educational Research Assn., 1230 17th St., NW, Washington, DC 20036. Quarterly. $20.00. ISSN: 0362-9791. 1976. Cosponsor: American Statistical Association.

319. Journal of Research and Development in Education. Univ. of Georgia, College of Education, Athens, GA 30602. Quarterly. $25.00. ISSN: 0022-426X. 1967.

320. Review of Educational Research. American Educational Research Assn., 1230 17th St., NW, Washington, DC 20036. Quarterly. $29.00. ISSN: 0034-6543. 1931.

Educational Technology/Media

Entries represent many aspects of technology and media—computer-assisted instruction, distance education, instructional systems, media services—although the field of computers in education dominates the section. Directories of media and software materials and works that "look to the future" are important in this field and several were included. Many educational/technical journals are published; a select few were chosen for inclusion.

Books

321. Administrative Uses of Computers in the Schools. Bluhm, Harry P. Prentice-Hall, 1987. 310p. LC: 86-25335. ISBN: 0-13-008467-0. $32.00.

Educators interested in becoming familiar with computers as an administrative tool will find this a useful resource with information on how a computer information system can help manage the educational program: basic issues such as the development, evaluation, and control of the system; instructional applications; computer software applications; and aspects of policy formation.

322. A Casebook for "Helping Teachers Teach". Edited by Turner, Philip M. Libraries Unlimited, 1988. 161p. LC: 88-22978. ISBN: 0-87287-615-2. $17.50.

A casebook created to demonstrate how school library media specialists can help teachers teach and consult with and plan for their instruction. Includes examples of 13 cases involving a school media specialist working with teachers at various levels and degrees of involvement.

Children and Computers Together in the Early Childhood Classroom *See* **RESOURCES FOR TEACHING (No. 779)**

323. Computers and Education. White, Charles Stitham and Hubbard, Guy. Macmillan, 1988. 240p. LC: 87-16831. ISBN: 0-02-427090-3. Contact publisher for price information.

Intended as a primary text for a course providing an overview of educational computing or for any use as a "general foundations" of educational computing. Early chapters cover the history of computing and how the hardware and software work; the remaining chapters address educational computing—state of the art and use of computers across disciplines.

Computers, Curriculum and Whole-Class Instruction: Issues and Ideas *See* **RESOURCES FOR TEACHING (No. 787)**

324. Computers in the Classroom. Edited by Kepner, Henry S. National Education Assn., 1986. 175p. LC: 85-31065. ISBN: 0-8106-1829-X. $10.95. 2nd edition.

This book is still useful as an introduction to the use of computers in the classroom even though it bears a 1986 publication date. Computer use by students is covered as is the use of computers across key subject areas and the future of educational computing from a teacher's perspective.

325. Computing and Change on Campus. Edited by Kiesler, Sara and Sproull, Lee. Cambridge Univ. Press, 1987. 255p. LC: 87-12491. ISBN: 0521-34431-X. $24.95.

A collection of systematic research studies of the computerization of Carnegie Mellon University and the social changes surrounding the introduction and expansion of computer technologies on campus. The research projects took place during the early 1980s on many parts of the campus; the experimental research is not included but the techniques and designs used are.

326. Constructivism in the Computer Age. Edited by Forman, George and Pufall, Peter B. (Jean Piaget Symposium Series). L. Erlbaum, 1988. 260p. LC: 87-25389. ISBN: 0-8058-0101-4. $39.95.

These essays evolved from a 1985 symposium sponsored by the Jean Piaget Society. Each addresses certain issues related to the use of the computer in knowledge construction and the nature of computer-based intellectual activity. Some of these issues are skill versus thinking, intuitive versus formal knowing, videodisc and video technology.

327. Critical Perspectives on Computers and Composition Instruction. Edited by Hawisher, Gail and Selfe, Cynthia L. (Computers and Education Series). Teachers College Press, 1989. 231p. LC: 88-295093. ISBN: 0-8077-2948-5. $29.95.

Contributors to the volume address the theory and research on computers and writing and current problems in computers and composition and explore new perspectives on using electronic media to help students learn to write.

328. Cultural Dimensions of Educational Computing: Understanding the Non-Neutrality of Technology. Bowers, C.A. (Advances in Contemporary Educational Thought, v. 1). Teachers College Press, 1988. 153p. LC: 88-12365. ISBN: 0-8077-2923-X. $19.95.

The author proposes reflecting on computing and education from a deep historical-cultural perspective and to view the computer as a cultural and not a technical device. Individual and cultural bias that may enter into programming and cultural forces at work in the learning environment are just two of the issues addressed.

329. Dictionary of Instructional Technology. Edited by Ellington, Henry and Harris, Duncan. (AETT Occasional Publication, No. 6). Nichols, 1986. 189p. LC: 85-28530. ISBN: 1-85091-072-3. $34.50.

The majority of the over 2,800 terms defined in the *Dictionary* are drawn from two areas: various branches of mainline instructional technology such as instructional design, assessment and evaluation, instructional media, and others and from the diverse fields that impinge upon or overlap with instructional technology such as educational psychology, film and television production, photography, etc.

330. Directory of Software Sources for Higher Education: A Resource Guide for Instructional Applications. Edited by Seiden, Peggy. Peterson's Guides, 1987. 169p. LC: 87-29123. ISBN: 0-87866-679-6. $29.95. Compiled by the Educational Software Library of Carnegie Mellon University for the EDUCOM Software Initiative.

Consolidates information from a large number of sources to assist those responsible for identifying software useful to a campus community. Focuses on software developed for instructional purposes at postsecondary institutions; professional software and other types are included if used in the higher education curriculum. Covers six source areas: commercial, noncommercial, directories, evaluation sources, journals and organizations. Contains subject, title, and organization indexes.

331. Educational Film/Video Locator of the Consortium of University Film Centers. Consortium of University Film Centers. R.R. Bowker, 1990. LC: 86-71233. ISBN: 0-8352-2179-2. $175.00 set. 2 volumes; 4th edition.

A listing of film and video titles held by the 52 member libraries of the Consortium; thousands of titles are added and deleted with each new edition. Bibliographical data for each entry in the title list consists of title, color, length, format, year, descriptive annotation, subject, audience level, production data, and sound designation. Subject and series access is also available.

332. Educational Media and Technology Yearbook. Libraries Unlimited, 1974-. LC: 85-643014. ISBN: 0-87287-772-8 (1989). $50.00 (1989). ISSN: 8755-2094.

This annual has been consistent in its content coverage since the first *Yearbook* in order to provide up-to-date information with each edition. Topical sections covered each year include a review of current trends, technological developments of the year, organizations and associations in North America, and a "Mediagraphy," a bibliography of recent articles and publications in the field.

333. The Educational Software Selector: T.E.S.S.. (Computers and Education Series). Teachers College Press, 1984-. LC: 87-644340. ISBN: Varies with edition. $34.95. ISSN: 8755-5107.

A source of thousands of educational software products available for schools and colleges for use on microcomputers. Sequenced by curriculum areas and within that by subject and in some cases further breakdowns. Classroom oriented software coverage is for all levels from nursery through graduate school, plus management aids for teachers and administrators. Aside from descriptive information for each entry, citations to reviews and evaluation ratings are provided.

334. Educational Technology: Its Creation, Development and Cross-Cultural Transfer. Edited by Thomas, R. Murray and Kobayashi, Victor N. (Comparative and International Education Series). Pergamon, 1987. 275p. LC: 87-14239. ISBN: 008-034-9935; 008-034-9943 (pbk.). $22.00 (pbk.); $52.00. Volume 4.

Papers presented at an international conference with the same title, divided into four areas of technology: electronic computers, television/radio, print media, and operating systems. For each area of technology its history is reviewed and the development of that technology in advanced industrial nations and the transfer of that technology are covered.

335. Electronic Learning, from Audiotape to Videodisc. Johnston, Jerome. L. Erlbaum, 1987. 118p. LC: 87-15424. ISBN: 0-8058-0012-3; 0-8058-0026-3 (pbk.). $24.95; $14.95 (pbk.).

Intended as an update of an earlier book by Chu and Schramm on learning from television and radio but also an expansion of that work in that it considers other recent technologies—electronic text, videodisc, and microprocessor-based technologies. Included are reviews of the literature in four electronic media—audio, video, electronic text and graphics, and videodisc.

336. Emerging School Library Media Program: Readings. Edited by McDonald, Frances Beck. Libraries Unlimited, 1988. 328p. LC: 88-6784. ISBN: 0-87287-660-8. $24.50.

A collection of readings illustrating the changing school library media program in the 1980s and the instructional and consulting roles of library media specialists and their contributions to the educational process. School libraries have changed to media centers with a multimedia, integrated approach to learning.

337. The Encyclopedia of Educational Media Communications and Technology. Edited by Unwin, Derick and McAleese, Ray. Greenwood, 1988. 568p. LC: 87-15049. ISBN: 0-313-23996-7. $125.00. 2nd edition.

The *Encyclopedia* has undergone extensive revision since the first edition because of the march of technology since 1977–78. The current edition contains 1,800 micro-entries (shorter definition-types) as against 900 previously; macro-entries (extended article-types) number 62 as against 28 previously. The policy to identify and include only those terms likely to be encountered in an educational context was continued.

338. Evaluating Educational Software. Coll, Carol Ann. American Library Assn., 1987. 87p. LC: 87-1417. ISBN: 0-8389-0474-2. $9.95.

Offers specific criteria to consider when evaluating educational microcomputer software: quality of information context, educational quality, instructional effectiveness, flexibility in use, quality of documentation accompanying software. A nine-page "Evaluation Checklist" summarizes the textual content.

339. Evaluating Educational Software: A Guide for Teachers. Sloane, Howard N. et al. Prentice-Hall, 1989. 89p. LC: 88-21561. ISBN: 0-13-298571-3. $15.00.

A very practical guide for anyone evaluating educational software from step one. Each of the eight chapters answers a question posed in the evaluation process; checklists to supplement the text content are found in the appendices. By completing all the checklists in evaluating a piece of software, a comprehensive evaluation is achieved.

340. Film and Video Finder. National Information Center for Educational Media. 1987. LC: 87-21405. ISBN: 0-89320-110-3. $295.00. ISSN: 0898-1582; 3 volumes.

A bibliographic guide to commercially produced 16mm films and videotapes for instruction, including documentaries and children's programs. Replaces the *NICEM Index to 16mm Educational Films* and the *NICEM Index to Educational Videotapes.* The 1987 edition contains some 90,000 entries. Volume I includes the "Index to Subject Headings" and "Directory of Producers/Distributors"; Volumes II and III have the main title (and series) entries where full bibliographic data are found.

341. Handbook of Educational Technology. Percival, Fred and Ellington, Henry. Nichols, 1988. 273p. LC: 87-31381. ISBN: 0-89397-297-5. $32.50.

Intended as a basic "primer" in the field of educational technology providing a simple overview of the field and how an ed-tech-based approach can help improve teaching; also identifies current trends in educational technology and products and their effect on education in the future. This second edition has been updated and revised. An extensive bibliography and glossary are included.

342. Information Power: Guidelines for School Library Media Programs. American Assn. of School Librarians. Assn. for Educational Communications and Technology, 1988. 171p. LC: 88-3480. ISBN: 0-8389-3352-1. $12.95. Prepared in conjunction with the American Library Association and the Association for Educational Communications and Technology.

Sets forth guidelines (serving as standards) for developing school library media programs that have become an integral part of the total instructional program in schools and not just a support service. The guidelines describe what can be expected in the way of media services in elementary and secondary schools.

343. Information Systems and School Improvement: Inventing the Future. Edited by Bank, Adrianne and Williams, Richard C. (Computers and Education Series). Teachers College Press, 1987. 252p. LC: 86-30148. ISBN: 0-8077-2842-X. $25.95.

Explores how computer-based information systems can be of assistance to instructional managers in the classroom, school or district-wide; these are referred to as Instructional Information Systems (IIS). Deals with such issues as the uses and abuses of an IIS, the capabilities of computer technologies to run IIS, persuading teachers to become dedicated users of an IIS. Presents a variety of IIS system models being developed.

344. Information Technologies and Basic Learning: Reading, Writing, Science and Mathematics. Edited by Center for Educational Research and Innovation. Organization for Economic Co-Operation and Development, 1987. 269p. ISBN: 92-64-13025-X. $32.00.

This report marks the completion of Phase II of a CERI project examining the issues inherent in the introduction of new information technologies in education. Specifically, the working groups formed by member countries examined the state of educational uses of new information technologies in the basic skills areas of reading, writing, mathematics, and science; their conclusions form this report.

345. Information Technology in the Delivery of Distance Education and Training. Winders, Ray. (Education and Human Communication Series). P. Francis, 1988. 192p. LC: GB87-54121. ISBN: 1-87016-703-1. $16.95.

Describes the application of information technology to distance learning including up-to-date case studies of systems operations in the United States, United Kingdom, Canada, and Australia. Covers such technologies as audioconferencing, videotex, viewdata, and satellite conferencing, and summarizes the potential of electronic communications in the future delivery of education at a distance.

Instructional Media and the New Technologies of Instruction *See* RESOURCES FOR TEACHING (No. 799)

346. Instructional Technology: Foundations. Edited by Gagne, Robert M. L. Erlbaum, 1987. 473p. LC: 86-6328. ISBN: 0-8985-9626-2; 0-8985-9878-8 (pbk.). $59.95; $24.95 (pbk.).

The scientific knowledge about and future prospects of instructional technology are linked in describing the foundations of the field in this collection of essays. The foundations of human learning and the conceptual design and development of instructional systems are covered. State-of-the-art topics include innovations in telecommunications, artificial intelligence, and educational delivery systems.

Integrating Computers into the Curriculum: A Handbook for Special Educators *See* SPECIAL EDUCATION (No. 856)

347. The Integration of Media into the Curriculum: An International Report Commissioned by the International Council for Educational Media. Edited by Tucker, Richard. Kogan Page, 1986. 182p. ISBN: 1-85091-214-9. $22.95.

Member countries of the International Council for Educational Media produced the individual national reports combined to form this collection. The models presented by each of the 13 countries cover decision-making about media and its implementation in a curriculum; production and distribution of media; information dissemination about media; use of media in schools; and additional areas in some reports.

348. Interactive Multimedia: Visions of Multimedia for Developers, Educators & Information Providers. Edited by Ambron, Sueann and Hooper, Kristina. (CD ROM Series). Microsoft Press, 1988. 339p. LC: 88-1449. ISBN: 1-55615-124-1. $24.95.

A collection of articles produced following a 1986 conference on "Multimedia in Education." Contributors from computer science, engineering education, television, and the publishing fields present a variety of multimedia projects and products from a multidisciplinary perspective with a glimpse at future multimedia learning environments.

349. Managing Media Services: Theory and Practice. Vlcek, Charles W. and Wiman, Raymond V. Libraries Unlimited, 1989. 426p. LC: 88-27360. ISBN: 0-87287-715-9. $35.00.

Provides information, ideas, and practices for managing media centers in business and industry as well as education. Following an overview and some philosophical perspectives, chapters cover management basics, computers in the media center, managing budgets, and personnel and other topics. Several appendices include organizational plans of exemplary programs and sample media selection policies.

350. Media Review Digest: The Only Complete Guide to Reviews of Non-Book Media. Edited by Regan, Lesley O. Pierian Press, 1973/74–. 915p., Volume 18, 1988/1989 LC: 73-172772. ISBN: 0-87650-232-X. $245, Volume 18 1988/1989.

An annual index to and digest of reviews, evaluations, and descriptions of non-book media appearing in some 132 periodicals and reviewing services. Primary emphasis is on educational, instructional, and information media in film, video, filmstrips, audio, and miscellaneous formats such as slides and posters. Full mediagraphic information appears for each entry and several indexes—video, general subject, alphabetical subject, geographical, reviewer—provide cross references.

351. Microcomputers in Early Childhood Education. Edited by Pardeck, John T. and Murphy, John W. (Special Aspects of Education, v. 9). Gordon and Breach, 1989. 147p. LC: 88-24429. ISBN: 0-677-21900-8. $34.00. ISSN: 0731-8413.

This collection of journal articles, primarily from *Early Child Development and Care*, provides an overview of the impact of computers in education. Discusses the influence of computers on the physical and cognitive environments in the classroom. The ramifications of computers in early childhood education are discussed from several viewpoints.

Modern Technology in Foreign Language Education: Applications and Projects *See* **RESOURCES FOR TEACHING (No. 803)**

352. Permissible Computing in Education: Values, Assumptions and Needs. Ragsdale, Ronald G. Praeger, 1988. 284p. LC: 87-35964. ISBN: 0-275-92894-2. $42.95.

The author explores some of the value bases that support the various uses of computers in education to encourage educators to make informed decisions about their use rather than using them because they are new and exciting. Some of the issues discussed include computer systems substituting for children's thinking skills, reducing human classroom interaction, and computers homogenizing the wide range of achievement in classrooms.

353. Power On: New Tools for Teaching and Learning. Edited by U.S. Office of Technology Assessment. U.S. Government Printing Office, 1988. 238p. LC: 88-60051. Contact publisher for price information. Stock no. 052-003-01125-5.

This government report examines developments in the use of computer-based technologies, analyzes key trends in hardware and software development, evaluates the capability of technology to improve learning in many areas, and explores ways to increase student access to technology. Reviews the role of the teacher in educational technology, the teacher's needs for training, and the impact of federal support for educational technology research and development.

354. Reading, Writing and Computers: Planning for Integration. Howie, Sherry Hill. Allyn & Bacon, 1989. 250p. LC: 88-27281. ISBN: 0-205-11965-4. $32.00.

Presents ideas for integrating reading and writing with computer use in the classroom in a well-planned curriculum. A theoretical base is provided but most of the book is designed for practical use by teachers with information on hardware and software, training and evaluation, and other areas; one chapter contains lesson plans for teachers at upper elementary, secondary, and college levels.

355. Schoolworlds/Microworlds: Computers and the Culture of the Classroom. Olson, John. Pergamon, 1988. 132p. LC: 88-11739. ISBN: 0-08-034985-4: 0-08-034984-6 (pbk.). $29.00; $14.50 (pbk.).

Clarifies what the computer revolution means for schools—how teachers are actually using computers in the classrooms; changes in classroom life and conceptual change in students as a result of computer experiences; implications for computer literacy; the potential of microcomputers to better schools. Illustrated by many case studies.

356. Selection and Use of Instructional Media: For Improved Classroom Teaching and for Interactive, Individualized Instruction. Romiszowski, A.J. Nichols, 1988. 396p. LC: 87-7962. ISBN: 0-89397-281-9. $41.50.

Intended as a handbook for educators or anyone faced with planning for the effective use of media and materials in the instructional process. Begins with a theoretical background to media selection and use and then moves to a discussion of presentation media used as instructional aids to transmit messages one-way, from instructor to learner and interactive media involving two-way communication. Many visuals enhance the text.

357. Software for Schools 1987–89: A Comprehensive Directory of Educational Software Grades Pre-K through 12. R.R. Bowker, 1987. 1085p. LC: 88-640969. ISBN: 0-8352-2369-8. $49.95.

A guide to instructional software products only; does not include software appropriate for home or recreational use. The main, descriptive entries are found in the "Title Index," alphabetically arranged. Two other indexes are included—"Classroom Software/Grade Level Index" listing software by computer first, then by title and grade level, and "Professional Software Index" listing products for the professional educator. Other features are a glossary and periodicals directory.

The Specialware Directory: A Guide to Software for Special Education *See* **SPECIAL EDUCATION (No. 885)**

358. Teachers and Machines: The Classroom Use of Technology since 1920. Cuban, Larry. Teachers College Press, 1986. 134p. LC: 85-14789. ISBN: 0-8077-2792-X. $10.95.

Teacher response to and usage of four technological devices is explored historically: film, radio, television, and computers. The author traces the acceptance and denial, enthusiasm and doubts of teachers and communities regarding the introduction of these technologies, with special emphasis on the influence and teacher use of computers.

359. Teaching and Learning with Computers: A Guide for College Faculty and Administrators. Heermann, Barry. (Jossey-Bass Higher Education Series). Jossey-Bass, 1988. 244p. LC: 87-46331. ISBN: 1-55542-084-2. $22.95.

A handbook intended to guide faculty and administrators through the practical steps for integrating computers with instruction. The first section addresses how (or whether) to enrich instruction with computers and the second how to create an environment for computer integration. Closes with a look at the future of academic computing.

360. Technology in Education: Looking Toward 2020. Edited by Nickerson, Raymond S. and Zodhiates, Philip P. L. Erlbaum, 1988. 330p. LC: 88-21126. ISBN: 0-8058-0214-2; 0-8058-0297-5 (pbk.). $49.95; $19.95 (pbk.).
Chapters originated as papers prepared for a "2020 Panel" of searchers, computer scientists, mathematicians, and educators convened to articulate a vision of technology's role in education in 2020 and to define the research, development, and related activities that would be needed to make it happen.

Using Computers in the Teaching of Reading *See* RESOURCES FOR TEACHING (No. 821)

361. What Curriculum for the Information Age?. Edited by White, Mary Alice. L. Erlbaum, 1987. 102p. LC: 87-6741. ISBN: 0-8985-9922-9. $19.95.
Published following a conference of the same title held at Teachers College, Columbia University. The book's (and conference) theme is that technologies are affecting very basic changes in curriculum and are more than an interesting adjunct to instruction. The very different approaches to what curriculum should be are represented in the five essays of the contributors. Questions posed at the conference are included.

Writing with Computers in the Early Grades *See* RESOURCES FOR TEACHING (No. 823)

Journals

AV Communication Review *See* E C & T J EDUCATIONAL TECHNOLOGY/MEDIA (No. 365)

362. Classroom Computer Learning: The Leading Magazine of Electronic Learning. Peter Li, Inc., 2451 E. River Rd., Dayton, OH 45439. 8/year. $22.50. ISSN: 0746-4223. 1983. Formerly *Classroom Computer News* (1980–1983).

Classroom Computer News *See* **Classroom Computer Learning** EDUCATIONAL TECHNOLOGY/MEDIA (No. 362)

363. Computers in the Schools: The Interdisciplinary Journal of Practice, Theory and Applied Research. Haworth Press, Inc., 12 W. 32nd St., New York, NY 10001. Quarterly. $36.00 institutions, $60.00 libraries. ISSN: 0738-0569. 1984.

364. The Computing Teacher. International Council for Computers in Education (ICCE), University of Oregon, 1787 Agate St., Eugene, OR 97403-9905. 9/year. $21.50. ISSN: 0278-9175. 1979.

365. E C & T J: Educational Communications and Technology Journal. Assn. for Educational Communications and Technology, 1126 16th St., NW, Washington, DC 20036. Quarterly. $24.00. ISSN: 0148-5806. 1953. Formerly *AV Communication Review.*

366. Educational Technology: The Magazine for Managers of Change in Education. Educational Technology Publications, 720 Palisade Ave., Englewood Cliffs, NJ 07632. Monthly. $99.00. ISSN: 0013-1962. 1961.

367. Electronic Learning. Scholastic, Inc., 730 Broadway, New York, NY 10003-9538. 8/year. $23.95. ISSN: 0278-3258. 1981.

368. Interface: The Computer Education Quarterly. Mitchell Publishing Co., Inc., 965 River St., Santa Cruz, CA 95060. Quarterly. $26.00. ISSN: 0163-6626. 1979.

369. Journal of Computer Assisted Learning. Blackwell Scientific Publications, 52 Beacon St., Boston, MA 02108. 3/year. $50.00. ISSN: 0266-4909. 1985.

370. Journal of Computer Based Instruction. Assn. for the Development of Computer-Based Instructional Systems, Western Washington University, Miller Hall, Bellingham, WA 98225. Quarterly. $36.00. ISSN: 0098-597X. 1974.

371. T.H.E. Journal: Technological Horizons in Education. Information Synergy, Inc., Box 17239, Irvine, CA 92713. 10/year. $29.00. ISSN: 0192-592X. 1973.

Mathematics and Computer Education *See* CONTENT AREAS (No. 81)

372. Media & Methods: Educational Products, Technologies & Programs for Schools & Universities. American Assn. of Media Specialists & Librarians, 1429 Walnut St., Philadelphia, PA 19102. 5/year. $29.00. ISSN: 0025-6897. 1964. Formerly *Teachers Guide to Media and Methods.*

Teachers Guide to Media and Methods *See* **Media & Methods** EDUCATIONAL TECHNOLOGY/MEDIA (No. 372)

Elementary/Secondary Education

Preschool education through grade 12 is included in this category. Reference sources on private schools, religious schools, special resources for schooling, and alternative methods of schooling are covered. General texts on early childhood education and elementary and secondary programs are also covered. Some information on effective schools is included in the book materials. Journals focus on levels of education, such as middle schools or early childhood education.

Books

373. Adolescent Literacy: What Works and Why. Davidson, Judith and Koppenhaver, David. (Garland Reference Library of the Social Sciences, vol. 442). Garland, 1988. 275p. LC: 88-5936. ISBN: 0-8420-1938-5. $37.00.

An investigation and in-depth descriptions of programs that demonstrate innovative and successful ways of reaching out to adolescents with literacy needs. These and other program sites (school and non-school) were visited by staff of the Project on Adolescent Literacy to collect data through observation and interviews. Chapter on "What Works and Why" highlights common elements of the successful programs.

374. A Better Start: New Choices for Early Learning. Edited by Hechinger, Fred M. Walker, 1986. 172p. LC: 86-15711. ISBN: 0-8027-0897-8. $16.95.

Advocates quality early childhood education tailored to the individual needs of the child. Of interest to parents and teachers, this book presents examples of successful early childhood programs. The focus is on providing a sound basis for school and subsequently life success for children, particularly those from disadvantaged backgrounds.

375. Changing Patterns of Secondary Education: An International Comparison. Edited by Lawson, Robert F. Univ. of Calgary Press, 1988. 313p. ISBN: 0-919813-40-2. Contact publisher for price information.

Development, change, and tensions in secondary education are at issue in this book. Compares secondary education at the international level and by selected states in the U.S. These comparisons are designed to provide the reader with an overview of the challenges, innovations, and reforms in progress at the secondary level on a worldwide basis. Implications of findings are related to secondary education in Canada.

376. The Classroom Observer: Developing Observation Skills in Early Childhood Settings. Boehm, Ann E. and Weinberg, Richard A. Teachers College Press, 1987. 154p. LC: 87-18036. ISBN: 0-8077-2874-8. $13.95 (pbk.). 2nd edition.

A practical text on developing observation skills necessary to effective teaching. Emphasis is on early childhood settings and the audience includes researchers, educators, and human service providers. Discusses systematic observation, the classroom setting, types of observation techniques, dangers of poor or biased observation activities, and ethical issues.

377. The Condition of Teaching: A State-by-State Analysis. (Carnegie Foundation Technical Report). Carnegie Foundation for the Advancement of Teaching/Princeton Univ. Press, 1988. 106p. LC: 85-26898. ISBN: 0-931050-35-9. $10.95.

Compilation and analysis of information from 1987 and 1988 national surveys about the nation's teachers. Data are prefaced with a foreword by Ernest Boyer, listing the problems related to and recommendations to improve the condition of teaching and education. Presents 83 tables of data on various aspects of U.S. teaching. Tables are arranged in six chapters, each introduced by a brief analysis.

378. Contemporary Approaches to Moral Education: An Annotated Bibliography and Guide to Research. Leming, James S. (Garland Bibliographies in Contemporary Education, v. 2/Garland Reference Library of Social Science, v. 117). Garland, 1983. 451p. LC: 81-48422. ISBN: 0-8240-9389-5. $60.00.

Bibliography of journal articles, reports, dissertations, and books primarily published from 1965 to 1981. Focuses on the practical implementation of moral instruction rather than its philosophical and historical basis. Contents are arranged by topic such as general analyses, cognitive development, value analysis, specific curricular areas, and specific settings. Special section on journals having theme issues on moral education is valuable aid to locating literature.

379. Curriculum and Aims. Walker, Decker F. and Soltis, Jonas F. (Thinking About Education Series). Teachers College Press, 1986. 116p. LC: 85-22274. ISBN: 0-8077-2788-1. $8.95 (pbk.).

Provides an overview of the purposes, content, design, and structure of educational programs. Presents issues and questions for debate and discussion by preservice teachers. Designed as a text for teacher preparation programs, *Curriculum and Aims* offers theory, research, and case studies to stimulate an exchange of ideas within the classroom or work setting.

380. Curriculum Design: A Handbook for Educators. Wulf, Kathleen M. and Schave, Barbara. Scott, Foresman, 1984. 177p. LC: 84-1294. ISBN: 0-673-16644-9. Contact publisher for price information.

Presents the procedural steps necessary in planning and developing a curriculum. Written for classroom teachers and education students, this handbook offers a systematic approach in designing and changing the school curriculum.

Discipline in the Secondary Classroom: A Problem-by-Problem Survival Guide *See* **RESOURCES FOR TEACHING (No. 791)**

Dynamics of Effective Teaching *See* **RESOURCES FOR TEACHING (No. 794)**

381. The Early Childhood Curriculum: A Review of Current Research. Edited by Seefeldt, Carol. (Early Childhood Education Series). Teachers College Press, 1987. 288p. LC: 86-14510. ISBN: 0-8077-2819-5. $25.95.

A compilation of research and theory in the early childhood curriculum content areas. Each chapter focuses on the theory, research, and implications for practice of a specific content area such as social studies or the visual arts. Advocates an integrated, child-centered curriculum. Final chapter suggests areas for future research and work.

382. Early Childhood Education in the Schools. Edited by Bauch, Jerold P. (NEA Aspects of Learning). Natl. Education Assn., 1988. 352p. LC: 88-19569. ISBN: 0-8106-1461-2. $19.95.

Presents a history of early childhood education, policy issues, challenges, controversial issues, parental involvement, and future directions. A provocative potpourri of articles reprinted from a variety of journals, all focusing on aspects of early childhood education. A diversity of viewpoints is provided. Most articles have extensive references.

383. Early Childhood Programs: Human Relationships and Learning. Read, Katherine H., Gardner, Pat and Mahler, Barbara Child. Holt, Rinehart, and Winston, 1987. 434p. LC: 86-25770. ISBN: 0-03-007172-0. Contact publisher for price information. 8th edition.

This revised edition of *The Nursery School and Kindergarten* provides information about all kinds of child care programs: day care, infant care, home care, and after school programs. Based on research, each chapter discusses a specific aspect, such as setting, teaching skills, behavior, and parent and teacher concerns. Comprehensive text on the issues facing child care providers.

384. Early Schooling: The National Debate. Edited by Kagan, Sharon L. and Zigler, Edward F. Yale Univ. Press, 1987. 236p. LC: 87-21763. ISBN: 0-300-04124-1. $10.95.

Discusses the reasons behind the demand for early schooling: specifically, the need for child care, research related to early education and disadvantaged children, and national reform efforts to improve education in general. Separately authored chapters address the debate about early schooling, accountability, public school responsibility, policy issues, curricula, and benefits/disadvantages to the child. Research is used to document the various positions taken by authors.

385. Educating the Infant and Toddler. White, Burton L. Lexington Books, 1988. 361p. LC: 86-45293. ISBN: 0-669-13137-7. $35.00.

Provides practical, reliable information about the learning process and working with parents of infants and toddlers. Based on extensive research and a project in Missouri on education for parenthood, this book discusses early childhood development, issues pertaining to child development, and an in-depth view of the Missouri project. Topics covered include sibling spacing, child care, social development, and bonding.

386. The Effects of Early Education: A Report from the Child Health and Education Study. Osborn, A.F. and Milbank, J.E. Clarendon, 1987. 294p. LC: 86-31186. ISBN: 0-19-827801-2. $47.00.

Describes a study of preschool education in Great Britain and investigates the long-term educational benefits of early education. Utilizes data from a national, longitudinal study in the U.K. and evaluates ordinary preschool programs rather than experimental ones in order to determine benefits of early schooling. A number of variables are examined to determine impact on educational success. Methodology and findings are useful to researchers and practitioners on both sides of the Atlantic.

387. El-Hi Textbooks and Serials in Print, 1990. R.R. Bowker, 1990. 1,224p. ISBN: 0-8352-2815-0. $99.95. Former title: *El-Hi Textbooks in Print* .

Published since 1963, this excellent source lists texts, workbooks, text series, journals, teaching aids, programmed learning materials, and other resources appropriate to the elementary and secondary classroom. Includes classroom resources from mainstream publishers as well as from small presses.

388. The Enquiring Classroom: An Approach to Understanding Children's Learning. Rowland, Stephen. Falmer, 1984. 162p. LC: 84-1480. ISBN: 0-905273-99-0. $16.00 (pbk.).

Discusses the importance of an open classroom in stimulating teacher/student interactions to the benefit of the learning environment. Uses a study of a British primary school to support theories of children's learning. Particular attention is given to how children influence and control the learning environment and their own learning activities.

389. The Essential Montessori. Hainstock, Elizabeth G. New American Library, 1986. 129p. LC: 85-29880. ISBN: 0-452-25808-1. $6.95 (pbk.). Updated edition.

Guide to the Montessori method includes excerpts from Montessori's writing, presents a biography of Montessori and a history of her movement, and evaluates the effectiveness of the Montessori method in the U.S. Provides information about Montessori organizations and programs and the availability of Montessori resource materials. Discusses the adaptability of the method and presents criticisms of the system. Includes bibliography.

First Lessons: A Report on Elementary Education in America
See EDUCATIONAL REFORM (No. 244)

Foundations of Early Childhood Education: Teaching Three, Four and Five-Year-Old Children *See* RESOURCES FOR TEACHING (No. 797)

390. Friendship and Peer Culture in the Early Years. Corsaro, William A. (Language and Learning for Human Service Professions, v.5). Ablex, 1985. 336p. LC: 84-28221. ISBN: 0-89391-174-7. $42.50.

Based on a detailed ethnography of peer interaction in a nursery school. Identifies several stable aspects of peer culture and examines the relation between peer culture and development of specific types of social knowledge. Concludes that children use sharing and group role play to gain control over their lives. Discusses the implications of the study's findings for early childhood education.

391. The Handbook of Private Schools: An Annual Descriptive Survey of Independent Education. (The Sargent Handbook Series). Porter Sargent, 1915-. 1445p. LC: 15-12869. ISBN: 0-87558-122-6. $50.00. Annual. (70th edition, 1989); ISSN: 0072-9884.

The 70th edition lists 1,765 private and independent schools, including military programs, elementary boarding schools, and coeducational facilities. Summer academic programs and summer camps are also listed. Arrangement is by geographical location.

High School: A Report on Secondary Education in America *See* EDUCATIONAL REFORM (No. 247)

392. High School Achievement: Public, Catholic, and Private Schools Compared. Coleman, James S., Hoffer, Thomas and Kilgore, Sally. Basic Books, 1982. 289p. LC: 81-68411. ISBN: 0-465-02956-6. $21.95.

Based on the 1980 study, High School and Beyond, from the National Center for Education Statistics, this report compares public and private schools, particularly in terms of academic achievement. Addresses public policy implications for the increased focus on open choice in schooling and educational organization in general.

393. Home Schools: An Alternative. Gorder, Cheryl. Blue Bird, 1987. 203p. LC: 85-4004. ISBN: 0-933025-10-6. $11.95 (pbk.). Rev. edition.

Presents information about home schooling, particularly the reasons why some parents choose home schooling. Explores the social, psychological, and emotional aspects of home schooling; religious and moral issues; academic advantages; historical and philosophical background; legal aspects and state laws; and resources for home school instruction. Home school organizations are listed in the appendix.

Horace's Compromise: The Dilemma of the American High School *See* EDUCATIONAL REFORM (No. 248)

394. Imagination and Education. Edited by Egan, Kieran and Nadaner, Dan. Teachers College Press, 1988. 268p. ISBN: 0-8077-2878-0. $31.95.

Explores the roles and values of imagination in education and the pitfalls of ignoring them. Attempts to clarify the role imagination has in the classroom. Specific examples of classroom instruction and imagination are presented. Pretend play in early childhood, scientific discovery, visual and musical imagination, and imagina-

tion as an aid to intercultural understanding are a few of the topics considered in this collection of edited papers.

395. Inside Schools: A Collaborative View. Atkin, J. Myron, Kennedy, Donald and Patrick, Cynthia L. (Stanford Series on Education and Public Policy). Falmer, 1989. 146p. ISBN: 1-85000-432-3. $33.00.

Describes and evaluates a collaborative effort between Stanford University and six nearby school districts to address educational reform. "The Study of Stanford and the Schools" focuses on secondary education and serves as a model for other collaborative efforts between schools and universities. The study utilized a research-oriented, data-based, yet pragmatic approach to involve the university and school communities in developing an understanding of the issues and desired outcomes.

The Invitational Elementary Classroom *See* RESOURCES FOR TEACHING (No. 802)

396. Just Playing? The Role and Status of Play in Early Childhood Education. Moyles, Janet R. Open Univ. Press., 1989. 190p. LC: 89-3327. ISBN: 0-335-09569-0. $65.00.

Presents theoretical background of play as a learning medium, and the need and importance of incorporating play into the curriculum. Specifically examines the impact of play on language problem solving and creativity. Emphasizes the need for play in the early childhood curriculum, but also considers constructive adult play.

The Last Little Citadel: American High Schools Since 1940 *See* HISTORY AND PHILOSOPHY OF EDUCATION (No. 648)

397. Little Earth School: Education, Discovery, Celebration. Munzenrider, Steven et al. Schocken Books, 1986. 274p. LC: 85-26206. ISBN: 0-8052-4012-8. $25.00 (pbk.).

Presents instructional material for preschool through third grade with special suggestions for parents doing home schooling. Chronicles the development of the Little Earth School in New Mexico. Discusses the philosophy of respect for children in a healthy, fun learning environment. Focuses on concrete activities for children based on the value of individual student contributions. Chapters on content areas are filled with appropriate learning activities.

398. Messages from Home: The Mother-Child Home Program and the Prevention of School Disadvantage. Levenstein, Phyllis. Ohio State Univ. Press, 1987. 247p. LC: 87-17315. ISBN: 0-8142-0447-3. $22.50.

Discusses the Verbal Interaction Project's Mother-Child Home Program. The research for this program indicates that low-income mothers can improve their child's future school performance by casual, positive verbal interactions. Describes the nonobtrusive, simple, inexpensive program as well as the systematic research evaluating its effectiveness.

399. Miseducation: Preschoolers at Risk. Elkind, David. Knopf, 1987. 221p. LC: 86-82790. ISBN: 0-394-55256-3. $18.45.

Theorizes that young children are being miseducated by parents anxious to have superkids—children with a competitive edge who will advance beyond their peers. Discusses the short- and long-term risks of miseducating children and presents alternative practices to implement in the school and home. Identifies the differences and overlaps with *The Hurried Child* by the same author.

400. Patterson's Elementary Education. Edited by Moody, Douglas. Educational Directories, Inc., 1989. 723p. ISBN: 0-910536-45-7. $57.50.

Contains 13,456 public school districts, 59,929 public elementary schools, and 10,508 private and church affiliated elementary schools. Includes middle schools but not junior high schools. Excludes special needs schools in this otherwise comprehensive directory.

The Piaget Handbook for Teachers and Parents: Children in the Age of Discovery, Preschool-Third Grade *See* RESOURCES FOR TEACHING (No. 804)

A Place Called School: Prospects for the Future *See* EDUCATIONAL REFORM (No. 265)

401. Professional Ethics in Education. Rich, John Martin. C.C. Thomas, 1984. 155p. LC: 84-2426. ISBN: 0-398-05017-1. $26.25.

A survey and assessment of the issues and problems of professional ethics in elementary, secondary, and higher education. Chapters cover the importance, characteristics, and justification of professional ethics; student rights; research ethics; faculty relations; community relations; and ethical codes. Codes of ethics for the National Education Association and the American Association of University Professors are reprinted. Includes an index.

402. Promoting Effective Student Motivation in School and Classroom: A Practitioner's Perspective. Grossnickle, Donald R. and Thiel, William B. Natl. Assn. of Secondary School Principals, 1988. 72p. ISBN: 0-88210-200-1. $6.00 (pbk.).

Designed to help practitioners improve student motivation by encouraging recognition of obstacles and developing ways to overcome them. Presents a systems model to promote classroom and school motivation; prevention, intervention, and resolution techniques; and methods for establishing schoolwide motivational programs and practices. Useful appendixes are included.

Public Schools USA: A Comparative Guide to School Districts *See* GENERAL SOURCES (No. 453)

403. Quality of Pupil Learning Experiences. Bennett, Neville, Desforges, Charles, Cockburn, Anne and Wilkinson, Betty. L. Erlbaum, 1984. 262p. ISBN: 0-86377-010-X. $29.95.

Based on a research study undertaken in Great Britain, this book attempts to address classroom learning as affected by task allocation and on-task activity. Explores also the issue of the intellectual demands on children made by teachers and how children avoid, meet, or adapt to these demands. Recognizes the complexity of classroom life and socialization as it refers to the learning process.

404. Religious Schools in America: A Selected Bibliography. Hunt, Thomas C., Carper, James C. and Kniker, Charles R. (Garland Reference Library of Social Science, vol. 338). Garland, 1986. 391p. LC: 86-12118. ISBN: 0-8240-8583-3. $47.00.

Selectively annotated bibliography covers private schools with religious affiliations at the kindergarten through high school level. Includes books, articles, dissertations, and reports. Seventeen religious groups are addressed in separate chapters. Historical and contemporary sections are provided for various denominations as well as general works. Chapter two is devoted to court decisions and government regulation of religious schools.

405. School Discipline: A Socially Literate Solution. Alschuler, Alfred S. McGraw-Hill, 1980. 215p. LC: 79-26621. ISBN: 0-001127-3. Contact publisher for price information.

Social literacy, based on the philosophy of Paulo Freire, offers increased democratic participation on the part of teachers, students, and administrators in the governance of schools. Using a problem solving approach, this book can be used as a manual to implement constructive discipline in the classroom. The appendixes include a guide to establishing a Social Literacy Group.

406. School Violence. Goldstein, Arnold P., Apter, Steven J. and Harootunian, Berj. Prentice-Hall, 1984. 246p. LC: 83-8670. ISBN: 0-13-794545-0. $36.00.

Advocates a systems approach to eliminating violence in the schools. Teaching prosocial values and behavior, using aggression control techniques, and involving the school and community are some of the recommendations described. Offers specific guidelines and programs to reduce school violence.

407. Schooling As a Ritual Performance: Towards a Political Economy of Educational Symbols and Gestures. McLaren, Peter. Routledge & Kegan Paul, 1986. 326p. LC: 85-2303. ISBN: 0-7102-0499-X. $16.95 (pbk.).

An ethnographic study based on the theory that schools prepare working-class students for the lower levels of occupational options. Demonstrates how this occurs within the cultural context of the school and shows how the ideologies imbedded in the various school rituals oppress students. Provides insight into the use of power through school rituals, and how that creates both dominated students and students who resist. Fascinating study of cultural domination explores the negative impact of schooling as well as some of the constructive alternatives to oppressive schooling.

408. Schooling the Daughters of Marianne: Textbooks and the Socialization of Girls in Modern French Primary Schools. Clark, Linda L. (European Social History Series). State Univ. of New York Press, 1984. 224p. LC: 83-5035. ISBN: 0-87395-787-3. $57.50.

Focuses on pedagogical literature used in French primary schools since 1880. Explains how primary education for girls differed from that of boys and the consequences for social and political issues. This well-researched study provides a fascinating insight into public education in France as well as the opportunity to compare bias in textbooks in another country to similar research currently being done on U.S. textbooks.

Skill Streaming the Elementary School Child: A Guide for Teaching Prosocial Skills *See* RESOURCES FOR TEACHING (No. 812)

409. Student Activities in the Secondary School: A Handbook and Guide. Sybouts, Ward and Krepel, Wayne J. Greenwood, 1984. 428p. LC: 83-18535. ISBN: 0-313-23379-9. $38.95.

Using the term "student activities" rather than "extracurricular activities," this volume offers a rationale and philosophy for their existence and describes practices in specific areas. These areas include drama, music, athletics, debate, and school publications. Activities covering governance, such as school council or honor societies and social events, are addressed in succeeding chapters. Financial, legal, and planning issues are explored as are questions and concerns expressed by opponents to extracurricular activities.

410. Study of Excellence in High School Education: Longitudinal Study, 1980–1982 Final Report. Educational Testing Service. Ofc. of Educational Research and Improvement, U.S. Dept. of Education, 1986. 721p. Contact publisher for price information. CS86-231.

A longitudinal analysis of high school sophomores from 1980 relating their growth and development to the school experiences from 1980 to 1982. Provides extensive statistical data to aid policymakers in identifying school and student factors that affect student outcomes. Methodology is described in narrative introduction. School dropouts were surveyed as well as continuing students.

411. Successful Schools and Competent Students. Garbarino, James, with the assistance of Asp, C. Elliott. Lexington Books, 1981. 170p. LC: 81-47004. ISBN: 0-669-04526-8. Contact publisher for price information.

Presents a social and developmental perspective on schooling and schools. Addresses the origin and meaning of school success at the elementary, secondary, and post-secondary level. Also discusses the utopian views of school and the reality in our present time. Issues such as school size and racial injustice are discussed briefly.

412. Teacher-Pupil Conflict in Secondary Schools: An Educational Approach. Cronk, K.A. (Issues in Education and Training Series, v. 9). Falmer, 1987. 232p. LC: 87-45768. ISBN: 1-85000-263-0. $40.00.

Advocates a person-centered approach to education and classroom conflict. Explores the important link between belief in the intrinsic morality of disruptive students and practicing a person-centered approach rather than controlling or manipulating students. Utilizes a case study to examine theory in a practical situation. Also addresses the relationship between classroom behavior and the curriculum.

413. Textbooks in School and Society: An Annotated Bibliography and Guide to Research. Edited by Woodward, Arthur, Elliott, David L. and Nagel, Kathleen Carter. (Garland Reference Library of Social Science, vol. 405/ Garland Bibliographies in Contemporary Education, vol. 6). Garland, 1988. 176p. LC: 87-35302. ISBN: 0-8240-8390-3. $25.00.

A classified arrangement of 471 entries with brief annotations. One section contains information about textbook producers and consumers; the other provides evaluation and criticism of textbooks. Entries include journal articles and books from the mid 1970s through 1989. Worthwhile introduction.

414. Toys for Growing: A Guide to Toys That Develop Skills. Sinker, Mary. Natl. Lekotek Center/Year Book Medical Publ., 1986. 170p. ISBN: 0-8151-7750-X. $9.95.

Designed to assist therapists, teachers, care providers, and parents in selecting the appropriate toy to enrich the child's environment. All toys have been field tested with children with special needs but are appropriate for any child. Toys are organized by developmental category. A resource guide at the back lists specialty toy companies. Many toys are available at general toy stores.

415. The World We Created at Hamilton High. Grant, Gerald. Harvard Univ. Press, 1988. 285p. LC: 87-26067. ISBN: 0-674-96200-1. $9.95 (pbk.).

Using Hamilton High as a focal point, the author shows the development of moral and intellectual ideals in schools, the decline and the subsequent rebuilding of these ideals. This case study addresses the need for moral education and a sense of community in educational reform. Hamilton High, a desegregated school, epitomizes many of the failures and successes of the reform movement.

Journals

416. American Secondary Education. Ohio Assn. of Secondary School Administrators, Rm. 319 Education Bldg., Bowling Green State Univ. Bowling Green, OH 43403. Quarterly. $15.00. ISSN: 0003-1003. 1970.

417. Childhood Education. Assn. for Childhood Education International, 11141 Georgia Ave., Suite 200, Wheaton, MD 20902. 5/year. $45.00. ISSN: 0009-4056. 1924. Subtitle: *A Journal for Teachers, Teachers-in-Training, Teacher Educators, Parents, Day Care Workers, Librarians, Pediatricians and Other Child Caregivers.*

418. The Clearing House: A Journal for Middle Schools, Junior and Senior High Schools. Heldref, 4000 Albemarle St., NW, Washington, DC 20016. 9/year. $38.00. ISSN: 0009-8655. 1920. Former titles: *Junior High Clearing House, Junior High School Clearing House, Junior-Senior High School Clearing House.*

419. Day Care and Early Education. Human Sciences Press, 72 Fifth Ave., New York, NY 10011. Quarterly. $58.00. ISSN: 0092-4199. 1973.

Early Years *See* **Early Years/K-8 ELEMENTARY/SECONDARY EDUCATION (No. 420)**

420. Early Years/K-8: A Magazine for Teachers of Preschool Through Grade 8. Allen Raymond, Inc., 40 Richards Ave., Norwalk, CT 06854-2309. 9/year. $18.00. 1971. Former title: *Early Years.*

421. Education Week. Editorial Projects in Education, 4301 Connecticut Ave., NW, Suite 250, Washington, DC 20008. 40/year. $49.94. ISSN: 0277-4232. 1981.

422. Elementary School Journal. Univ. of Chicago Press, 5720 S. Woodlawn Ave., Chicago, IL 60637. Bi-monthly. $43.00. ISSN: 0013-5984. 1900.

423. High School Journal. Univ. of North Carolina Press, Box 2288, Chapel Hill, NC 27514. 4/year. $17.00. ISSN: 0018-1498. 1917.

424. Journal of Curriculum and Supervision. Assn. for Supervision and Development, 125 N. West St., Alexandria, VA 22314. Quarterly. $30.00. ISSN: 0882-1232. 1985.

Junior High Clearing House *See* **The Clearing House ELEMENTARY/SECONDARY EDUCATION (No. 418)**

Junior-Senior High School Clearing House *See* **The Clearing House ELEMENTARY/SECONDARY EDUCATION (No. 418)**

425. Middle School Journal. National Middle School Assn., 4807 Evanswood Dr., Columbus, OH 43229. Quarterly. $20.00. ISSN: 0094-0771. 1970. Former title: *Midwest Middle School Journal.*

Midwest Middle School Journal *See* **Middle School Journal ELEMENTARY/SECONDARY EDUCATION (No. 425)**

426. Urban Education. Sage, 2111 West Hillcrest Dr., Newbury Park, CA 91320. Quarterly. $98.00. ISSN: 0042-0859. 1966.

General Sources

Only general sources relevant to education, useful to professionals and students in education, are considered in this section; general social science reference sources that pertain to education as well as other disciplines, e.g., *National Faculty Directory* or *Historical Statistics of the United States*, are not included. The many guides to colleges and universities, such as *Comparative Guide to American Colleges* or *Lovejoy's*, have also been omitted.

Books

427. Academic Year Abroad. Edited by Howard, E. Marguerite. Institute of International Education, 1989. 391p. LC: 88-21913. ISBN: 87206-167-1. $24.95. 18th edition.
Describes over 1,800 postsecondary programs offered in other countries during the academic year. The programs listed in the first part are sponsored or cosponsored by colleges and universities accredited in the United States; those in the second part are programs offered by institutions without U.S. accreditation. Arrangement is by geographic region providing program information on sponsor, host institution, dates, courses of study, available credit, eligibility, and costs.

428. Adult Literacy/Illiteracy in the United States: A Handbook for Reference and Research. Costa, Marie. (Contemporary World Issues Series). ABC-Clio, 1988. 167p. LC: 87-31696. ISBN: 0-87436-492-2. $34.95.
Provides a foundation for understanding adult literacy/illiteracy by providing basic information in such areas as history and chronology of the field, biography, facts and data, and identifying resources such as organizations and agencies, printed materials, and computer resources. Includes a glossary of literacy-related terms, a list of references, and a combined author, subject, title index.

429. American Education: A Guide to Information Sources. Durning, Richard G. (American Studies Information Guide, v.14). Gale, 1982. 264p. LC: 82-15387. ISBN: 0-8103-1265-4. $68.00.
A selective, annotated (some very brief) bibliography covering the field of education from early childhood through graduate studies and beyond in 107 subject chapters. Opens with a bibliographical essay tying together significant developments, movements, concerns, and themes in the history of American education with important books and sources that appeared at the time. An alphabetic name index includes all persons mentioned in the essay and the bibliography.

430. American Educators' Encyclopedia. Dejnozka, Edward L. and Kapel, David E. Greenwood, 1982. 634p. LC: 81-6664. ISBN: 0-313-20954-5. $85.00.
Provides almost 2,000 short articles based on the names and terms frequently found in the literature of professional education and written by the two authors; basic information on a subject entry is given with follow-up sources for more information covered in the individual bibliographies. Authorities in the 22 broad areas covered were asked to review and evaluate all of the entries for accuracy, comprehensiveness of information, and the relevance of the references included. Encompasses elementary, secondary, and higher education.

431. American Universities and Colleges. Walter de Gruyter, 1987. 2024p. LC: 28-5598. ISBN: 0-89925-179-X. $119.50. 13th edition; ISSN: 0066-0922.
A standard directory of approximately 2,000 colleges and universities that grant the baccalaureate or higher degrees. Following some general informational chapters on higher education in Part 1 and the listing of accrediting agencies in Part 2, the major portion presents the usual descriptive information for the institutions but also includes information on publications of an institution, library collections, etc. *Commonwealth Universities Yearbook* and *International Handbook of Universities and . . . Higher Education* are standard directories for Commonwealth countries and countries outside the U.S.

432. ARBA Guide to Education. Edited by Brewer, Deborah J. Libraries Unlimited, 1985. 232p. LC: 85-23150. ISBN: 0-87287-490-7. $23.50.
Special compilation of education reference works reviewed in *American Reference Books Annual* from 1970–1985; coverage for 1986+ continues in the yearly edition of ARBA for individual years. Arranged by type of work—bibliographies, indexes, dictionaries—with each type arranged by subject. Covers sources of bibliographic information, sources of factual information, and sources on special topics such as instructional media, special education, and others.

433. Bibliographic Guide to Education. (Bibliographic Guides Series). G.K. Hall, 1978–. 470p., 1987 LC: 79-643170. ISBN: 0-8161-7-67-3, 1987. $250.00.

An annual bibliographic guide on all aspects of education covering books cataloged at Columbia University's Teachers College Library, supplemented by selected titles from the New York Public Library. The equivalent of a card catalog in book format, it provides full bibliographic data for the main entry and access by added entries, titles, series titles, and subjects for most of what is published in the United States in education, excluding serials.

434. Catalog of Federal Domestic Assistance. Government Printing Office, 1965–. LC: 73-600118. $38.00, 1989. 23rd edition; Stock no. 922009-00000-7.

A directory of information on programs under which communities and individuals may be able to obtain federal assistance in various forms (financial and nonfinancial)—grants, loans, surplus government property, technical advice, and information. The 1989 *Catalog* contains more than 1,100 different assistance programs in many areas of education—adult education, higher education, special education. Program information is cross referenced by subject, applicant, deadlines.

435. Childhood Information Resources. Woodbury, Marda. Information Resources Press, 1985. 593p. LC: 84-80534. ISBN: 0-87815-051-X. $45.00.

A compilation of major information sources on all aspects of childhood from different disciplines covered under three sections—Printed Reference Works, Nonprint Sources on the Child, and Special Subjects. Emphasizes current sources on American children from conception through age 12, a few sources on children worldwide, and some historical sources. Types of materials include bibliographies, periodicals, audiovisuals, and databases.

436. The College Blue Book: Scholarships, Fellowships, Grants and Loans. Macmillan, 1979–. LC: 79-66191. ISBN: 0-02-695969-0. $200 set. Contact publisher for price information for single volume. 5 volumes; 22nd edition.

Lists private sources of financial aid in the form of scholarships, fellowships, grants, and loans for funding a college education. Information is provided under nine broad subject areas, further subdivided; a "general" section lists sponsors who do not restrict awards to specific subject areas. The other volumes in the *College Blue Book* set are—*Degrees Offered by College and Subject, Narrative Descriptions,* and *Tabular Data.*

437. Dictionary of Educational Acronyms, Abbreviations, and Initialisms. Palmer, James C. and Colby, Anita Y. Oryx, 1985. 97p. LC: 84-42814. ISBN: 0-89774-165-X. $27.50. 2nd edition.

The two sections in this useful resource are an alphabetically arranged list of acronyms identifying the initials of each entry and a reverse list of acronyms arranged alphabetically by their unabbreviated forms. Each entry includes only the acronym and the terminology it represents. All entries are drawn from such sources as *Resources in Education,* education journals, college catalogs, and the *Encyclopedia of Associations.*

438. Directory of Curriculum Materials Centers. Edited by Lehman, Lois J. and Kiewitt, Eva L. Assn. of College and Research Libraries, American Library Assn., 1985. 196p. LC: 86-143852. ISBN: 0-8389-6917-8. $20.00.

This guide describes the collections of some 170 curriculum centers, representing 42 states and 5 Canadian locations. Information included for each location includes holdings, classification system, budget, types of materials, and contact person.

439. Directory of Research Grants. Oryx, annual. 1200p. LC: 76-47074. $118.00. ISSN: 0146-7336.

The *Directory* is the printed complement to the GRANTS database. Lists programs offering nonrepayable research funding for projects in medicine, the physical and social sciences, the humanities, and the arts. Each annotation describes the program's focus and goals, requirements, restrictions, contacts, deadlines, and funding amounts. Subject, sponsoring organization, and type of sponsoring organization indexes are provided. The GRANTS database should be searched to update information in the *Directory.*

440. Don't Miss Out: The Ambitious Student's Guide to Financial Aid 1989–90. Leider, Robert and Leider, Anna. Caroline House, 1988. 96p. LC: 79-3000. ISBN: 0-945981-00-7. $5.00. 13th edition.

A handy comprehensive guide to strategies available to those students seeking financial aid for college. This booklet size work is concise and straightforward on how to play the financial aid game in getting money from many sources—colleges, employers, federal government, etc., with a special section for minorities, women, and athletes. An addition to the collection that should also include *Chronicle Student Aid Annual* and the *College Cost Book* or *Peterson's College Money Handbook* for information on institutional financial aid offerings.

441. Education: A Guide to Reference and Information Sources. Buttlar, Lois. (Reference Sources in the Social Sciences Series, no.2). Libraries Unlimited, 1989. 258p. LC: 89-2651. ISBN: 0-87287-619-5. $35.00.

Part of an important series covering major sources within the social sciences, including this volume in education and related fields. The 900 sources, almost all published after 1980, include major English-language printed guides, bibliographies, indexes, and abstracts, and nonprint sources such as databases, organizations, and others. General reference sources are covered first, then specific areas of education.

442. Education Journals and Serials: An Analytical Guide. Collins, Mary Ellen. (Annotated Bibliographies of Serials: A Subject Approach, no.12). Greenwood, 1988. 355p. LC: 87-31442. ISBN: 0-313-24514-2. $49.95.

Identifies, with annotations, currently published English-language, national and international serials in the major fields of education. The 803 entries are subdivided into general education areas, levels of education, teaching methods, curriculum and professional issues, and 17 topical areas. Types of sources cover association publications, review journals, newsletters, state and regional publications, and selected government publications.

443. Educator's Desk Reference (EDR): A Sourcebook of Educational Information and Research. Freed, Melvin N., Hess, Robert K. and Ryan, Joseph M. American Council on Education/Macmillan, 1989. 536p. LC: 88-9249. ISBN: 0-02-910740-7. $70.00.

A reference handbook providing information for the professional educator on the academic field of "education" to satisfy practical, research oriented and nonresearch inquiries. Areas covered include: important reference books, publishers and producers of software, profiles of standardized tests, directory of education organizations, and various research designs. Referrals are made to other sources for more complete information.

Encyclopedia of Special Education: A Reference for the Education of the Handicapped and Other Exceptional Children and Adults *See* SPECIAL EDUCATION (No. 841)

444. The Facts on File Dictionary of Education. Edited by Shafritz, Jay M., Koeppe, Richard P. and Soper, Elizabeth W. Facts on File, 1988. 503p. LC: 88-24554. ISBN: 0-8160-1636-4. $40.00.

Contains definitions of words, terms, phrases, processes, names, laws and court cases, and biographical and organization entries and test descriptions that are central to current concerns of education and with which those concerned with education would be familiar. Two types of definitions are provided: brief glossary descriptions and more comprehensive coverage.

445. Foundation Grants to Individuals. Edited by Olson, Stanley. Foundation Center, 1988. 288p. LC: 81-70303. ISBN: 0-87954-238-1. $24.00. 6th edition.

A listing of 1,041 private United States foundations that provide financial assistance to individuals; 183 programs are new to this edition. Describes giving for scholarships, student loans, fellowships, foreign recipients, travel, internships, residencies, arts and cultural projects, and general welfare. A bibliography of reference guides to alternative funding other than foundations is provided. Information on funding programs for non-profit organizations and institutions is available in *The Foundation Directory* and *Source Book Profiles*.

446. The Gourman Report: A Rating of Graduate and Professional Programs in American and International Universities. Gourman, Jack. National Educational Standards, 1989. 267p. LC: 88-063477. ISBN: 0-918192-13-7. $14.95. 5th edition.

This volume and *The Gourman Report* for *Rating of Undergraduate Programs* are intended as guides for evaluating the effectiveness of programs and comparing one program against another "taking into account a wide variety of empirical data." Ratings are assigned to quality of faculty, standards of instruction, students' scholastic work, and the records of graduates. Much has been written about the validity of the "Gourman reports" in the literature; this information should also be consulted.

447. The Grants Register 1989–1991. Edited by Lerner, Craig A. St. Martin's, 1988. 779p. LC: 77-12055. ISBN: 0-312-02118-6. Contact publisher for price information. 11th edition.

A standard resource listing the following kinds of assistance for students pursuing graduate or postgraduate education: scholarships, fellowships, grants, exchange opportunities, vacation study and travel grants; also describes opportunities for administrative and academic staff of educational institutions. Many awards are international in scope. The *Register* is published every two years.

448. A Guide to Sources of Educational Information. Woodbury, Marda. Information Resources Press, 1982. 430p. LC: 82-80549. ISBN: 0-87815-041-2. $39.95. 2nd edition.

A very useful guide still in print. Descriptions of some 700 print and non-print sources of educational information are collected under three sections: Printed Research Tools, Special Subjects, and Nonprint Sources. A preliminary section on effective research and a final follow-through chapter on reporting the results of an information search are included.

The HEP Higher Education Directory *See* HIGHER AND CONTINUING EDUCATION (No. 550)

449. International Encyclopedia of Education: Research and Studies. Edited by Husen, Torsten and Postlethwaite, T. Neville. Pergamon, 1985. 5648p. LC: 84-20750. ISBN: 0-08-028119-2. $2,150.00.

This ten-volume set is an attempt to present an "up-to-date overview of scholarship brought to bear on educational problems, practices and institutions all over the world" through approximately 1,500 longer and shorter articles authored by international scholars. A separate "Subject Index" volume is an important access point for a work of this size; an Author Index and Classified List of Entries is included. A supplementary "Volume 1" was published in 1988 and listed in *Books in Print*.

450. International Who's Who in Education. Edited by Kay, Ernest. Taylor & Francis, 1986. 715p. ISBN: 0-90033-287-5. $185.00. 3rd edition.

A biographical dictionary of the world's leading teachers and university staff, education advisers and writers, and administrators. No criteria are given for selection of individuals except the "selection is made on the grounds of interest to the general reader as well as to those within the teaching profession." Biographies included are from as many different countries as possible and as many educational levels as space will allow. Photographs are now included with some biographies.

451. Learning Independently. Edited by Wassermann, Steven, O'Brien, Jacqueline W. and Applebaum, Edmond L. Gale, 1987. 437p. LC: 82-3006. ISBN: 0-8103-0362-0. $220.00. 3rd edition.

"A directory of approximately 4,000 self-instruction resources including correspondence courses, programmed learning products, audio and videocassette, films and filmstrips, games and simulations, multi-media kits and conventional learning materials such as books intended for non-formal education." The 3,997 entries exclude products that require an instructor working with a class or group interaction.

452. Peterson's Guide to Graduate Programs in Business, Education, Health and Law. (Peterson's Annual Guides to Graduate Study Series: Book 6). Peterson's Guides, 1988–. 1619p. LC: 89-645335. ISBN: 0-87866-753-9. $19.95. ISSN: 0897-6023; 23rd edition.

A new volume in the series, for 1989, covering graduate and professional programs in business, health, education, and law, offered by accredited colleges and universities in the United States and Canada. Information presented includes profiles, announcements, and full descriptions of the programs written by the graduate school and program administrators. Book 1 of the series offers an overview of the institutions, as a whole; the remainder, books 2–6, are specific to other academic and professional fields. Available online as *GRADLINE*.

453. Public Schools USA: A Comparative Guide to School Districts. Harrison, Charles. Williamson, 1988. 366p. LC: 87-34313. ISBN: 0-913589-36-5. $17.95.

Profiles approximately 500 school districts with enrollments of 2,500+ students located in major metropolitan areas. Comparisons of the school districts can be made based on 22 statistics including enrollment, current expense per student, teacher salaries, and other factors. Using the statistical profile, an "Effective Schools Index" was computed for each district, rating it in each category against the national average; this Index is very helpful in comparing districts. A useful guide for anyone concerned with the comparative merits of public schools.

454. Teach Overseas: The Educators World-Wide Handbook and Directory to International Teaching in Overseas Schools, Colleges and Universities. Webster, Steve. Maple Tree, 1984. 420p. LC: 83-23866. ISBN: 0-915387-01-8. $12.95.

Following some general comments on teaching overseas, the text presents information on teaching in countries and territories from A to Z. Each entry provides an overview; a brief history; a listing of government positions; and the addresses of schools, colleges, and universities.

455. The Teacher's Almanac 1988–89. Harris, Sherwood and Harris, Lorna B. Facts on File, 1988. 320p. LC: 87-647888. ISBN: 0-8160-1986-X. $35.00. ISSN: 0889-079X.

A compilation of information of "greatest usefulness and interest to teachers" and educational researchers from a variety of sources such as the Department of Education and professional associations in education; the volume is valuable for its convenience. Contains 11 sections with many subsections covering teacher salaries and jobs, state rankings, the teacher's year, and specific topics such as "State Teacher of the Year" and "State Textbook Adoption Schedule."

456. The World of Learning. Gale, 1989. 1925p. LC: 47-30172. ISBN: 0-9466-5346-1. $255.00. 39th edition; ISSN: 0084-2117.

The standard international directory of scholarly organizations covering universities, colleges, technical institutions, libraries, museums, learned societies, and research institutes. Listings vary by type of institution/organization but all include name, address, and key officials.

457. Yearbook. National Society for the Study of Education. National Society for the Study of Education. Univ. of Chicago Press, 1902–. Annual.

The Society's monograph-yearbooks have been published annually since 1902, most recently in two or three parts on different significant topics—*Schooling and Disability* (1989), *Culture, Literacy and the Idea of General Education* (1988), *Ecology of School Renewal* (1987). Each *Yearbook* is a scholarly contribution to current educational thought and practice compiled under the direction of a different editor. Indexed in *Education Index*.

Journals

458. American Journal of Education. Univ. of Chicago Press, Journals Division, 5720 S. Woodlawn Ave., Chicago, IL 60637. Quarterly. $38.00. ISSN: 0195-6744. 1979. Formerly *School Review* (1893–1979).

459. Current Index to Journals in Education. Oryx Press, 4041 N. Central at Indian School Rd., Phoenix, AZ 85012. Monthly index/semiannual cumulations. $207 monthly/$198 semiannual cumulations. ISSN: 0011-3565. March 1969. A monthly indexing and abstracting journal to more than 750 primary journals in social and behavioral education-related disciplines. Coverage is comprehensive, indexed by subject terms (descriptors) from the *The-*

saurus of ERIC Descriptors. Brief annotations are provided as are author and alphabetic journal-contents indexes. Semiannual cumulations. Also available online and in compact disk through several vendors.

460. Education. Project Innovation of Mobile, P.O. Box 8508, Spring Hill Station, Mobile, AL 36608. Quarterly. $21.00. ISSN: 0013-1172. 1980.

461. Education Digest. Prakken Publications, Inc., 416 Longshore Dr., Box 8623, Ann Arbor, MI 48107. 9/year. $24.00. ISSN: 0013-127X. 1935.

462. Education Index. H.W. Wilson, 950 University Ave., Bronx, NY 10452. 10/year with annual cumulations. Price based on size of institution's educational periodical collection. ISSN: 0013-1385. 1929. Serves as a basic index to a selected list of approximately 400 English-language education periodicals and proceedings, yearbooks, monographs, bulletins and some government publications in education. Authors and subjects are combined in one alphabetic index.

463. Educational Forum. Kappa Delta Pi Intl. Honor Society in Education, P.O. Box A, 1601 W. State St., West Lafayette, IN 47906. Quarterly. $12.00. ISSN: 0013-1725. 1936.

464. Educational Horizons. Pi Lambda Theta, 4101 East Third St., Bloomington, IN 47401. Quarterly. $15.00. ISSN: 0013-175X. 1921.

465. Educational Studies. American Educational Studies Assn., John E. Carter, Editor, School of Education, Indiana State Univ., Terre Haute, IN 47809. Quarterly. $25.00. ISSN: 0013-1946. 1970.

466. Harvard Educational Review. Graduate School of Education, Longfellow Hall, 13 Appian Way, Cambridge, MA 02138. Quarterly. $55.00. ISSN: 0017-8055. 1937.

467. Peabody Journal of Education. Peabody College for Teachers/Vanderbilt Univ., Box 41, Nashville, TN 37203. Quarterly. $40.00. ISSN: 0031-3432. 1923.

468. Phi Delta Kappan. Phi Delta Kappa Inc., P.O. Box 789, Bloomington, IN 47402-0789. 10/year. $20.00. ISSN: 0031-7217. 1915.

469. Resources in Education (RIE). U. S. Dept. of Education, Office of Educational Research and Improvement, Educational Resources Information Center, 2440 Research Blvd., Suite 550, Rockville, MD 20850. Monthly index/semiannual cumulations. $70.00 monthly/$21.00 semiannual. ISSN: 0098-0897. 1966. A monthly index with abstracts to documents processed by a network of clearinghouses in ERIC (Educational Resources Information Center) located throughout the country. Covers reports of federally funded projects, technical and research reports, conference proceedings, documents from school districts, etc., the hard-to-find, peripheral materials produced in education. Indexed by subject terms (descriptors) from the *Thesaurus of ERIC Descriptors.* Author and institution indexes also. Also available online and in compact disk through several vendors. Also annual cumulation published by The Oryx Press.

470. Review of Education. Redgrave Publishing Co., Box 67, South Salem, NY 10590. Quarterly. $34.00. ISSN: 0098-5597. 1975.

School Review *See* American Journal of Education GEN-
ERAL SOURCES (No. 458)

471. Theory into Practice. Ohio State University, College of
Education, 174 Arps Hall, 1945 N. High St., Columbus,
OH 43210. Quarterly. $30.00. ISSN: 0040-5841. 1962.

472. Times Educational Supplement. Times Newspaper, Ltd.,
Priory House, St. John's Lane, London EC1M 4BX, United Kingdom. Weekly. $75.00. ISSN: 0040-7887. 1910.

473. Urban Review: Issues and Ideas in Public Education.
Agathon Press, Inc., 111 8th Ave., New York, NY 10011.
Quarterly. $44.00. ISSN: 0042-0972. 1966.

Health/Physical Education

A mixture of titles in physical and health education and sports are provided—research in these areas, historical coverage, law and sports, developing instructional programs, health practices, safety issues, etc. Contemporary issues are also dealt with—AIDS, women in sports, drug and alcohol education—although there are not very many education-related titles in these areas or in an area such as child abuse from an educational perspective. Textbooks are inevitable since they are the primary vehicle for conveying content information in these areas. Journals cover all levels of health and physical education.

Books

474. Advancing Health Through Education; A Case Study Approach. Edited by Cleary, Helen P., Kichen, Jeffrey M. and Ensor, Phyllis G. Mayfield, 1985. 395p. LC: 84-060884. ISBN: 0-87484-569-6. $29.95.

A textbook in health education using a case study approach. The selected case studies illustrate health education practices in school settings, medical care settings, community settings, and worksite settings; each study concludes with an analysis and discussion questions. For students, educators, practitioners, and administrators in health education.

475. AIDS Challenge: Prevention Education for Young People. Edited by Quackenbush, Marcia, Nelson, Mary and Clark, Kay. Network Publications, 1988. 526p. LC: 88-19509. ISBN: 0-941816-54-0; 0-941816-53-2 (pbk.). $34.95; $24.95 (pbk.).

Brings together current knowledge about AIDS education for young people with chapters by national and international experts on AIDS. Covers all bases of information—the human element, the science of AIDS, essential elements for prevention education in the classroom and a religious setting, controversial issues, and AIDS risks for minorities and special populations. Guidelines for building an effective preschool-Grade 12 AIDS prevention education program are provided.

476. Business of Physical Education: Future of the Profession. Ellis, Michael J. Human Kinetics, 1988. 222p. LC: 87-17344. ISBN: 0-87322-127-3. $28.00.

The author's goal is to predict the future nature of the physical education profession by relating it to the political, economic, and demographic factors of society. Discussion covers the problems for physical education in society at large, changes occurring in the physical education field and models for physical education.

477. Comparative Physical Education and Sport, Volume 5. Edited by Broom, Eric F. et al. (International Seminar on Comparative Physical Education and Sport, 5th). Human Kinetics, 1988. 292p. LC: 87-37821. ISBN: 0-87322-047-1. $38.00. Proceedings of the Fifth International Seminar on Comparative Physical Education and Sport, May 22–31, 1986, University of British Columbia.

Although no theme is indicated for this international seminar-related collection of papers, most of the contributor's works are comparative studies of some aspect of sport, fitness, or physical education in their country or cross-national comparisons of countries. Topics include international perspectives of aerobic dance, the state of physical education in and between various countries, and changes in women's intercollegiate sports.

478. Completed Research in Health, Physical Education, Recreation and Dance, Including International Sources. Edited by Freedson, Patty S. and Moffatt, Robert. American Alliance for Health, Physical Education, Recreation and Dance, 1959–. ISBN: 0-88314-386-0 (Vol. 19, 1988). Contact publisher for price information. 0516-916X.

An annual compilation of research completed in the areas of health, physical education, recreation, dance and allied areas during a given year, i.e., 1988 covers 1987. Four sections are: "Index to Abstracts" arranged by subject headings; "Theses Abstracts" from institutions producing master's and doctor's theses in alphabetical order according to institution; "Bibliography" of research published in periodicals reviewed; "Institutions Reporting" their research.

Developmental/Adapted Physical Education: Making Ability Count *See* **RESOURCES FOR TEACHING (No. 790)**

479. Drug Abuse. Edited by Reitz, Raymond J. (Hot Topics Series). Center on Evaluation Development and Research/Phi Delta Kappa, 1987. 310p. Contact publisher for price information.

A collection of articles providing educators with practical information on the prevalence of drug abuse; determinants of drug abuse; effects of drug abuse on students, schools, and parents; and characteristics of school-based prevention programs designed to prevent drug abuse.

Drug Education: Content and Methods *See* **RESOURCES FOR TEACHING (No. 792)**

Dynamic Physical Education for Elementary School Children *See* **RESOURCES FOR TEACHING (No. 793)**

480. Education, Movement, and the Curriculum. Arnold, Peter J. Taylor & Francis, 1988. 175p. LC: 88-24389. ISBN: 1-85000-413-7. $19.00.
A philosophical exploration of the relationship between education and movement and what implications are evident for the teacher and for curriculum planning and its evaluation. The author's definition of "movement" refers to, collectively, the family of physical activities comprised of games, swimming, dance, athletics, gymnastics, and outdoor pursuits. A "Three Dimensional Model of the Movement Curriculum" is proposed.

481. Effects of Physical Activity on Children: A Special Tribute to Mabel Lee. Edited by Stull, G. Alan. (American Academy of Physical Education Papers, No. 19). Human Kinetics, 1986. 167p. ISBN: 0-87322-049-8. $14.00. ISSN: 0741-4633; American Academy of Physical Education, Fifty-Seventh Annual Meeting, April 15–16, 1985, Atlanta, Georgia.
Papers summarize existing research on the effects of physical activity and exercise on factors such as moral, social, emotional, intellectual and physical development of children; weight control, physical fitness, motor learning and coronary risk factors in children. An introductory chapter offers a tribute to Mabel Lee, a prominent female pioneer and leader in the field of physical education.

482. Encyclopedia of Physical Education, Fitness and Sports. Edited by Cureton, Thomas K. American Alliance for Health, Physical Education, Recreation and Dance, 1977–1985. LC: 76-46608. ISBN: 0-88314-239-7.
A four-volume compendium of information related to physical education, sport, and fitness. The set covers: Volume 1, Philosophy, Programs and History; Volume 2, Training, Environment, Nutrition and Fitness; Volume 3, Sports, Dance and Related Activities; Volume 4, Human Performance: Efficiency and Improvements Sports, Exercise and Fitness. Volumes 2 and 4 are still available in *Books in Print*.

483. From Fair Sex to Feminism: Sport and the Socialization of Women in the Industrial and Post-Industrial Eras. Edited by Mangan, J.A. and Park, Roberta. Frank Cass and Co., 1987. 312p. LC: 86-17529. ISBN: 0-7146-3288-0; 0-7146-4049-2 (pbk.). $29.50; $14.95 (pbk.).
Presents an overview of major attitudes toward women and physical education and sports in both Old and New Worlds; physical education from British perspectives during Victorian times and the twentieth century; aspects of health, physical education, leisure pursuits and sports for American women from the late seventeenth to twentieth centuries. Some of the papers have been published elsewhere and rewritten for reproduction.

484. Health in Elementary Schools. Cornacchia, Larry K., Olsen, Larry K. and Nickerson, Carl J. Times Mirror/Mosby College Publications, 1988. 479p. LC: 87-17996. ISBN: 0-8016-1120-2. $26.95. 7th edition.

Like other texts in this field, this title deals with a healthful school environment, health services, and health education; the latter area forms the bulk of the text covering the status of health education today and programs, organization, materials, methods, and evaluation issues.

485. History of Physical Education and Sport. Zeigler, Earle F. et al. Stipes, 1988. 311p. ISBN: 0-87563-309-0. $21.80. Revised edition.
Provides a history of physical education and sport in early societies, in the Middle Ages, in modern times, in the United States and Canada. The author places physical education and sport in a different historical perspective by viewing some of the persistent problems and social forces recurring throughout history as they relate to physical education and sport e.g., values, politics, religion, use of leisure.

486. How Healthy Is Your School?: Guidelines for Evaluating School Health Promotion. Nelson, Steven. NCHE Press, 1986. 240p. LC: 86-16323. ISBN: 0-914617-02-8. $11.95.
A practical, non-technical manual providing methods and resources for school personnel to evaluate health-related activities in a school. Presents an overview of what comprises school health, health services, and a healthful school environment; provides a basic evaluation framework and emphasizes the planning and implementation of school health programs along with student outcomes. Many forms and charts included.

Instructional Strategies for Secondary School Physical Education *See* **RESOURCES FOR TEACHING (No. 800)**

487. Introduction to Research in Health, Physical Education, Recreation and Dance. Thomas, Herry R. and Nelson, Jack K. Human Kinetics, 1985. 414p. LC: 84-25251. ISBN: 0-93125-093-5. $27.00.
Intended primarily for beginning graduate students in physical education, since most illustrations applying research are in physical education. Basic areas are covered: overview of the research process, statistical concepts in research, types of research, measurement, and writing the research report.

488. Law in Sport and Physical Activity. Clement, Annie. Benchmark, 1988. 214p. LC: 87-70299. ISBN: 0-936157-21-6. $18.95.
Aside from on-the-job precautions that physical activity professionals need to maintain, this book provides the legal literacy that these professionals should acquire. Legal concepts deliberated are followed by a discussion of the concepts related to human movement and their relevancy in real court cases. Legal principles of contract and employment are considered as are civil rights issues, an important part of future litigation in school environments.

489. Leading the Way: Amy Morris Homans and the Beginning of Professional Education for Women. Spears, Betty. (Contributions in Women's Studies, no. 64). Greenwood, 1986. 179p. LC: 85-21872. ISBN: 0-313-25107-X. $35.00.
As per Ms. Homans' wishes, this book is not biographical in nature; it relates Amy Homans' struggles to gain the acceptance of physical education as a profession for women and her unique approach to educating women leaders for that profession.

490. Learning by Heart: AIDS and Schoolchildren in America's Communities. Kirp, David L. et al. Rutgers Univ. Press, 1989. 304p. LC: 88-29789. ISBN: 0-8135-1396-0. $22.95.

Chronicles the conflicts that occurred across American communities where schoolchildren with AIDS attempted to attend school. Begins with a chapter discussing the political and social dimensions of the question of whether a child with AIDS belongs in school. Each of the next chapters reports on the public and personal experiences of AIDS schoolchildren, their families, and the communities confronted with that question.

491. Management of Physical Education and Athletic Programs. Bucher, Charles A. Times Mirror/Mosby College Publications, 1987. 438p. LC: 86-16391. ISBN: 0-801-60908-9. $31.95. 9th edition.

This ninth edition remains much the same as previous editions covering administrative theory of management, management considerations in physical education instructional programs, and management functions; new material includes information on management tasks via computers, marketing physical education, and other areas. Instructor's manual available.

492. Measurement for Evaluation in Physical Education and Exercise Science. Baumgartner, Ted A. and Jackson, Andrew S. William C. Brown, 1987. 470p. LC: 86-71261. ISBN: 0-697-00916-5. Contact publisher for price information. 3rd edition.

Both theoretical and practical information are presented following a "mastery approach" in chapter organization—instructional objectives at the beginning of each chapter and test questions at the end. Measurement areas covered are quantitative aspects, performance testing, cognitive and affective testing, and psychological dimensions of physical education. Includes new material on the use of microcomputers in measurement.

493. Methods of Research in Physical Education. Thorpe, JoAnne L. C.C. Thomas, 1986. 308p. LC: 85-14841. ISBN: 0-398-05174-7. $40.25.

A guide to conducting research in physical education beginning with some introductory material and chapters on research in general: writing the research report, basic statistics, techniques for gathering data, and study designs. The remainder of the text deals with methods of research specifically applied to physical education.

494. New Directions in Health Education: School Health Education and the Community in Western Europe and the United States. Edited by Campbell, George. (New Directions Series, Falmer Press). Falmer, 1985. 238p. LC: 84-18718. ISBN: 0-90527-358-3; 0-90527-357-5 (pbk.). $33.00; $18.00 (pbk.).

Papers written by leading health educators in Western Europe and the United States on the school-community interface theme in health education. Examines constraints on school-community interaction and strategies and methods of overcoming the constraints. Describes post-1981 developments in professional training for health education in various countries with special emphasis on the United Kingdom.

495. Organization of School Health Programs. Redican, Kerry J., Olsen, Larry K. and Baffi, Charles R. Macmillan, 1986. 500p. LC: 84-25039. ISBN: 0-02-398870-3. Contact publisher for price information.

Provides information needed to develop and organize a sound school health program or to evaluate existing or emerging school health programs. Organized in four sections: Foundations—basics necessary for developing a sound program; Environment—prerequisites for physical plant, maintenance, and emotional climate; Services—appraisal, screening and referral of students, and other areas; Instruction—content and activities for the school health curricula. Supporting documents for program development provided in the appendices.

496. Physical Education and Curriculum Study: A Critical Introduction. Kirk, David. Croom Helm, 1988. 179p. LC: GB87-49356. ISBN: 0-70993-126-3.

As the result of dissatisfaction with other curriculum texts in physical education, the author offers this introduction to some of the standard topics/issues in curriculum studies as they apply in a physical education context and at the same time offers a discussion of alternate ways of looking at these topics. Some topics are recent developments in physical education, curriculum content, and the hidden curriculum.

497. Physical Education and Health: Selected Works of James H. Humphrey. Humphrey, James Harry. (AMS Studies in Education, no. 8). AMS Press, 1987. LC: 86-47843. ISBN: 0-404-12669-3. $75.00 set. ISSN: 0882-348X; 2 Volumes.

A collection of selected works of James Humphrey, writer, scholar, researcher, and professor emeritus in the field of physical education. Volume 1 is devoted to writings in "Physical Education" and Dr. Humphrey's pioneer efforts to promote physical education for young children and their learning through motor activity. Volume 2, "Health," includes essays on alcohol and drug abuse and the problem of stress in children.

498. Physical Education Index. Edited by Kirby, Ronald F. BenOak Publishing, 1978–. LC: 80-2013. $150.00. 0191-9202.

Subject index to 186 English-language, domestic (national and state), and foreign periodicals in these major subject areas: dance, health, physical education, physical therapy, recreation, sports and sportsmedicine. Indexes articles pertinent to professionals, legislation in these areas, reports of associations and conventions, and biographies and obituaries of physical education professionals.

Principles of Safety in Physical Education and Sport *See* RESOURCES FOR TEACHING (No. 805)

499. Program Design in Physical Education: A Guide to the Development of Exemplary Programs. Vogel, Paul and Seefeldt, Vern. Benchmark, 1988. 84p. LC: 88-070144. ISBN: 0-936157-29-1. $12.95.

A guide to planning, implementing, and evaluating physical education programs to facilitate obtaining evidence of the effectiveness of these programs regarding student outcomes and benefits; the authors propose that greater public support and resources would result. Supplementary materials available in the chapters and appendices.

500. School Health Practice. Creswell, William H. and Newman, Ian M. Times Mirror/Mosby College Publications, 1989. 482p. LC: 88-31547. ISBN: 0-8016-2560-2. $33.95. 9th edition.

A revised edition that includes greater emphasis on contemporary issues and health problems of students, such as substance use, sexual behavior, eating disorders, and the trend toward establishing school-based clinics for comprehensive school health programs. For teachers the problem of child abuse is recognized and addressed. A "Self-Appraisal Checklist for School Health Programs" is appended.

501. School Phobia and Its Treatment. Blagg, Nigel. Routledge, Chapman & Hall, 1987. 228p. LC: 87-13444. ISBN: 0-709-93938-8. $49.95.

Drawing on extensive research studies, the author first reviews what is known about a condition called school phobia and its treatment through a critical review of the literature. The "rapid behavioral treatment" approach used in the author's research is described and illustrated with six case studies. A "School Phobia Record Form" is included.

502. Sports and Physical Education: A Guide to the Reference Sources. Gratch, Bonnie, Chan, Betty and Lingenfelter, Judith. Greenwood, 1983. 198p. LC: 82-24159. ISBN: 0313-23433-7. $36.95.

Guide to English-language reference sources in sports, physical education, and certain allied fields such as sports medicine, history of sports, women and sports, physical fitness, adapted physical education, sports for the handicapped, and other areas. Commercial monographs and serials, ERIC documents, and some government publications are indexed.

503. Sports Law for Educational Institutions. Wade, Steven C. and Hay, Robert D. Quorum Books, 1988. 207p. LC: 87-37573. ISBN: 0-89930-335-8. $39.95.

Explores the relationship of law to organized sports in secondary schools and colleges providing edited texts of leading judicial opinions on legal cases involving organized athletics at these levels; explanatory notes and comments supplement the judicial opinions. Covers equal opportunity for participation, civil rights of participants versus disciplinary authority, products liability of equipment manufacturers, and tort liability of program sponsors.

504. Student Drug and Alcohol Abuse. Towers, Richard L. (NEA Professional Library/How Schools Can Help Combat Series). National Education Assn., 1987. 224p. LC: 86-16471. ISBN: 0-8106-3292-6; 0-8106-3291-8. $19.95; $10.95.

Major purpose is to provide methods of preventing student abuse of drugs and alcohol and what to do when abuse occurs. The emphasis throughout is on the importance of schools sharing in a partnership with the home and community to combat the student drug abuse problem. Covers activities and materials used successfully by schools; vocabulary of the drug scene; types of treatment programs; school's role in aftercare and reentry for recovering abusers.

505. Teaching Children to Relax. Humphrey, James Harry. C.C. Thomas, 1988. 164p. LC: 88-16075. ISBN: 0-398-05512-2.

The "Father of Stress," childhood stress, is providing information for educators to help relieve children of the stress and tension of the school day with periodic relaxation programs. Following some discussion on childhood emotions and the extent of stress in the school environment, relaxation practices that have been field-tested with children are recommended; some are physiological and some psychological in nature.

506. Trends Toward the Future in Physical Education. Edited by Massengale, John D. Human Kinetics, 1987. 190p. LC: 86-34282. ISBN: 0-87322-103-6. $24.00.

Each of the contributors to this anthology explores trends toward the future of physical education in education beginning with the same frame of reference—the state of contemporary education. Some issues examined are scholarship, professional development, women in physical education, sport management, and wellness programs.

What, When & How to Talk to Students About Alcohol & Other Drugs: A Guide for Teachers *See* **RESOURCES FOR TEACHING (No. 822)**

507. What Works: Schools Without Drugs. United States, Department of Education. U.S. Government Printing Office, 1989. 87p. Free.

A revised edition of a popular, 1986 government publication featuring research-based information about the effects of drugs, alcohol, tobacco, and steroids use in schools, with information on implementing drug prevention programs and examples of successful school programs. Emphasizes the concept of the student-school-parent-community partnership as the most promising approach to drug use prevention.

Journals

American Alliance for Health, Physical Education and Recreation HEALTH/PHYSICAL EDUCATION (No. 517)

American College Health Association Journal *See* **Journal of American College Health HEALTH/PHYSICAL EDUCATION (No. 510)**

508. Health Education. American Alliance for Health, Physical Education, Recreation and Dance, 1900 Association Drive, Reston, VA 22091. 6/year. $50.00. ISSN: 0097-0050. 1970. Formerly *School Health Review.*

509. Journal of Alcohol and Drug Education. Alcohol and Drug Problems Assn. of North America, c/o MICAP, Box 10212, Lansing, MI 48901. 3/year. $250.00. ISSN: 0090-1482. 1972. Formerly *Journal of Alcohol Education* (1955–1972).

Journal of Alcohol Education *See* **Journal of Alcohol and Drug Education HEALTH/PHYSICAL EDUCATION (No. 509)**

510. Journal of American College Health. American College Health Assn., Heldref Publishers, 4000 Albemarle St., NW, Washington, DC 20016. 6/year. $46.00. ISSN: 0744-8481. 1982. Formerly *American College Health Association Journal* (1952–1982); published by American College Health Assn., distributed by Heldref.

Journal of Health, Physical Education, Recreation *See* **Journal of Physical Education, Recreation and Dance HEALTH/PHYSICAL EDUCATION (No. 513)**

511. Journal of Leisure Research. National Recreation and Park Assn., 3101 Park Center Dr., Alexandria, VA 22302. Quarterly. $30.00. ISSN: 0022-2216. 1968.

512. Journal of Outdoor Education. Northern Illinois Univ., Dept. of Outdoor Teacher Education, Taft Field Campus, Box 299, Oregon, IL 61061. Annual. Free. ISSN: 0022-3336. 1966.

Journal of Physical Education and Recreation *See* **Journal of Physical Education, Recreation and Dance HEALTH/ PHYSICAL EDUCATION (No. 513)**

513. **Journal of Physical Education, Recreation and Dance.** American Alliance for Health, Physical Education, Recreation and Dance, 1900 Association Dr., Reston, VA 22091. 10/year. $545.00. ISSN: 0730-3084. 1981. Formerly *Journal of Physical Education and Recreation* (1975–1981) and *Journal of Health, Physical Education, Recreation* (1896–1975).

514. **Journal of School Health.** American School Health Assn., P.O. Box 708, Kent, OH 44240. 10/year. $65.00. ISSN: 0022-4391. 1937.

515. **Physical Educator: A Magazine for the Profession.** Phi Epsilon Kappa Fraternity, 901 W. New York St., Indianapolis, IN 46223. Quarterly. $15.00. ISSN: 0031-8981. 1940.

516. **Quest.** National Assn. for Physical Education in Higher Education, Human Kinetics Publishers, Inc., 1607 N. Market St., Box 5076, Champaign, IL 61820. 3/year. $30.00. ISSN: 0033-6297. 1963. Distributed by Human Kinetics.

Research Quarterly *See* **Research Quarterly for Exercise and Sport HEALTH/PHYSICAL EDUCATION (No. 517)**

517. **Research Quarterly for Exercise and Sport.** American Alliance for Health, Physical Education, Recreation and Dance, 1900 Association Dr., Reston, VA 22091. Quarterly. $50.00. ISSN: 0270-1367. 1980. Formerly *American Alliance for Health, Physical Education and Recreation. Research Quarterly.*

School Health Review *See* **Health Education HEALTH/ PHYSICAL EDUCATION (No. 508)**

Higher and Continuing Education

An attempt has been made to cover a wide range of topics in this broad category: assessment in higher education, curriculum, history and criticism of teacher training institutions, business and higher education, and more. The focus is also on adult/continuing education as well as higher education. Most titles are recent, but some important, standard titles, still in print, have been included. Reference works about higher education are considered; those that are guides to higher education areas are found under **General Sources**. For the history of higher education, see the **History and Philosophy of Education** section.

Books

518. The Academic Ethic: The Report of a Study Group of the International Council on the Future of the University. Hersch, Jeanne et al. Univ. of Chicago Press, 1984. 104p. LC: 84-6. ISBN: 0-226-75330-1. Contact publisher for price information. Reprinted from *Minerva*, vol. 20:1–2.
Culmination of the work of a study group of the International Council on the Future of the University. Addressed to all the academic profession in universities in the Western tradition, this report focuses on the attitudes of university instructors. Intended to provoke discussion and reflection on the traditional obligations of teachers to make a difference for good in all their academic endeavors and responsibilities.

519. Academic Freedom and Catholic Higher Education. Annarelli, James John. (Contributions to the Study of Education, no. 21). Greenwood, 1987. 236p. LC: 86-27152. ISBN: 0-313-25425-7. $37.95.
Addresses the problem of finding a model of academic freedom applicable to American Roman Catholic colleges and universities as religious institutions as well as institutions devoted to the free pursuit of truth; current Catholic models are inadequate guides according to the author. Following critical examinations of these models and the American secular model of academic freedom, criteria for the interpretation of academic freedom in the American Roman Catholic university are generated.

520. The Academic Life: Small Worlds, Different Worlds. Clark, Burton R. (A Carnegie Foundation Special Report). Carnegie Foundation for the Advancement of Teaching/ Princeton University Press, 1987. 360p. LC: 87-15068. ISBN: 0-931050-31-6. $28.50.
Examines the teaching and research function in higher education. Includes a history of higher education, results from research interviews conducted in the mid-1980s about the academic profession, and examines the diversity necessary to a healthy academic community.

Academic Preparation for College: What Students Need to Know and Be Able to Do See EDUCATIONAL REFORM (No. 228)

Academic Revolution See HISTORY AND PHILOSOPHY OF EDUCATION (No. 603)

Academic Science, Higher Education and the Federal Government, 1950–1983 See HISTORY AND PHILOSOPHY OF EDUCATION (No. 604)

Academic Women: Working Towards Equality See HISTORY AND PHILOSOPHY OF EDUCATION (No. 605)

521. Adult Literacy: A Source Book and Guide. French, Joyce N. (Garland Reference of Social Science, vol. 346/Source Books on Education, vol. 14). Garland, 1987. 435p. LC: 87-21075. ISBN: 0-8340-8574-4.
Examines adult literacy and illiteracy in a variety of relevant contexts, from a theoretical perspective and a practical one. That discussion is followed by an annotated bibliography for each area examined: adult basic literacy, literacy and the older adult, the speaker of English as a second language, and literacy in the workplace, in postsecondary education and around the world.

The American College and the Culture of Aspiration, 1915–1940 See HISTORY AND PHILOSOPHY OF EDUCATION (No. 607)

522. Assessing Basic Academic Skills in Higher Education: The Texas Approach. Edited by Alpert, Richard T., Gorth, William P. and Allan, Richard G. L. Erlbaum, 1989. 274p. LC: 88-31005. ISBN: 0-8058-0336-X. $27.50.
Although the greater portion of this book focuses on the Texas Academic Skills Program, the first part is devoted to discussions on general issues related to the assessment of basic academic skills in higher education. Several documents that form the components of the TASP have been reproduced in the volume.

523. Assessment in Higher Education. Heywood, John. Wiley, 1989. 416p. LC: 88-14423. ISBN: 0-471-92032-0. $76.95. 2nd edition.

A study of assessment and its many forms in higher education in the United States and Great Britain. A multi-strategy approach assessing institutions and the individuals within them is proposed in discussion under these areas: grades and grading, testing in coursework, self-assessment in teaching, perception and learning, objective tests and others.

524. Beyond the Open Door: New Students to Higher Education. Cross, Patricia K. Jossey-Bass, 1971. 200p. LC: 77-170212. ISBN: 0-87589-111-X. $25.95.

There was a "new student" in higher education in the 1960s defined here as one in the lowest third academically. The central purpose is to show how higher education institutions were not prepared to educate these new students and to help educators improve educational programs. The argument is supported by a large database developed from major research conducted between 1960–69 representing large samples of students—Project Talent, SCOPE, Comparative Guidance and Placement Program.

Blue Ribbon Commissions and Higher Education: Changing Academe from the Outside *See* EDUCATIONAL REFORM (No. 234)

525. Campus Life: Undergraduate Cultures from the End of the Eighteenth Century to the Present. Horowitz, Helen Lefkowitz. Knopf, 1987. 330p. LC: 86-21345. ISBN: 0-394-54997-X. $24.45.

In tracing the evolution of the concept of college life, three different "types" of undergraduates emerged—college men and women, outsiders, and rebels—as competing subcultures. College life emerged as a particular subculture shared by only a minority of these types of students who partake of it. Research also describes how undergraduates define themselves, view their teachers and their peers, and form associations and codes of behavior.

526. The Character of American Higher Education and Intercollegiate Sport. Chu, Donald. (SUNY Frontiers in Education Series). State Univ. of New York Press, 1989. 252p. LC: 87-34015. ISBN: 0-88706-791-3; 0-88706-793-X (pbk.). $39.50; $12.95 (pbk.).

Explores the connection between higher education institutions and athletics as a peculiar characteristic of American colleges and universities. Following a historical account of the rise of intercollegiate sports, the book presents the rationale for the existence of sports in higher education, the effects of sports on individual participants, and the economic effects of campus sports.

527. China's Universities and the Open Door. Hayhoe, Ruth. M.E. Sharpe, 1989. 249p. LC: 88-18347. ISBN: 0-87332-501-X. $37.50.

Reflections on the ways in which knowledge has been constituted in the modern Chinese higher education curriculum and the role of Chinese universities in China's reintegration into the international political economy. The investigation moves from describing the internal constitution of knowledge-power relations to external issues of China's knowledge participation in global relationships.

528. A Classification of Institutions of Higher Education. (Carnegie Foundation Technical Report). Carnegie Foundation for the Advancement of Teaching, 1987. 148p. LC: 85-28030. ISBN: 0-931050-26-X. $6.50.

An inexpensive guide to institutions by categories, based on the highest degree offered and the comprehensiveness of the mission; doctorate-granting institutions, comprehensive universities and colleges, two-year colleges, and non-traditional schools. No descriptive information.

The Closing of the American Mind: Education and the Crisis of Reason *See* EDUCATIONAL REFORM (No. 236)

College and the Learning Disabled Student: Program Development, Implementation, and Selection *See* SPECIAL EDUCATION (No. 830)

529. College: The Undergraduate Experience in America. Boyer, Ernest L. Harper & Row, 1987. 328p. LC: 85-45182. ISBN: 0-06-015507-08. $9.95.

Sponsored by the Carnegie Foundation for the Advancement of Teaching, this report serves as a companion to an earlier study, *High School.* Describes the current status of the college experience by identifying strengths and problem areas referred to as eight points of tension, the quality of campus life for example. Suggests ways in which institutions might be strengthened.

Colleges and Universities for Change: America's Comprehensive Public State Colleges and Universities *See* HISTORY AND PHILOSOPHY OF EDUCATION (No. 614)

530. Community College Fact Book. Edited by El-Khawas, Elaine and Carter, Deborah J. (American Council on Education/American Association of Community and Junior Colleges/Macmillan Series on Higher Education). American Council on Education/Macmillan, 1988. 87-37232 ISBN: 0-02-900941-3. $29.95.

Highlights current data on community, technical, and junior colleges. General statistics in the first section cover enrollment trends, student characteristics, student outcomes, institutional finances, and staffing patterns. Planning information data are included in Section II on population growth, employment, educational attainment, etc.

A Comparative Survey of Seven Adult Functional Literacy Programs in Sub-Saharan Africa *See* COMPARATIVE EDUCATION (No. 7)

Comparing Adult Education Worldwide *See* COMPARATIVE EDUCATION (No. 8)

531. Conducting Interinstitutional Comparisons. Edited by Brinkman, Paul T. (New Directions for Institutional Research, no. 53). Jossey-Bass, 1987. 112p. ISBN: 1-55542-964-5. $9.95. ISSN: 0271-0579.

Practical guide to conducting interinstitutional comparisons in higher education: choosing institutions to compare; obtaining, analyzing and using comparative data; organizing ongoing data exchanges; a sample case study on the use of comparative data to set new funding targets.

532. The Craft of Teaching: A Guide to Mastering the Professor's Art. Eble, Kenneth E. Jossey-Bass, 1988. 247p. LC: 87-46351. ISBN: 1-55542-088-5. $21.95. 2nd edition.

This second edition, by a master teacher, has been revised but still focuses on college teaching—philosophical aspects and the mythology of teaching as well as "grubby stuff and dirty work."

Democracy's College: The Land-Grant Movement in the Formative State *See* HISTORY AND PHILOSOPHY OF EDUCATION (No. 618)

533. Designing and Improving Courses and Curricula in Higher Education: A Systematic Approach. Diamond, Robert M. (Jossey-Bass Higher Education Series). Jossey-Bass, 1989. 88-28433 ISBN: 1-55542-129-6. $26.95.

A model for approaching curricula change and course and program design in higher education is offered; the model has been applied at the author's institution for many years. Step-by-step information, with illustrative case studies in a variety of disciplines, is provided for implementing and administering the model.

534. Distance Education and the Mainstream Convergence in Education. Edited by Smith, Peter and Kelly, Mavis. Routledge, Kegan & Paul, 1987. 207p. LC: 87-21717. ISBN: 0-7099-4499-3. $49.95.

Each of the ten contributors discusses how convergence is beginning to occur and blur the boundaries between distance education (off-campus) and mainstream education (campus-based) in theory and practice in higher education systems in Australia, Kenya, Canada, and the United States.

The Diverted Dream: Community Colleges and the Promise of Educational Opportunity in America, 1900–1985 *See* HISTORY AND PHILOSOPHY OF EDUCATION (No. 622)

535. Dollars and Scholars: An Inquiry into the Impact of Faculty Income Upon the Function and Future of the Academy. Edited by Linnell, Robert H. Univ. of Southern California Press, 1982. 142p. LC: 82-051020. ISBN: 0-88474-106-0. $12.00.

Explores the relationship of economics and ethics in higher education. Particular attention is given to outside work taken on by faculty because of low salaries, and the potential for conflicts of interest. Ethical dilemmas, intellectual property rights, government support, and academic earnings are discussed and supported by numerous references. Final chapter offers recommendations and suggested policies.

536. Ed School: A Brief for Professional Education. Clifford, Geraldine Joncich and Guthrie, James W. Univ. of Chicago Press, 1988. 413p. LC: 87-30147. ISBN: 0-226-11017-6. $24.95.

Focuses on normal schools in a university—their origins, historical evolution, continuing problems, and future prospects—by concentrating on case studies of a select few schools of education. The author addresses the need for reform of schools of education ensnared in the politics of their institutions and ignoring their professional allegiances to the education professions and to improving the quality of teaching.

537. Educating America: Lessons Learned in the Nation's Corporations. Bowsher, Jack E. Wiley, 1989. 245p. LC: 88-39747. ISBN: 0-471-60066-0. $22.95.

Describes how education can be restructured to make dramatic improvements in the process of education by transferring lessons learned in restructuring employee education in industry to education systems; the author is former director of education for IBM. Using the case-study method, changes taking place in employee education in the business world are described.

538. Educating the Majority: Women Challenge Tradition in Higher Education. Edited by Pearson, Carol S., Shavlik, Donna L. and Touchton, Judith G. (American Council on Education/MacMillan Series in Higher Education). Collier Macmillan, 1989. 491p. LC: 88-31508. ISBN: 0-02-924810-8. $24.95.

A collection of 36 essays implying that the needs of women students are not well served by higher education and advancing the claim for fuller representation of women in all levels of higher education than is currently the case. Focuses on structural, emotional, and intellectual changes needed in higher education institutions to address the diversity and commonalities among women students.

539. Education's Smoking Gun: How Teachers Colleges Have Destroyed Education in America. Damerell, Reginald G. Freundlich Books, 1985. 312p. LC: 85-10113. ISBN: 0-88191-025-2. $17.95.

Much of the text is an indictment of public school education and teachers, especially, but the blame for the "destruction of our schools" is laid at the doorstep of our schools of education. "False notions, fads and trivia," in lieu of a body of knowledge, are "taught" to prospective teachers in schools of education; "visual literacy" is an example. The author advocates the abolition of schools of education.

540. The Effective College President. Fisher, James L., Tack, Martha W. and Wheeler, Karen J. American Council on Education/Macmillan, 1988. 209p. LC: 88-5107. ISBN: 0-02-910321-5. $24.95.

Describes the characteristics and backgrounds of effective college presidents, based on a national survey and utilization of the Fisher/Tack Effective Leadership Inventory. Effective college presidents were compared to representative college presidents and corporate executives for leadership traits. Several appendices chart the results of the inventory.

541. Essays on the Closing of the American Mind. Edited by Stone, Robert L. Chicago Review Press, 1989. 382p. LC: 89-771. ISBN: 1-55652-052-2. $11.95.

A collection of 62 essays by journalists and educators responding to Bloom's controversial book *The Closing of the American Mind.* Drawn from publications which praise, blame, criticize, and challenge Bloom in the classroom as an elitist, a Nihilist, anti-feminist, and for his views on the role of the university in a democratic society.

542. Ethical Dilemmas for Academic Professionals. Edited by Payne, Stephen L. and Charnov, Bruce H. C.C. Thomas, 1987. 241p. LC: 86-30173. ISBN: 0-398-05319-7. $32.75.

Each chapter focuses on a particular dilemma facing faculty or doctoral students and is followed by sample cases and related questions with responses from academicians. Dilemmas include consulting, grading, involvement in professional organizations, and the publication process. This work will raise the ethical consciousness of readers.

543. Ethical Principles, Practices, and Problems in Higher Education. Edited by Baca, M. Carlota and Stein, Ronald H. C.C. Thomas, 1983. 272p. LC: 83-4783. ISBN: 0-398-04865-7. $33.50.

Analyzes ethical principles in higher education and the codification of these principles. Focuses on the ethical component of problem solving rather than resolution of the problem itself. Issues addressed include personal ethics vs. responsibility to the institution, conflicts of interest, admissions, collective bargaining, and teaching of ethics. Codes of ethics from different organizations are appended.

544. Ethics and the Professor: An Annotated Bibliography, 1970–1985. Herring, Mark Youngblood. (Garland Reference Library of the Humanities, v. 742). Garland, 1988. 605p. LC: 87-17800. ISBN: 0-8240-8491-8. Contact publisher for price information.

Divided into topical chapters such as Science and Ethics, with several sections in each chapter, this bibliography addresses the major issues in higher education. Each chapter begins with an overview followed by annotated entries. Comprehensive listing of books and articles addressing copyright laws to educational malpractice and the related ethical issues.

545. Exploring Common Ground: A Report on Business/Academic Partnerships. American Association of State Colleges and Universities. University Pub. Associates, 1987. 206p. LC: 87-27068. ISBN: 0-88044-090-2; 0-88044-089-9 (pbk.). $24.00; $9.75 (pbk.).

A report exploring the variety of ways in which corporate-university relationships exist in the member colleges and universities of the AASCU. Thirty-six examples are given in five different areas: communication processes, curriculum and instruction, direct delivery of services, facilities and equipment sharing, and comprehensive programs. The concluding chapter offers some strategies for those administrators interested in pursuing corporate partnering.

546. Fact Book on Higher Education. American Council on Education, Division of Policy Analysis and Research. American Council on Education/Macmillan, 1958–. LC: 87-655587. ISBN: 0-02-897511-1 (1989–90). $41.95 (1989–90). ISSN: 0363-6720.

Data are condensed into tables that emphasize trends in higher education and provide baseline information that makes comparisons over time possible; some data can be traced back to the 1940s. Many documentary sources such as National Center for Education Statistics and Census unpublished datatapes are used to present data on demographic and economic trends, enrollments, institutions, student aid, etc.

547. A Free and Ordered Space: The Real World of the University. Giamatti, A. Bartlett. W.W. Norton, 1988. 306p. LC: 88-10013. ISBN: 0-393-02622-1. $19.95.

Essays written by the former President of Yale University between the late seventies and eighties concerned with three areas: the nature and purpose of the American university, the principles of a liberal undergraduate education, and the pressures and affiliations connecting the university and our society.

548. Grants for Higher Education. The Foundation Center. 1987. 314p. ISBN: 0-87954-204-7. $38.00.

Covers grants to colleges and universities in the United States and abroad for research, fellowships, scholarships, and programs in all disciplines. Lists over 10,000 grants made by 410 foundations in the areas of student aid, faculty development, teacher training, continuing education, and others. Keyword and geographic indexes available. One of several subject publications produced from the *Foundation Grants Index*.

Growth of an American Invention: A Documentary History of the Junior and Community College Movement *See* HISTORY AND PHILOSOPHY OF EDUCATION (No. 639)

Handbook for Educational Fund Raising: A Guide to Successful Principles and Practices for Colleges, Universities and Schools *See* EDUCATIONAL ADMINISTRATION AND LAW (No. 147)

Handbook of Counseling in Higher Education *See* EDUCATIONAL PSYCHOLOGY/GUIDANCE/COUNSELING (No. 197)

549. Handbook on Continuing Higher Education. Gessner, Quentin H. (American Council on Education/Macmillan Series in Higher Education). American Council on Education/Macmillan, 1987. 261p. LC: 86-16308. ISBN: 0-02-911620-1. $24.95.

A sourcebook providing an overview of the current state of continuing education within postsecondary institutions. Attention is given to essays on the history of continuing education, issues in the field, organizational models, sources of funding, program planned models, needs assessment, delivery systems, marketing plans, research and evaluation.

550. The HEP Higher Education Directory. Higher Education Publications, 1989. 558p. LC: 83-641119. ISBN: 0-914927-10-8. Contact publisher for price information. ISSN: 0736-0797; 7th edition.

Provides information on accredited institutions of postsecondary education that meet the U.S. Department of Education eligibility requirements; information is solicited and the *Directory* claims a 99.9% institutional response rate. A "Prologue" lists accrediting agencies, higher education associations, and statewide agencies of higher education. The directory portion has four parts: listings of institutions by state with institutional characteristics; index by accrediting agencies; index of key administrators; and alphabetical index of entries. *Peterson's Higher Education Directory* is a similar directory.

551. Higher Education: A Bibliographic Handbook. Edited by Halstead, D. Kent. Government Printing Office, 1984. 750p., Volume 1; 641p. Volume 2 LC: 83-237987. $14.00, Volumes 1 and 2. Stock 065-000-00215-9; 2 Volumes.

The purpose of this and future editions of this bibliography is to identify high-quality references in higher education encompassing all major activities of colleges and universities; programs and organizations; resources employed; and approaches used to study the field. Issued in two volumes covering publications issued from 1968 through 1981—the first deals with subjects generally approached from an aggregate state or national perspective; the second embraces topics usually studied at the individual institutional level.

552. Higher Education and Employment: An International Comparative Analysis. Sanyal, Bikas C. (An IIEP Research Project). Falmer, 1987. 237p. LC: 87-10699. ISBN: 1-85000-251-7; 1-85000-252-5 (pbk.). $40.00; $21.00 (pbk.).

Synthesizes the issues and findings of an extensive research project that studied the relationship of higher education within a country to the changing needs of the employment market. Twenty-one national case studies provided a database with information on the demand for higher education in a country, the transition from higher education to work, and the operation of the world of work. Important implications for higher education planning.

553. Higher Education Bibliography Yearbook 1987. Edited by Halstead, Kent. Research Associates of Washington, May 1987. 348p. LC: 87-655773. Contact publisher for price information. ISSN: 0893-3154.

This first yearbook identifies selective higher education books and journal articles of greatest interest and value published yearly; each *Yearbook* to cover the preceding calendar year. Six major categories are covered: academic enterprise, students, institutions, state and national, discipline approaches, and sectors. The subject index further divides the categories into 34 topics, 100 subtopics. Very long annotations and summaries provided.

554. Higher Education Finance: An Annotated Bibliography and Guide to Research. Hines, Edward R. and McCarthy, John R. (Garland Bibliographies in Contemporary Education, Vol. 4/Garland Reference Library of Social Science, Vol. 198). Garland, 1985. 357p. LC: 83-48212. ISBN: 0-8240-9054-3. $50.00.

Annotated bibliography of the literature dealing with the support of higher education. The selected works extend from 1970 to 1983, include published books, monographs, journal articles, reports, and studies covered under these major areas: fiscal planning and budgets; government fiscal support; external funding; student financial aid; institutional management; retrenchment; economics of higher education.

555. Higher Education: Handbook of Theory and Research. Edited by Smart, John C. Agathon Press, 1985–. ISBN: 0-87586-080-X (1987, Volume III). $48.00 (1987, Volume III). Published under the sponsorship of the American Educational Research Association.

A handbook series intended to provide "an annual compendium of exhaustive and integrative literature reviews on a diverse array of topics" that reflect the scholarly and policy inquiries in higher education for a year. Each contributor reviews the research on a selected topic, critiques that research, and provides an agenda for future research. Handbooks I, II, and III have been published.

556. Higher Education in a Learning Society: Meeting New Demands for Education and Training. Apps, Jerold W. (Jossey-Bass Higher Education Series). Jossey-Bass, 1988. 241p. LC: 88-42775. ISBN: 1-55542-115-6. $22.95.

As stated in the preface, this book is a theoretical formulation of the problems higher education faces. Offers practical analysis and planning strategies for colleges and universities and provides extensive examples of how institutions are coping with the demands of continuing, adult, and higher education.

557. Higher Education in American Life, 1636–1986: A Bibliography of Dissertations and Theses. Young, Arthur P. (Bibliographies and Indexes in Education, no. 5). Greenwood, 1988. 431p. LC: 88-10996. ISBN: 0-313-25352-8. $49.95. ISSN: 0742-6917.

A comprehensive undertaking produced in two sections: Part One, dissertation citations arranged alphabetically by state then subdivided by institution; Part Two, topical coverage in 69 areas. The majority of the 4,570 entries are studies of individual institutions, biographies, and topical works. Only dissertations with extensive historical orientation were selected; follow-up studies of

graduates were omitted. Some profile data on dissertation production is available.

558. Higher Education in American Society. Edited by Altbach, Philip G. and Berdahl, Robert O. Prometheus, 1987. 351p. LC: 87-25790. ISBN: 0-87975-420-6. $15.95. Revised edition.

Contributors to this collection all deal with contemporary American higher education's relations with society. Major "external" constituencies that act to influence or control higher education are discussed; the reactions of major "internal" constituencies to the increasing external pressures are presented.

Higher Education in Transition: A History of American Colleges and Universities, 1636–1976 *See* HISTORY AND PHILOSOPHY OF EDUCATION (No. 640)

559. The Higher Education System: Academic Organization in Cross-National Perspective. Clark, Burton R. Univ. of California Press, 1983. 315p. LC: 82-13521. ISBN: 0-520-04841-5; 0-520-05892-5 (pbk.). $40.00; $11.95 (pbk.).

Details the basic elements of the higher education system from an organizational perspective: arrangement of work, distribution of authority, systems changes, etc. How those elements vary across nations or where a commonality of elements exists is explored by cross-national comparisons of the United States, United Kingdom, Sweden, Japan, Italy, Federal Republic of Germany, Poland, Mexico, and Thailand.

560. Higher Learning. Bok, Derek. Harvard Univ. Press, 1986. 206p. LC: 86-9876. ISBN: 0-674-39175-6. $16.50.

Describes our American system of higher education and how universities evolve, stimulated by competition and the constant pressure to respond to society's needs. Considers the status of the liberal arts college and professional schools such as law, business, and medicine; describes current developments in higher education such as advanced technology in teaching and interest in mid-career education.

Humanities in America: A Report to the President, the Congress, and the American People *See* EDUCATIONAL REFORM (No. 249)

561. Illiteracy in America: Extent Causes and Suggested Solutions. National Advisory Council on Adult Education, Literacy Committee. U.S. Government Printing Office, 1986. 93p. LC: 86-602565. $4.75. Stock no. 065-000-00253-1.

The Council, charged with developing recommendations on adult basic education, compiled this more extensive report to determine first the extent of adult illiteracy before exploring the causes and what could be done to prevent it. Recommendations for reducing illiteracy are offered as well as the reasons for the recommendations. Concludes that educators themselves are largely responsible for many of the literacy problems.

562. Improving Higher Education Environments for Adults: Responsive Programs and Services from Entry to Departure. Schlossberg, Nancy, Lynch, Ann Q. and Chickering, Arthur. (Jossey-Bass Higher Education Series). Jossey-Bass, 1989. 281p. LC: 88-32049. ISBN: 1-55542-136-9. $22.95.

Pulls together the literature, research, and theory on the new challenge facing higher education—creating an educational environment responsive to adults trying to use the resources of higher education institutions. Follows adult learners as they move through educational programs at institutions and provides recommendations for setting up introductory, supporting, and culminating adult programs.

563. In Pursuit of Equality in Higher Education. Edited by Pruitt, Anne S. General Hall, 1987. 226p. LC: 86-080125. ISBN: 0-930390-68-7. $28.95.

Reports on research that investigated higher education issues in instances where minorities were affected. Most studies, however, focus on issues relative to the *Adams vs. Richardson* suit, a landmark civil rights case regarding the equality of opportunity for access of students, faculty, and administrators in higher education. Investigations cover enrollments and success of black students in undergraduate and graduate education, aspirations and career choices of black students, and other areas.

564. Innovation for Excellence: The Paracollege Model. Brown, J. Wesley. Univ. Press of America, 1989. 123p. LC: 88-30208. ISBN: 0-8191-7244-8. $10.25.

The Paracollege is an innovation in higher education that was constructed in the late 1960s as an alternative college in response to the concern for individual development and fulfillment and a general education. The 20-year experiment at St. Olaf College in Minnesota is described in terms of student, faculty, and curriculum development and institutional change and assessment of the paracollege's effectiveness.

565. Investment in Learning: The Individual and Social Value of American Higher Education. Edited by Bowen, Howard. Jossey-Bass, 1977. 507p. LC: 77-82069. ISBN: 0-87589-341-4. $29.95. Prepared with support of the Sloan Foundation and issued by the Carnegie Council on Policy Studies in Higher Education.

A comprehensive study about the outcomes of American higher education. Information and an enormous amount of data were assembled, interpreted, and analyzed and judgments reached as to whether American higher education is worth what it costs.

566. Leaving College: Rethinking the Causes and Cures of Student Attrition. Tinto, Vincent. Univ. of Chicago Press, 1987. 246p. LC: 86-11379. ISBN: 0-226-80446-1. $19.95.

Two goals are focused on—proposing a theory of student departure that describes the role institutions play in the social and intellectual development of students and what can be done to increase student retention in higher education. A synthesis of research on the multiple causes of student leaving and successful retention programs is offered. A course of action that can be employed in a variety of settings to confront the student departure problem is presented.

567. Libraries and the Search for Academic Excellence. Edited by Breivik, Patricia Senn. Scarecrow, 1988. 213p. LC: 88-15855. ISBN: 0-8108-2157-5. $25.00.

These papers were commissioned for a national Symposium on Libraries and the Search for Academic Excellence to address the overriding themes of the educational reform reports and to explore how institutions were using or could use their libraries to achieve related campus objectives. Topics include networks, fostering research, libraries, and the humanities.

568. Lifelong Education for Adults: An International Handbook. Edited by Titmus, Colin. Pergamon, 1989. 590p. LC: 88-36623. ISBN: 0-08-030581-1. Contact publisher for price information.

A series of subsets of *The International Encyclopedia of Education* is to be published on specific aspects of educational research; this *Handbook* is among them. The 117 contributors from 23 countries have covered the concepts, principles, purposes, practices, people, organization, and scholarship of adult education throughout the world, seen from the point of view of lifelong education. Should be of interest to anyone engaged in educational activities for adults.

569. The Moral Collapse of the University. Wilshire, Bruce W. (SUNY Series in the Philosophy of Education). State Univ. of New York Press, 1990. 287p. LC: 89-4455. ISBN: 0-7914-0196-0; 0-7914-0197-9 (pbk.). $29.50; $14.95.

The author creates a picture of the twentieth-century "multiversity," a research institution that is a loose grouping of disciplines, each caught up in its own research and publishing interests. He describes how academic professionalism has taken precedence over teaching and excluded the education of students.

570. A New Academic Marketplace. Burke, Dolores L. (Contributions to the Study of Education, no. 30). Greenwood, 1988. 198p. LC: 88-15445. ISBN: 0-313-26383-3. $37.95. ISSN: 0196-707X.

This book grew out of a 1958 study, *Academic Marketplace*, appraising change in the academic personnel processes in the research university. The "new" marketplace studies the academic labor market fitting the universities of the 1980s into the earlier framework. Interview data collected in 1985–86 are discussed in the bulk of the text covering issues such as market characteristics and institutional policies, the faculty search and selection process, and the separation process. Detailed methodology available.

571. New Perspectives on the Education of Adults in the United States. Long, Huey. Nichols, 1987. 263p. LC: 86-21738. ISBN: 0-89397-263-0. $31.50.

A personal perspective on the current growth and development in education for and of adults by a prominent adult educator, reexamining older ideas to discover new and future applications and perspectives. Some issues covered include adult education philosophies, purposes, research, and theory; the clientele of adult education such as the elderly and those in corporate settings are also discussed.

572. None of the Above: Behind the Myth of Scholastic Aptitude. Owen, David. Houghton Mifflin, 1985. 327p. LC: 84-25262. ISBN: 0-395-35540-0. $7.95.

This book has an important message in the context of our national test mania and an excessive "reverence" for test scores. The discussion covers standardized testing and other general test issues but focuses on the Educational Testing Service and its "scientific mystique" and the Scholastic Aptitude Test in particular. Getting rid of the SAT (and ETS) is wishfully proposed but more realistic halfway measures are offered.

573. The Organization and Planning of Adult Education. Kowalski, Theodore J. State Univ. of New York Press, 1988. 218p. LC: 87-34014. ISBN: 0-88706-798-0; 0-88706-799-9 (pbk.). $39.50; $12.95 (pbk.).

Organization-related topics are explored in the first half of the text: relationship between the sponsoring agency and the dynamics of structured learning activities, organizational climate, and conflict resolution. The second half covers the planning process of adult education including needs assessment, advisory councils, budgeting, and technical models.

The Path to Excellence: Quality Assurance in Higher Education *See* **EDUCATIONAL REFORM (No. 264)**

574. Profscam: Professors and the Demise of Higher Education. Sykes, Charles J. Regency Gateway, 1988. 304p. LC: 88-21942. ISBN: 0-89526-559-1. $18.95.

The author begins with an overview of his indictment of university professors' crimes against higher education, and in the chapters following details his bill of indictment against the "Professorus Americanus." Included are how professors have seized control of higher learning and what they have done with that power, the world of academic research and publishing, "sabotage" of the curriculum, and "What can be done to save our universities".

575. Quality Control in Higher Education. Hogarth, Charles P. Univ. Press of America, 1987. 145p. LC: 87-2055. ISBN: 0-8191-6174-8; 0-8191-6175-6 (pbk.). $24.75; $11.50 (pbk.).

A brief text on what kind of quality controls exist for colleges and universities and what more should be done to improve the quality of the product. The quality controls outside the institution are covered first—accrediting, governmental and other groups; the controls existing inside the operations of higher education are covered next—structure, finance, personnel, program and support services, and other areas.

Raising Academic Standards: A Guide to Learning Improvement *See* **EDUCATIONAL REFORM (No. 267)**

576. Recruitment and Retention of Black Students in Higher Education. Johnson, Niba and Norman, Regina. Univ. Press of America, 1989. 135p. LC: 88-38113. ISBN: 0-8191-7292-8; 0-8191-7293-6 (pbk.). $18.50; $9.75 (pbk.).

Presents six essays offering workable solutions and mechanisms for encouraging retention (persistence to graduation) and combating the problem of dropping out of minority students. Some of the issues examined are financial aid and tuition, strategic planning models to achieve excellence, and cognitive styles and multicultural populations.

577. The Report of the President's Commission on Campus Unrest. United States. President's Commission on Campus Unrest. Ayer, 1970. 537p. LC: 71-139710. ISBN: 0-405-01712-X. $5.95. Reprint edition.

A report commissioned in 1970 following the tragedies at Kent State University in Ohio and Jackson State College in Mississippi. It was compiled following the Commission staff's extensive three-month investigation.

578. Research in Higher Education: A Guide to Source Bibliographies. Quay, Richard H. Oryx, 1985. 133p. LC: 85-18745. ISBN: 0-89774-194-3. $32.00. 2nd edition.

A revised edition of a bibliography of bibliographies on higher education-related topics. This work cites approximately 900 references under 15 chapter/categories, including: history and philosophy of higher education, administrative behavior, social and political issues, comparative higher education, adult and lifelong education. The *Thesaurus of ERIC Descriptors* was used to create the subject index.

579. A Resource Guide on Blacks in Higher Education. National Assn. for Equal Opportunity. Univ. Press of America/NAFEO Research Institute, 1988. 44p. LC: 88-834. ISBN: 0-819-1694-8. $8.00.

A guide to sources of data that measure the participation and success of blacks in higher education. Thirty-eight data collection/analysis organizations, which conduct surveys of higher education populations and institutions, are described. Address, phone, activities, publications, type of data collected, and contact person are provided. A "Matrix of Data Sources" is appended.

580. The Rights of Youth: American Colleges and Student Revolt, 1798–1815. Novak, Steven J. Harvard Univ. Press, 1977. 218p. LC: 76-43109. ISBN: 0-674-77016-1. $15.00.

Examines the first major wave of college student revolts that occurred between 1798 and 1815 and the events leading up to that rebellious period. Several case studies of early institutions—William and Mary, Princeton—are included to describe the actual effects of student resistance on institutions. In addition to records and newspaper accounts, a primary source of information was the correspondence between members of the academic community.

581. Roots of Special Interests in American Higher Education: A Social Psychological Historical Perspective. Wallenfeldt, E.C. Univ. Press of America, 1986. 224p. LC: 86-9234. ISBN: 0-8191-5415-6; 0-8191-5416-4 (pbk.). $22.74; $13.00 (pbk.).

Demonstrates that special interest group perspectives, influencing directions in American colleges and universities, have been in operation a long time. The current situation and the influence of special interests historically are examined against six dimensions of higher education: governance, institutional funding, evolution of curriculum and research, origin and growth of professional schools, concept of public service, and the development of the community college.

582. Saints and Scamps: Ethics in Academia. Cahn, Steven M. Rowman & Littlefield, 1986. 112p. LC: 86-13859. ISBN: 0-8476-7517-3. $15.95.

Filled with sample cases exemplifying "saints and scamps" in academe, this very readable book covers everything from sexual harassment to poorly prepared exams. The ethics involved in such situations as well as the need for standards and ethics in higher education are discussed.

The School and the University: An International Perspective *See* **COMPARATIVE EDUCATION (No. 38)**

583. Sexual Harassment on Campus: A Legal Compendium. National Association of College University Attorneys. 1988. 195p. Contact publisher for price information.

In addition to reprints of law review and journal articles pertaining to sexual harassment in higher education, this work contains sexual harassment policies and procedures from various universities and organizations. A selected bibliography and useful guidelines for drafting sexual harassment policies are included.

584. Stalking the Academic Communist: Intellectual Freedom and the Firing of Alex Novikoff. Holmes, David R. Univ. Press of New England, 1989. 288p. LC: 88-40129. ISBN: 0-87451-466-5; 0-87451-469-X (pbk.). $25.00; $14.95 (pbk.).

An intensive study of an individual case of dismissal of a university biologist during the spread of McCarthyism in the 1950s. Using materials from private papers, interviews, FBI files, university archives, and the local press, the author provides a detailed account of the political evolution and professional career of Alex Novikoff. The study explores how the university came to a decision to dismiss him and how McCarthyism operated.

585. State Higher Education Profiles: A Comparison of State Higher Education Data. National Center for Education Statistics, Postsecondary Education Statistics Division, Special Surveys and Analysis Branch. U.S. Government Printing Office, 1987–. LC: 88-655086. $25.00 (1988). Stock 065-000-00357-1.
These annual profiles present a combination of statistics and indicators of higher education for the nation, and the 50 states including the District of Columbia. The data, related to state involvement, support, and performance in higher education, are collected by NCES through its "Higher Education General Information Survey (HEGIS)." Each state statistic is indexed to a national average; the indexing allows states to be ranked on selected statistics.

To Secure the Blessings of Liberty: Report of the National Commission on the Role and Future of State Colleges and Universities *See* **EDUCATIONAL REFORM (No. 277)**

Towards a History of Adult Education in America: the Search for a Unifying Principle *See* **HISTORY AND PHILOSOPHY OF EDUCATION (No. 670)**

586. Universities Under Scrutiny. Organization for Economic Co-Operation and Development, 1987. 113p. ISBN: 92-64-12922-7. $18.00. Written by William Taylor, Vice-Chancellor, Hull University, United Kingdom.
A report having its origin in the recommendations of the OECD "Intergovernmental Conference on Policies for Higher Education in the 1980s," calling for a reappraisal of the special position of the university. Concludes that universities cannot remain aloof and immune to the pressures of the changing world and must participate more fully in social and economic development while maintaining their strengths as centers of excellence.

587. The University and the City: From Medieval Origins to the Present. Edited by Bender, Thomas. Oxford Univ. Press, 1988. 316p. LC: 88-1411. ISBN: 0-19-505273-0. $34.50.
Essays based on a conference called to celebrate the centennial of the Graduate School of Arts and Sciences at New York University. Various viewpoints illuminate and define the relationship between universities and cities during: medieval origins, early modern revitalization, the development of the metropolitan university and the modern university. The modern urban university emerges dependent on its host city in contrast to the independence of early universities.

588. When Dreams and Heroes Died: A Portrait of Today's College Student. Levine, Arthur. (Carnegie Council on Policy Studies in Higher Education). Jossey-Bass, 1981. 157p. LC: 80-8005. ISBN: 0-87589-481-X. $19.95.
Intended as a technical report, the book uses data and figures collected by the Carnegie Council to describe the college students of the 1970s: their politics, intelligence, social life and personal futures; the effects of family, government, and the media on the shift to "meism"; the stereotypes generally used to conceptualize the 1970s college generation. Also presents a retrospective look at characteristics common to college students over 300 years and some future prospects.

589. Women of Academe: Outsiders in the Sacred Grove. Aisenberg, Nadya and Harrington, Mona. Univ. of Massachusetts Press, 1988. 207p. LC: 87-30067. ISBN: 0-87023-606-7; 0-87023-607-5 (pbk.). $30.00; $11.95 (pbk.).
Studies the experience of women in the academic profession and those who were deflected from their expected academic careers. Following interviews of 37 women off their normal career track and 25 tenured women, the data was analyzed for recurrences of experiences that were clustered as related issues and form the basis for the thematic chapters: old societal norms, various transformations in women's lives, formal and informal rules of the game, etc. The epilogue presents four stories in which the themes function in actual academic women's lives.

590. Yearbook of American Universities and Colleges, Academic Year, 1986–1987. Edited by Kurian, George Thomas. Garland, 1988. 653p. LC: 88-654750. ISBN: 0-8240-7942-6. $60.00. ISSN: 0896-1034.
Intended as an annual report on the condition of higher education in the United States drawn from a variety of sources: reports, essays, statistics, speeches and documents, major court decisions. Most of the material has been published previously, although some is original. Sections cover major sectors of higher education, issues, statistics, major speeches of the year, collective bargaining, corporate aid.

Journals

Adult Education *See* **Adult Education Quarterly HIGHER AND CONTINUING EDUCATION (No. 591)**

591. Adult Education Quarterly. American Assn. for Adult and Continuing Education, 1112 16th St., NW, Suite 420, Washington, DC 20036. Quarterly. $36.00. ISSN: 0741-7136. 1983. Formerly *Adult Education.*

Adult Leadership *See* **Lifelong Learning HIGHER AND CONTINUING EDUCATION (No. 601)**

592. ASHE-ERIC Higher Education Reports. Assn. for the Study of Higher Education, ASHE-ERIC Higher Education Reports, George Washington Univ., One Dupont Circle, Suite 630, Washington, DC 20036. 8/year. $80.00. ISSN: 0884-0040. 1972.

Change in Higher Education *See* **Change HIGHER AND CONTINUING EDUCATION (No. 593)**

593. Change: The Magazine of Higher Learning. American Assn. of Higher Education, Heldref Publishers, 4000 Albemarle St., NW, Washington, DC 20016. 6/year. $40.00. ISSN: 0009-1383. 1972. Formerly *Change in Higher Education* (1968–1972).

594. The Chronicle of Higher Education. Chronicle of Higher Education, 1255 23rd St., NW, 700, Washington, DC 20037. 48/year. $55.00. ISSN: 0009-5982. 1966.

College Student Personnel Abstacts *See* **Higher Education Abstracts HIGHER AND CONTINUING EDUCATION (No. 597)**

595. Community College Review. Dept. of Adult and Community College Education, North Carolina State Univ., Box 7801, Raleigh, NC 27695-7801. Quarterly. $28.00. ISSN: 0091-5521. 1973.

596. Continuing Higher Education Review. National Univ. Continuing Education Assn., One Dupont Circle, NW, Suite 420, Washington, DC 20036. 3/year. $26.00. ISSN: 0162-4024. 1986. Formerly *Continuum* and *EA Spectator* .

Continuum *See* **Continuing Higher Education Review HIGHER AND CONTINUING EDUCATION (No. 596)**

EA Spectator *See* **Continuing Higher Education Review HIGHER AND CONTINUING EDUCATION (No. 596)**

597. Higher Education Abstracts: Abstracts of Periodical Literature, Monographs and Conference Papers on College Students, Faculty and Administration. Claremont Graduate School, Claremont, CA 91711. Quarterly. $90.00. ISSN: 0748-4364. 1984. Formerly *College Student Personnel Abstracts* (1965–1984).

Journal of College and University Law *See* **EDUCATIONAL ADMINISTRATION AND LAW (No. 175)**

Journal of Developmental and Remedial Education *See* **Journal of Developmental Education HIGHER AND CONTINUING EDUCATION (No. 598)**

598. Journal of Developmental Education. National Center for Developmental Education, Appalachian State Univ., Boone, NC 28608. 3/year. $24.00. ISSN: 0738-9701. 1983. Formerly *Journal of Developmental and Remedial Education.*

599. Journal of General Education. Pennsylvania State Univ. Press, 215 Wagner Building, University Park, PA 16802. Quarterly. $28.00. ISSN: 0021-3667. 1946.

Journal of the College and University Personnel Association *See* **EDUCATIONAL PSYCHOLOGY/GUIDANCE/COUNSELING (No. 223)**

600. Liberal Education. Assn. of American Colleges, 1818 R St., NW, Washington, DC 20009. 5/year. $36.00. ISSN: 0024-1822. 1958.

601. Lifelong Learning; An Omnibus of Practice and Research. American Assn. for Adult and Continuing Education, 1112 16th St., NW, Suite 420, Washington, DC 20036. 8/year. $37.00. ISSN: 0740-0578. 1982. Formerly *Lifelong Learning: The Adult Years* and *Adult Leadership.*

602. New Directions for Higher Education. Jossey-Bass, Inc. Publishers, 433 California St., San Francisco, CA 94104. Quarterly. $52.00. ISSN: 0271-0560. 1973. Other *New Directions* series are available in higher education areas such as continuing education, community colleges, institutional research, and student services.

History and Philosophy of Education

The emphasis in this section is on recently published titles, but some classics, still in print, have been included. Historical coverage of many areas of education is provided—higher education, curriculum, literacy, childhood, women in teaching, adult education, education and government—along with various historical periods and educational trends such as liberalism and twentieth-century reforms. Philosophical works cover the major philosophers and theories spanning the early years through the 1980s.

Books

603. Academic Revolution. Jencks, Christopher and Riesman, David. Univ. of Chicago Press, 1977. 580p. LC: 68-15597. ISBN: 0-226-39628-2. $7.95.

The original edition, published in 1968 during the college enrollment growth and disturbances of the 1960s, focused on the rise to power of the academic profession. This 1977 edition, while exploring the developments of the 1970s—greater intrusiveness of government, specialized versus liberal education, collective bargaining—repeatedly returns to that focus and its consequences for graduate and undergraduate education.

604. Academic Science, Higher Education and the Federal Government, 1950–1983. Wilson, John T. Univ. of Illinois Press, 1983. 116p. LC: 83-17964. ISBN: 0-226-90051-7. $10.00.

An essay highlighting the events of some 30 years experience in the relationship between government and higher education, particularly as regards academic science. Begins with the period following World War II, when government support of academic science was high and continues through the early 1980s by examining the Reagan administration's policies and support of higher education and academic scholarship.

605. Academic Women: Working Towards Equality. Simeone, Angela. Bergin & Garvey, 1987. 161p. LC: 86-26436. ISBN: 0-89789-111-2; 0-89789-114-7 (pbk.). $29.95; $10.95 (pbk.).

A study of women in higher education replicating the method used in Bernard's 1964 *Academic Women* and updating the status of women in academia since that publication; in addition the results of 25 in-depth interviews of female faculty members were added to the findings. Investigated the impact of networking of academic women, why women choose or do not choose academic careers, and how women fare on indicators of status and other areas. Concludes that while conditions have improved for academic women, the overall picture remains basically unchanged.

606. Academic Work and Educational Excellence: Raising Student Productivity. Edited by Tomlinson, Tommy M. and Walberg, Herbert J. McCutchan, 1986. 307p. LC: 85-62682. ISBN: 0-8211-1908-7. $24.00.

Many position papers, from noted educators, were commissioned by the National Commission on Excellence in Education as part of the preparation of the well-known and controversial report *A Nation at Risk*. Some of the background papers were collected for publication in this volume reflecting the themes of the report, especially the concept of academic work as an important dimension of educational excellence.

607. The American College and the Culture of Aspiration, 1915–1940. Levine, David O. Cornell Univ. Press, 1986. 281p. LC: 86-4169. ISBN: 0-8014-1884-4. $32.50.

In the years between the world wars, 1915 to 1940, the culture of aspiration stimulated the demand for higher education as a symbol of economic and social mobility, although universal access was still not a reality. This era of unprecedented access to higher educational opportunity is traced, using extensive supporting references.

608. American Education in the Twentieth Century: A Documentary History. Edited by Lazerson, Marvin. (Classics in Education, no. 52). Teachers College Press, 1987. 205p. LC: 86-30147. ISBN: 0-8088-2852-7; 0-8077-2851-9 (pbk.). $20.00; $11.00 (pbk.).

The history of American education is reviewed in the first half of this text, referring to a series of 34 documents reprinted in the second half of the twentieth century. The tensions between pride in and criticism of American education are a central theme as is the constant swing between commitments to equality and excellence during this century.

609. American Education: The Metropolitan Experience, 1876–1980. Cremin, Lawrence A. Harper & Row, 1988. 781p. LC: 87-45040. ISBN: 0-0601-5804-2. $35.00.

This work completes a three-volume series begun with *American Education: The Colonial Experience, 1607–1783* and continued with *American Education: The*

National Experience, 1783–1876 in presenting a scholarly account of the history of American education by a well-known authority in educational history. *The Metropolitan Experience* traces the transformation of education institutions, libraries, museums, and other cultural agencies as the United States became a metropolitan society.

610. American Educational History: A Guide to Information Sources. Sedlak, Michael and Walsh, Timothy. (American Government and History Information Guide Series, v. 10). Gale, 1981. 265p. LC: 80-19646. ISBN: 0-8103-1478-9. $68.00.
A selective list of materials relating to the history of American education, compiled and annotated to meet the needs of "undergraduates and interested educators." The nine chapters cover different aspects of educational history: pedagogy, higher education, outsiders, families, and cities. A guide to further research and index are included.

611. The American School 1642–1985: Varieties of Historical Interpretation of the Foundations and Development of American Education. Spring, Joel. Longman, 1986. 347p. LC: 85-19749. ISBN: 0-582-28571-2. $18.95.
For each period of American educational history covered, the major interpretations of events for that period are explored. For example, in covering the common school era, the interpretations of major educational historians such as Cubberley, Katz, Kaestle, and others are discussed.

612. A Bibliography of American Educational History: An Annotated and Classified Guide. Edited by Cordasco, Francesco and Brickman, William W. AMS Press, 1975. 394p. LC: 74-29140. ISBN: 0-404-12661-8. $47.50.
A specialized bibliography of some 3,000 entries on the history of American education covering general sources, and topical sources under such headings as elementary and secondary education, state-by-state education, higher education, and education of women. A chronological listing is included as is an author index.

613. A Class Divided: Then and Now. Peters, William. Yale Univ. Press, 1987. 172p. LC: 87-50411. ISBN: 0-3000-3666-3; 0-3000-4048-2 (pbk.). $25.00; $8.95 (pbk.). Expanded edition.
In the original edition reprinted here, Jane Elliott, in an attempt to counter the teaching of hatred, conducted a social experiment (dividing her class by eye color) with her third graders that became newsworthy and televised as the "Eye of the Storm." This expanded edition covers a reunion of the original third graders and a replication of the experiment with adult employees. A new hour-long documentary has been produced covering the earlier and later experiments.

614. Colleges and Universities for Change: America's Comprehensive Public State Colleges and Universities. Harcleroad, Fred F. and Ostar, Allan W. AASCU Press/University Pub. Associates, 1987. 226p. LC: 87-19277. ISBN: 0-88044-085-6; 0-88044-086-1 (pbk.). $24.50; $11.75 (pbk.).
Presents the historical development of a new type of higher education institution—the state college and university. The process of adaptation and change in American liberal arts colleges and research-oriented universities to form this modern mutation is chronicled into the twentieth century. The establishment of the American Association of State Colleges and Universities for-malized the new type of institution; attention is also focused on the AASCU.

615. The Colonial Colleges in the War for American Independence. Roche, John F. (National University Publications). Associated Faculty Press, 1986. 210p. LC: 83-24372. ISBN: 0-8046-9350-1. $24.95.
The evidence collected for this study supports the conclusion that American colonial colleges' involvement in the Revolution was modest in scale; they did not serve as major centers of revolutionary activity. Focuses on the activities of faculty and students in the early war years, the impact of wartime shocks on the college and their operations, and the problems the colleges faced following the Revolution—separation from Britain, financial problems.

616. Culture Wars: School and Society in the Conservative Restoration, 1969–1984. Shor, Ira. (Critical Social Thought Series). Routledge, Kegan & Paul, 1986. 238p. LC: 85-2305. ISBN: 0-710-20637-2; 0-710-20649-6 (pbk.). $25.00; $12.95 (pbk.).
The political nature of education becomes evident as the author analyzes three major waves of school reform: 1971–75, which focused on career and vocational education; 1975–82, the back-to-basics and literacy crisis; 1983+, the reforms launched by the commission on excellence calling for more discipline, academic subjects, and hi-tech. Each phase of school reform corresponds to a specific political intention of safeguarding the establishment from the denunciations and crises of the 1960s.

617. The Curriculum: Problems, Politics and Possibilities. Edited by Beyer, Landon E. and Apple, Michael W. (SUNY Series, Frontiers in Education). State Univ. of New York Press, 1988. 368p. LC: 87-33556. ISBN: 0-88706-818-9. $16.95.
A major goal of this text is to stimulate thoughtful practice and more politically sensitive curriculum inquiry around six thematic issues that form the major divisions of the book: history of the curriculum in a social and political context, curriculum planning, knowledge selection and curriculum, curriculum and teaching, technology and curriculum, programs and politics of evaluation.

618. Democracy's College: The Land-Grant Movement in the Formative State. Ross, Earle Dudley. (American Education: Its Men, Ideas and Institution Series). Ayer, 1969. 267p. LC: 74-89226. ISBN: 0-405-01463-5. $12.00. Reprint edition.
A comprehensive history tracing the development of the land-grant institutions over several decades. Extensive use of primary sources.

619. The Development and Structure of the English School System. Evans, Keith. (Studies in Teaching and Learning). Hodder and Stoughton, 1985. 275p. LC: 85-116944. ISBN: 0-34035-905-6. $24.95.
Concentrates on the development and structure of the statutory system of schooling in England and Wales. Schooling is considered in the wider societal context and for the nineteenth and twentieth centuries giving extra weighting to the post-war years and the last decade; attention given to elementary, secondary, and special education; curriculum and testing; teacher training. Intended for teacher training students with a summary and systematic type presentation.

620. Dewey, Russell, Whitehead: Philosophers as Educators. Hendley, Brian Patrick. Southern Illinois Univ. Press, 1986. 177p. LC: 85-2148. ISBN: 0-8093-1229-8. $10.95.

A study of three twentieth-century educational philosophers intended to encourage a redirection in the educational philosophy of today to go beyond the preoccupation with conceptual analysis to develop theories of education based on what is happening in the classroom. The educational ideas of Dewey, Russell, and Whitehead provide models for this in their application of philosophical insights to concrete educational situations—Dewey's Laboratory School, Russell's Beacon Hill School, and Whitehead's theory of the rhythm of education.

621. The Dialectic of Freedom. Greene, Maxine. Teachers College Press, 1988. 151p. LC: 88-2228. ISBN: 0-8077-2898-5; 0-8077-2897-7 (pbk.). $17.95; $9.95 (pbk.).

An exploration of the problem of freedom and the ways it has been understood and acted on in our American history. Develops a conception of education for freedom (not liberty) that takes into account our political and social realities as well as the human condition itself and that encourages inquiry, discovery, and making choices. Originally began as a John Dewey Lecture.

622. The Diverted Dream: Community Colleges and the Promise of Educational Opportunity in America, 1900–1985. Brint, Steven and Karabel, Jerome. Oxford Univ. Press, 1989. 312p. LC: 89-2891. ISBN: 0-19-504815-6. $24.95.

Explores the growth and transformation of the American two-year (junior or community) college. Focuses on origins, regional character and later diffusion nationally, transformation from the junior college into predominantly vocational institutions, and place in the larger system of higher education. A detailed case study of the development of community colleges in Massachusetts is presented as representative of the national development and trends.

623. Doctrines of the Great Educators. Rusk, Robert R. and Scotland, James. St. Martin's, 1979. 310p. LC: 78-12874. ISBN: 0-312-21492-8. $25.00.

Author Scotland has made some changes in this fifth edition of Rusk's original work defining the features that distinguish a "great educator" and why choices were made for those included—Plato, Quintilian, Loyola, Comenius, Locke, Rousseau, Pestalozzi, Herbart, Froebel, Montessori, Dewey. Extensive notes, short biographies of the educators, and other material included.

624. Education and the City: Theory, History and Contemporary Practice. Edited by Grace, Gerald. Routledge, Kegan & Paul, 1984. 302p. LC: 83-22983. ISBN: 0-710-09918-5. $16.95.

Contributed essays cover theory and history of and contemporary practice in urban education in the United States and Great Britain. The focus of the collection is to show that understanding contemporary urban education requires delving into its history and putting urban schooling in the context of a theory of society.

625. Education and the U.S. Government. Sharpes, Donald K. St. Martin's, 1987. 190p. LC: 86-29839. ISBN: 0-312-00467-2. $30.00.

A historical approach to the study of the federal government's role in education and how it was and is determined by the federal judiciary, the U.S. Congress, and the federal executive. Describes the "Origins of Federal Education," assessing contributions made by key political figures, and compares and analyzes the educational statements of other selected national constitutions.

626. Education as History: Interpreting Nineteenth and Twentieth-Century Education. Silver, Harold. Routledge, Kegan & Paul, 1984. 305p. LC: 82-20853. ISBN: 0-416-33320. $13.95.

A collection of essays on the social history of education in the nineteenth and twentieth centuries focusing on the methodologies used (and misused) by educational historians. Some of the methodological issues raised are violation of self-evident rules of method, ignoring the fluctuations in the social history of educational opinion, and a failure to write the social history of education from a comparative perspective.

627. Education: Assumptions Versus History: Collected Papers. Sowell, Thomas. Hoover Institution Press, Stanford Univ., 1986. 203p. LC: 85-18131. ISBN: 0-8179-8112-8. $8.95.

Essays, studies, and other writings of the author over several years have been reprinted, focusing on a central theme that policies and innovations in education should be supported on facts of the past and present and not on the basis of assumptions. Some of these assumptions are race and IQ, tuition tax credits, and the open university.

628. Education in a Free Society: An American History. Edited by Rippa, S. Alexander. Longman, 1988. 448p. LC: 87-3053. ISBN: 0-801-30127-0. $18.95. 6th edition.

A chronological social history of American education covered in three time periods: 1607–1865, the formative period; a transition period, 1865–1919; and modern society from 1919 to the present. This sixth edition provides a fresh look at some old topics—status of women in education and business, ours as an information society—plus new material on Jean Piaget's contributions, education of American Indians, and attention to revisionist historians.

629. Education in the United States: A Documentary History. Edited by Cohen, Sol. Greenwood, 1974. LC: 73-3099. ISBN: 0-313-20141-2. $225.00 set. 5 Volumes.

A five-volume collection of significant documents in the field of American education from the sixteenth century to the early 1970s. An overview of the period begins each volume wherein documents are arranged chronologically within topical chapters. Includes early essays by Erasmus and Rousseau and continues through the colonial period until the present with excerpts from Dewey's work, John Kennedy, and the Civil Rights Act of 1964.

630. Education in the United States: An Historical Perspective. Gutek, Gerald Lee. Prentice-Hall, 1986. 367p. LC: 85-20991. ISBN: 0-13-235680-5. Contact publisher for price information.

An undergraduate textbook on the history of American education from colonial America through the development of lower and upper levels of education, the evolution of America's system of education through several wars, concluding with chapters on the 1960s, 1970s, and 1980s. Each chapter contains discussion questions and research topics.

631. The Education of Nations: A Comparison in Historical Perspective. Ulich, Robert. Harvard Univ. Press, 1967. 365p. LC: 67-27094. ISBN: 0-674-23900-8. $27.00. Revised edition.

Revised edition of the 1961 text with an additional chapter on new developments in the educational policies of the major nations described in the book. First presents an overview of the major periods of early history through the era of technology and then the distinguishing evolution of education in England, France, Germany, Russia and the United States.

632. Education & the American Dream: Conservatives, Liberals & Radicals Debate the Future of Education. Edited by Holtz, Harvey et al. (Critical Studies in Education Series). Bergin & Garvey, 1989. 246p. LC: 88-7554. ISBN: 0-89789-177-5; 0-89789-176-7 (pbk.). $44.95; $16.95 (pbk.).

Features some highlights from a symposium entitled the "National Debate About the Future of Education" held at Indiana University of Pennsylvania. Among the contributors are educators, union officials, and activists from the right, center, and left approaches to education so that the views presented are conflicting ideologies. Issues debated are values, social inequality, computers, curriculum, pedagogy, teachers, reform.

633. Educational Roots and Routes in Western Europe. Brickman, William W. Emeritus, 1985. 404p. LC: 85-70176. ISBN: 0-943594-01-9. $20.00.

A collection of research studies and essays covering the educational history, problems, and literature of Western Europe, focusing on these countries: England, Denmark, France, German Federal Republic, Italy, Netherlands, Spain, Sweden, Switzerland, and Turkey. Several select bibliographies included.

634. Educational Theory as Theory of Conduct: From Aristotle to Dewey. Chambliss, Joseph James. State Univ. of New York Press, 1987. 172p. LC: 86-14540. ISBN: 0-88706-463-9; 0-88706-464-7 (pbk.). $49.50; $16.95 (pbk.).

The ideas of some of the great classic writers/philosophers are considered and discussed as they support the theory of education as a theory of conduct: Plato, Aristotle, Augustine, Clement, John of Salisbury, John Locke, Dewey, Watts, Rousseau. The exploration of thinking about conduct is a way of thinking about education and teaching as "conducting."

635. Educational Thought of the Classical Political Economists. O'Donnell, Margaret. Univ. Press of America, 1985. 156p. LC: 85-13487. ISBN: 0-8191-4817-2; 0-8191-4818-0 (pbk.). $26.25; $11.50 (pbk.).

Most of the political economists discussed in this book wrote during the nineteenth century. Their writings were examined for their educational philosophy, macroeconomic and microeconomic effects of education on the society, and demand and supply theory for education.

636. Elements of a Post-Liberal Theory of Education. Bowers, C.A. Teachers College Press, 1987. 187p. LC: 86-30135. ISBN: 0-8077-2849-7; 0-8077-2848-9 (pbk.). $27.95; $16.95 (pbk.).

A post-liberal approach to educational empowerment going beyond the thinkers who laid the foundations for modern liberalism (i.e. post-liberal) by taking into account developments in contemporary social theory and the problems of modernization. Recommendations are made on how the reform of curriculum and pedagogy can contribute to empowerment. The chief characteristics of four archetypal forms of educational liberalism are examined—John Dewey, Paulo Freire, B.F. Skinner, and Carl Rogers.

637. The Formation of School Subjects: The Struggle for Creating an American Institution. Edited by Popkewitz, Thomas S. (Studies in Curriculum History). Falmer, 1987. 310p. LC: 86-29347. ISBN: 1-85000-169-3; 1-85000-170-7 (pbk.). $38.00; $24.00 (pbk.).

A collection of essays focusing on the formation of the contemporary school curriculum to understand the social origins, cultural/political implications, and economic consequences affecting the emergence of subject matter in the American school. Each essay on the history of a subject—art, reading, writing, biology, mathematics, social studies, special education—is concerned with social dynamics that shaped curriculum. The range of time considered varies with each essay.

638. Founders: Innovators in Education, 1830–1980. Stabler, Ernest. Univ. of Nebraska Press, 1987. 306p. LC: C86-091443-7. ISBN: 0-88864-114-1. $24.95.

Some of the innovators in education and their institutional innovation are studied: N.F.S. Grundtvig, who started the Danish folk high schools; Horace Mann, who supported the development of public elementary schools; Mary Lyon, founder of Mt. Holyoke College for women; and the developers of the British Open University. Stresses the need to explore the economic and social environment surrounding innovative movements such as these.

The Great School Debate: Which Way for American Education? *See* **EDUCATIONAL REFORM (No. 246)**

639. Growth of an American Invention: A Documentary History of the Junior and Community College Movement. Diener, Thomas. (Contributions to the Study of Education, no. 16). Greenwood, 1986. 249p. LC: 85-9832. ISBN: 0-313-24993-8. $35.00. ISSN: 0196-707X.

The author has pulled together carefully selected documents representative of the growth and development of the American junior and community college movements. The chronological history unfolds in four parts: challenging the educational status quo and sowing the seeds of junior college education; early junior college developments; from junior college to community college; the golden age of the 1960s and 1970s.

640. Higher Education in Transition: A History of American Colleges and Universities, 1636–1976. Brubacher, John S. and Rudy, Willis. Harper & Row, 1976. 536p. LC: 75-6331. ISBN: 0-0601-0548-8. $32.45.

With the publication of this third edition, the authors update their classic history of higher education to coincide with the celebration of the 1976 bicentennial. Five parts chronicle the history of higher education from the colonial college through the nineteenth century to the twentieth century. Some 100 pages of notes provide extensive references to many primary sources.

641. The History of American Education: A Guide to Information Sources. Cordasco, Francesco, Alloway, David N. and Friedman, Marjorie S. (Education Information Guide Series, v. 7). Gale, 1979. 328p. LC: 79-23010. ISBN: 0-8103-1382-0. $68.00.

This bibliography is addressed to many "constituencies" researching the field of the history of American education. Some of the 2,495 entries are annotated. First few sections cover general works, periodicals, and source collections. Separate chapters are then devoted to the historiography of American education, the American college and university, major historical periods, and the history of textbooks, teaching, and curriculum. Author, title, and subject indexes are provided.

642. The History of Childhood: The Untold Story of Child Abuse. Edited by deMause, Lloyd. Harper & Row, 1988. 450p. LC: 87-35166. ISBN: 0-8722-6181-6; 0-8722-6203-0 (pbk.). $25.00; $12.00 (pbk.).

A systematic investigation of the attitudes and practices of parents towards their children; traces the history of childhood in the West beginning with the Roman period and continuing through the Middle Ages up through the nineteenth century. The depressing results tell a "long and mournful story" of the abuse of children from the earliest times to the present day—children looked upon as burdens, the practice of infanticide, abandonment, neglect, swaddling, solitary confinement.

643. How Teachers Taught: Constancy and Change in American Classrooms, 1890–1980. Cuban, Larry. Longman, 1984. 292p. LC: 83-1755. ISBN: 0-582-28481-3; 0-801-30037-1 (pbk.). $31.95; $16.95 (pbk.).

The author gathered data informally through many years of experience in public schools and more deliberately for this study to ascertain "how did teachers teach?" The central research issue here is which teaching behaviors have persisted over time, which have changed and why. The data were collected in five categories: organization of classroom space, ratio of teacher to student talk, instructional grouping, presence of learning or interest centers, student movement. Case studies include schools in New York City, Denver, and Washington, D.C.

644. The Imperfect Panacea: American Faith in Education, 1865–1976. Perkinson, Henry. McGraw, 1977. 257p. LC: 76-45395. ISBN: 0-07-553674-9. $12.95. 2nd edition.

Replaces the original 1968 edition with an "Epilogue" updating the events of the last decade, but still supporting the thesis that schools are not the panacea for all social problems. Examines how schools had failed to solve multiple problems during 1865–1976, shaking American faith in the power of the school.

645. Individual, Society and Education: A History of American Educational Ideas. Karier, Clarence J. Univ. of Illinois Press, 1986. 459p. LC: 85-24547. ISBN: 0-252-01290-9; 0-252-01309-3 (pbk.). $34.95; $14.94 (pbk.). 2nd edition.

A second revised edition of the earlier title *Man, Society and Education.* Updates to cover the intervening years, 1967–1986, include a chapter on the post-World War II period, a section on the women's movement, and a follow-up chapter on the Supreme Court and its increasing attention to cases in education.

646. John Dewey's Reconstruction in Philosophy. Peterson, Forrest H. Philosophical Library, 1987. 96p. LC: 86-12285. ISBN: 0-8022-2515-2. $8.50.

The author's purpose is to clarify John Dewey's role in the development of public education. His philosophy of education was not readily applied in schools because many educators did not understand what his message was. Drawing primarily from Dewey's works, *Democracy and Education* and *Reconstruction in Philosophy* some of his expressions and phraseology are analyzed to help the reader comprehend Dewey's message.

647. The Labyrinths of Literacy: Reflections on Literacy Past and Present. Graff, Harvey J. Taylor & Francis, 1987. 264p. LC: 86-29351. ISBN: 1-85000-163-4. $22.00.

Brings together essays that either examine or challenge the social and economic contexts into which literacy came, linking historical and present issues: industrialization and the workplace, criminality, human fertility, economic development for individuals and nations.

648. The Last Little Citadel: American High Schools Since 1940. Hampel, Robert. (A Study of High Schools). Houghton Mifflin, 1986. 209p. LC: 85-27028. ISBN: 0-395-36451-5. $15.95. Co-sponsored by the National Association of Secondary School Principals and the Commission on Educational Issues of the National Association of Independent Schools.

An examination of the transformation of the educational citadel concept of the high school to a shopping mall high school nation. While tracing the developments and changes that occurred in high schools from 1940 to 1984, the book focuses on the reallocation and shifting of power and decision making of the educators inside and outside the "citadels."

649. Law and the Shaping of Public Education, 1785–1954. Tyack, David, James, Thomas and Benavot, Aaron. Univ. of Wisconsin Press, 1987. 259p. LC: 86-400062. ISBN: 0-299-10880-5. $25.00.

A historical look at how law has shaped schooling from three vantage points: state constitutions, statutes, and court decisions. The interaction of state government and education and not the federal government is the focus of analysis. Examines how law was used to build common schools in the new states and the relationship between majority rule and minority rights in education; three case studies are presented.

650. Learning from Our Mistakes. Perkinson, Henry. Greenwood, 1984. 209p. LC: 83-26670. ISBN: 0-313-24239-9. $35.00.

Describes a new theory of education, a Darwinian theory called a "Metatheory" that reinterprets earlier theories that have produced successful educational practices. The theorists reinterpreted are Karl Popper, Jean Piaget, B.F. Skinner, Maria Montessori, and A.S. Neill.

651. Life in Schools: An Introduction to Critical Pedagogy in the Foundations of Education. McLaren, Peter. Longman, 1989. 258p. LC: 88-551. ISBN: 0-582-28683-2. $11.15.

A critical analysis of schooling in the inner city intended to provide educators with the critical skills and conceptual means to analyze the goals of schooling and their own teaching. Explores the social problems besetting schools and society and introduces basic theoretical concepts of Kozol, Dewey, and Giroux with which to analyze the process of schooling. A journal transcription of the day-to-day challenges and demands of the author's inner-city teaching is offered for discussion.

652. Modern School Movement, Anarchism and Education in the United States. Avrich, Paul. Princeton Univ. Press, 1980. 447p. LC: 79-3188. ISBN: 0-691-04669-7; 0-691-10094-2 (pbk.). $49.50; $17.95 (pbk.).

Explores the history of the Modern School Movement from 1910 to 1960 analyzing its successes and failures in an attempt to create a new culture and new life through a new educational establishment. Extensive use of primary sources and personal testimony, since the approach is largely biographical.

653. The Myth of the Common School. Glenn, Charles Leslie. Univ. of Massachusetts Press, 1988. 369p. LC: 87-19183. ISBN: 0-87023-602-4; 0-87023-603-2 (pbk.). $37.50; $13.95 (pbk.).

This is not the history of a period but rather the history of a complex of ideas called a "myth" of the common or public school. The study covers the controversies over public education in France, Netherlands, and Massachusetts and what were the intentions of education reformers and their critics and supporters in organizing common schools. The comparative nature of this study makes it unique.

The New Servants of Power: A Critique of the 1980s School Reform Movement *See* **EDUCATIONAL REFORM (No. 261)**

654. Of Human Potential: An Essay in the Philosophy of Education. Scheffler, Israel. Routledge, Kegan & Paul, 1985. 141p. LC: 85-2140. ISBN: 0-710-20571-6. $18.95.

The Harvard Graduate School of Education Project on Human Potential was established to develop a theoretical framework for conceiving human potential that would be practically valuable for the guidance of education. The results of the work are to appear in four volumes; this volume, the second to be published, details the philosophical and conceptual aspects of the inquiry beginning with a background of the concept of potential in educational practice.

655. Opening Up of American Education. Teeter, Ruskin. Univ. Press of America, 1983. 146p. LC: 83-3647. ISBN: 0-8191-3137-7; 0-8191-3136-9 (pbk.). $12.00 (pbk.); $30.00.

An examination of 350 years of schooling in America portraying the "opening up" process of education repeated over many generations. Some lesser known developments toward a public, democratic form of education are chronicled in a readable style—marm's schools, Charles Houston's efforts in the civil rights struggle, Peabody Fund for Southern Education.

656. Outside In: Minorities and the Transformation of American Education. Fass, Paula S. Oxford Univ. Press, 1989. 308p. LC: 88-31953. ISBN: 0-19-503790-1. $29.95.

How schooling in the United States has dealt with outsiders in the early twentieth century and how it has been shaped through this response is the central issue in this historical study. The outsiders referred to are the immigrants, blacks, women, and Catholics who were outside the mainstream culture and school power networks in the early twentieth century.

657. Philosophy of Education in Historical Perspective. Dupuis, Adrian M. Univ. Press of America, 1985. 302p. LC: 85-9084. ISBN: 0-8191-4729-X. $13.25.

An introductory text in the philosophy of education with a historical perspective; issues are treated within the context of educational conservatism and liberalism. These philosophical views are covered: Plato, the Romans, the early Christians, the Renaissance, Dewey and other liberal philosophies, contemporary neoconservative philosophies, and the Soviet philosophy of education.

658. The Politics of Federal Reorganization: Creating the U.S. Department of Education. Radin, Beryl A. and Hawley, Willis D. (Pergamon Government & Politics Series). Pergamon, 1988. 253p. LC: 87-6972. ISBN: 0-08-033978-6; 0-08-033977-8 (pbk.). $32.50; $14.95 (pbk.).

Examines the creation and implementation of the new Department of Education through a case study in narrative form. Five themes are woven in the unfolding of this complex study: stages of policy process; politics and internal tensions in the executive branch; the culture of analysis versus the culture of politics; the role of interest groups and issue networks; the continuing uncertainty about the federal role in education. Extensive use of primary sources and personal interviews.

659. Politics of School Reform, 1870–1940. Peterson, Paul E. Univ. of Chicago Press, 1985. 241p. LC: 85-1042. ISBN: 0-226-66294-2; 0-226-66295-0 (pbk.). $27.50; $11.95 (pbk.).

School reform in urban education is the focus in this text. Discusses the forming of urban schools and the effects of pluralistic politics of urban America on the schools; urban educational reform and the effects of political and economic characteristics in spawning reform movements. Atlanta is the major focus but Chicago and San Francisco are also highlighted as examples.

660. Power and the Promise of School Reform: Grassroots Movements During the Progressive Era. Reese, William J. (Critical Social Thought Series). Routledge, Kegan & Paul, 1986. 342p. LC: 85-14250. ISBN: 0-710-09952-5.

Several cities were studied to construct the book's basic thesis on the importance of grassroots, community-oriented reformers in the history of schooling during the Progressive era: Rochester, New York; Toledo, Ohio; Milwaukee, Wisconsin; Kansas City, Missouri. Many primary sources were studied including school board minutes and proceedings, annual school reports, newspapers, and various manuscript collections.

661. Research in Educational History. Brickman, William W. Bern Porter, 1985. 332p. LC: 82-71738. ISBN: 0-317-19974-9. $64.50. Reprint edition.

The original (1949) edition appeared as the *Guide to Research in Education History*; the 1973 edition was an "Augmented" edition of the first titled *Research in Educational History*. In 1982 an edition with the title *Educational Historiography* was published which the author considered a third edition of the original *Guide*. The difference between this and earlier editions was the addition of two essays on educational historiography; the basic text is still an excellent guide to conducting historical research in education from start (research) to finish (report).

662. Social Goals and Educational Reform: American Schools in the Twentieth Century. Edited by Willie, Charles V. and Miller, Inabeth. (Contributions to the Study of Education, no. 27). Greenwood, 1988. 176p. LC: 88-217. ISBN: 0-313-24781-1. $37.95.

Presents a multidisciplinary perspective on the development of educational policy and practice in the U.S. during the twentieth century. Essays are divided by two major themes: to aid in the interpretation of the reports, federal statutes and Supreme Court cases regarding educational reform in American secondary schools; how education may have a two-fold goal of individual enhancement and community advancement.

663. The Social History of American Education. McClellan, B. Edward and Reese, William J. Univ. of Illinois Press, 1988. 370p. LC: 87-5893. ISBN: 0-252-01461-8; 0-252-01462-6 (pbk.). $34.95; $11.95 (pbk.).

A collection of selected articles published in the *History of Education Quarterly* over the years, reflecting some of the best essays produced on the social history of American education; works cover both popular and higher education.

664. The Sorting Machine Revisited: National Educational Policy Since 1945. Spring, Joel. Longman, 1989. LC: 88-11907. ISBN: 0-801-30279-X. Contact publisher for price information. Revised edition.

In this updated version of the 1976 edition the two themes remain the same—struggle for the control of educational policy since the 1940s by military, corporate, scientific, and political spheres, and the schools' selection and training of students for the labor market, i.e., the sorting machine, to serve the interests of the business community. A "Postscript" chapter updates educational events since 1976, using Ravitch's *Troubled Crusade* and Shor's *Culture Wars*, two very different educational historical orientations.

665. The State and the Non–Public School, 1825-1925. Jorgenson, Lloyd P. Univ. of Missouri Press, 1987. 235p. LC: 86-30776. ISBN: 0-8262-0633-6. $29.00.

In a broad sense this is the history of the split of education into public and non-public sectors and the struggles between proponents of these sectors in the nineteenth century. In a narrower sense, this history reviews the origins of the "School Question"—the political and legal principles that non-public schools are ineligible for public aid, and the exclusion of religious observances, Bible reading, and prayer from public schools.

666. A Subject Bibliography of the History of American Higher Education. Beach, Mark. Greenwood, 1984. 165p. LC: 83-22565. ISBN: 0-313-23276-8. $36.95.

A companion volume to an earlier bibliography, the 1975 *Bibliographic Guide to American Colleges and Universities*, providing 1,325 sources of materials about the history of higher education, arranged topically. Includes books, articles, and dissertations.

667. Theories of Education: Studies of Significant Innovation in Western Educational Thought. Bowen, James and Hobson, Peter R. Wiley, 1987. 478p. ISBN: 0-471-33420-0. $23.50. 2nd edition.

This revised edition contains an outline of major developments in Western educational thought since the 1974 edition and some modifications to the original text covering the theories of nine major educational thinkers: Plato, Aristotle, Rousseau, Dewey, Makarenko, Skinner, Neil, Peters, and Illich. Peters, Illich, and Freire are brought up-to-date and current positions of traditional and radical theories are examined. All bibliographies have been updated and revised.

668. The Thirteenth Man: A Reagan Cabinet Memoir. Bell, Terrel Howard. Free Press, 1988. 195p. LC: 87-25992. ISBN: 0-02-902351-3. $19.95.

A biographical account of Terrell Bell's four-year term as the Secretary of Education, the "thirteenth man" (based on the order of creation of departments and cabinet rank) in Reagan's first cabinet. He describes problems encountered in battling for support for the Department of Education; in a lack of commitment to federal leadership in carrying out recommendations of *A Nation at Risk*; in confrontations with other members of the Cabinet and Reagan's staff; and in combatting proposed budget slashes.

669. Three Thousand Years of Educational Wisdom: Selections from Great Documents. Ulich, Robert. Harvard Univ. Press, 1954. 668p. LC: 54-12764. ISBN: 0-674-89072-8. $16.00. 2nd edition.

Selections from the educational writings of great men and great works of these times and places: Asia, Greek and Roman Antiquity (Plato, Aristotle), Ancient and Medieval Christianity (Saint Augustine), Islam, Humanist Evolution (Jesuit Order), New Method of Thinking (Descartes), Development of Modern Education (Comenius), and Judaic Tradition.

670. Towards a History of Adult Education in America: the Search for a Unifying Principle. Stubblefield, Harold W. (Croom Helm Series on Theory and Practices of Adult Education in North America). Routledge, Kegan & Paul, 1988. 186p. LC: 87-30558. ISBN: 0-709-94463-2. $35.00.

A historical study of American adult education in the 1920s and 1930s. The focus is on the well-known adult educators who were influential at that time as the first generation theorists of adult education as a social practice. Their writings and agendas for adult education are treated under one of three unifying principles: the diffusion of knowledge and culture; liberal education; or social education.

671. The Troubled Crusade: American Education, 1945–1980. Ravitch, Diane. Basic Books, 1983. 384p. LC: 83-70750. ISBN: 0-465-08756-6. $19.95.

Beginning with the immediate postwar (1945) years, the author reports on the state of the crusade for equal educational opportunity in the American educational history. Essays on postwar initiatives, race, and education, from Berkeley to Kent State, reflect the view that American education is in trouble because of the belief that schooling can solve most social problems.

672. Truth and Credibility: The Citizen's Dilemma. Broudy, Harry S. (The John Dewey Society Lecture Series, no. 17). Longman, 1981. 164p. LC: 80-28305. ISBN: 0-582-28208-X. Contact publisher for price information.

Explores the conflict between faith and reason that is prevalent in our modern society. A philosophical discussion of credibility, truth, moral responsibility, and rational action within the context of education is presented by the author.

673. Understanding History of Education. Edited by Sherman, Robert R. Schenkman, 1984. 345p. LC: 84-23588. ISBN: 0-87073-338-9. $18.95. 2nd revised edition.

Revised edition of the 1976 title of the same name focusing on the study of the history of education, especially the role it should play in teacher preparation. The same essay format contains some new materials; updated references and stylistic changes from the first edition.

674. Visions of Childhood: Influential Models from Locke to Spock. Cleverly, John and Phillips, D.C. Teachers College Press, 1986. 166p. LC: 85-30359. ISBN: 0-8077-2801-2. $18.95.

A two-way analysis of theories of childhood is put forward: focusing on major ideas, themes, and models traditional to Western thought, and concentrating on leading individuals and how they owed much to earlier theoretical constructs in shaping their thoughts on paradigms of childhood. The aim is to sensitize readers to the influence of these major theories in our daily lives.

675. Voice of Liberal Learning: Michael Oakeshott on Education. Oakeshott, Michael J. Yale Univ. Press, 1989. 166p. LC: 88-27811. ISBN: 0-3000-4344-9. $20.00.

Oakeshott's reflections on teaching and learning in higher education are presented in this reprinted collection of his essays spanning the late 1940s to the mid 1970s. In the essays Oakeshott evokes the idea of liberal learning, offering a corrective to the current cultural barrier to liberal learning, espousing the metaphor of conversation, which is central to his ideas of philosophy and education.

676. What's Worth Teaching: Selecting, Organizing and Integrating Knowledge. Brady, Marion. (SUNY Series in the Philosophy of Education). SUNY Press, 1989. 147p. LC: 87-33636. ISBN: 0-88706-815-4; 0-88706-816-2 (pbk.). $39.50; $12.95 (pbk.).

Argues for a new theoretical base for the general education curriculum, one that expands an understanding of reality and presents a formal model for the study of the concept of culture; most of the book is devoted to discussing the kind of content likely to grow out of a curriculum structured by a formal model of the concept. Two appendices provide advice on teaching based on an understanding of sociocultural systems and illustrations of instructional material based on the concept of culture.

677. Women Teachers on the Frontier. Kaufman, Polly Welts. Yale Univ. Press, 1984. 270p. LC: 83-14699. ISBN: 0-3000-3043-6. $9.95.

Sent by the National Board of Popular Education in the 1800s, several hundred single women journeyed to teach in the western frontier; the diversity among them, the differences in the perceptions and conditions of some are chronicled here. The letters, reminiscences, and diaries researched for this text allow these women to tell their own remarkable stories as opposed to the usual stereotyped character of the eastern schoolmistress in the West.

Journals

678. Educational Theory: A Medium of Expression for the John Dewey Society and the Philosophy of Education Society. Univ. of Illinois, College of Education, 1310 S. Sixth St., Champaign, IL 61820. Quarterly. $20.00. ISSN: 0013-2004. 1951.

679. History of Education Quarterly. History of Education Society, Indiana Univ., School of Education, 3rd and Jordan, Bloomington, IN 47405. Quarterly. $47.00. ISSN: 0018-2680. 1961.

Humanistic Educator *See* **Journal of Humanistic Education and Development HISTORY AND PHILOSOPHY OF EDUCATION (No. 682)**

Interdisciplinary Perspectives *See* **Perspectives HISTORY AND PHILOSOPHY OF EDUCATION (No. 683)**

680. J E T: Journal of Educational Thought/Revue De La Pensee Educative. Faculty of Education, Univ. of Calgary, Room 502, Education Tower, Calgary, Alberta T2N 1N4 Canada. 3/year. $27.00 Canadian. ISSN: 0022-0701. 1967. Formerly *Journal of Educational Thought.*

681. Journal of Aesthetic Education. Univ. of Illinois Press, 54 E. Gregory Drive, Champaign, IL 61820. Quarterly. $30.00. ISSN: 0021-8510. 1966.

Journal of Educational Thought *See* **JET HISTORY AND PHILOSOPHY OF EDUCATION (No. 680)**

682. Journal of Humanistic Education and Development. American Assn. for Counseling and Development, Assn. for Humanistic Education and Development, 5999 Stevenson Ave., Alexandria, VA 22304. Quarterly. $12.00. ISSN: 0735-6846. 1982. Formerly *Humanistic Educator* (1962–1982).

Journal of Teaching and Learning *See* **Teaching and Learning HISTORY AND PHILOSOPHY OF EDUCATION (No. 685)**

683. Perspectives: The Journal of the Association for General and Liberal Studies. Assn. for General and Liberal Studies, c/o Bruce Busby, Editor, Ohio Dominican College, 1216 Sunbury Rd., Columbus, OH 43219-2099. 3/year. $15.00. ISSN: 0890-9792. 1982. Formerly *Interdisciplinary Perspectives* (1976–1981).

684. Philosophy of Education: Proceedings of the Annual Meeting. Philosophy of Education Society, c/o Thomas Nelson, Editor, Illinois State Univ., Dept. of E.A.F., Normal, IL 61761. Annual. $20.00. ISSN: 8756-6575. 1958.

685. Teaching and Learning: The Journal of Natural Inquiry. Center for Teaching and Learning, Univ. of North Dakota, Box 8158, Grand Forks, ND 58202. 3/year. $12.00. ISSN: 0887-9486. 1986. Formerly *Journal of Teaching and Learning.*

Measurement

This section contains resources on tests and testing. Reference sources, handbooks, some introductory textbooks, and research materials are included. *Testing Information Sources for Educators*, which appears below, provides additional information about databases and organizations. Information about the process of measurement as well as criticism of standardized testing is included for balance in this section. *FairTest Examiner* is an example of a journal that monitors the activities of the testing industry. Related materials may also be found in the section on **Educational Psychology/Guidance/Counseling.**

Books

686. Arthur Jensen: Consensus and Controversy. Edited by Modgil, Sohan and Modgil, Celia. (Falmer International Masterminds Challenged, v. 4). Falmer, 1987. 420p. LC: 86-14931. ISBN: 1-8500-093-X. $77.00.
   One in a series of books on major figures in education and psychology, such as Lawrence Kohlberg, Eysenck, and B.F. Skinner. Evaluates elements of Jensen's work from a variety of perspectives. Provides positive and negative evaluation of Jensen's theories by a number of reputable scholars. A concluding chapter by Jensen himself highlights this provocative compilation on Jensen and test bias.

687. Assessing Children's Language in Naturalistic Context. Lund, Nancy and Duchan, Judith F. Prentice-Hall, 1988. 366p. LC: 87-11579. ISBN: 0-13-049736-3. Contact publisher for price information. 2nd edition.
   Designed for the student teacher and practicing clinician as a guide to assessing the communication between language learners and their conversational partners. Discusses assessment procedures, phonology, morphology, syntax, semantics, and discourse within the context of communicative competence. Specific types of tests are reviewed for possible application.

688. Assessing Educational Achievement. Edited by Nuttall, Desmond L. (Contemporary Analysis in Education Series, Vol. 10). Falmer, 1986. 220p. LC: 85-20679. ISBN: 1-85000-056-5. $17.00.
   Collected essays examine individual assessment and its relationship to the performance of the educational system. England, Wales, France, Australia, the USA and Canada are among the systems examined. Reviews content developments and future prospects for public examinations. A historical background for educational assessment is provided, as well as a critical look at future directions.

689. Assessing School and Classroom Climate: A Consumers Guide. Arter, Judith A. Northwest Regional Educational Laboratory, 1987. 83p. ISBN: 0-317-66077-2. $9.75.
   Developed to assist educators in evaluating educational climate by providing reviews and descriptions of the major tests and surveys of classroom climate. Discusses the needs for assessing educational climate and methodology. Includes definitions, selection criteria, and a list of additional resources.

Assessment in Special and Remedial Education *See* SPECIAL EDUCATION (No. 824)

690. Behavioral Assessment in School Psychology. Shapiro, Edward S. (School Psychology Series). L. Erlbaum, 1987. 255p. LC: 86-24375. ISBN: 0-89859-881-8. $34.50.
   Provides school psychologists with a background on the procedures and concepts of behavioral assessment. Individual assessment in the school setting is the primary focus. Useful as a handbook as well as a college text, this volume includes examples, models, suggested methodology, and research background.

Classroom Measurement and Evaluation *See* RESOURCES FOR TEACHING (No. 786)

691. Constructing Test Items. Osterlind, Steven J. (Evaluation in Education and Human Services). Kluwer Academic, 1989. 343p. LC: 89-8152. ISBN: 0-7923-9012-1. $59.95.
   A basic, thorough presentation of the complexities of item-writing and test construction. Directed to teachers, researchers, and students, this work includes sample items with evaluative information indexes and a bibliography.

Creative Classroom Testing *See* RESOURCES FOR TEACHING (No. 788)

692. Designing Tests for Evaluating Student Achievement. Cangelosi, James S. Longman, 1990. 230p. LC: 89-30279. ISBN: 0-8013-0263-3. Contact publisher for price information.

Designed to assist teachers in applying state-of-the-art strategies for evaluating student achievements. Chapters address selection and design of tests, validity and reliability, types of tests, ethics of testing, and interpretation of test scores. Supplemented by a glossary of test-related terms.

693. Developing Observation Skills. Cartwright, Carol A. and Cartwright, G. Phillip. (McGraw-Hill Series in Special Education). McGraw-Hill, 1984. 163p. LC: 83-13583. ISBN: 0-07-010185-X. $22.95. 2nd edition.

The importance of observation techniques in identifying characteristics and behaviors is addressed in a practical way in this manual. The necessity of observation, particularly as mandated by Public Law 94-142, the types of observation methods, and descriptions of commercially available instruments are well-covered. Useful to a wide audience including child development specialists, therapists, social workers, school psychologists, and nurses.

694. Directory of Selected National Testing Programs. Test Collection, Educational Testing Service. Oryx Press, 1987. 280p. LC: 86-43112. ISBN: 0-89774-386-5. $35.00.

Provides information about a wide variety of educational testing programs. Covers fee-based tests offered at designated testing centers. Includes three categories: selection and admissions, academic credit, and certification and licensing.

695. Directory of Unpublished Experimental Mental Measures. Goldman, Bert Arthur et al. Human Sciences Press, 1974–. 639 p. (v.5, 1990) LC: 73-17342. ISBN: 0-87705-130-5 (v.1); 0-87705-300-6 (v.2); 0-89885-095-9 (v.3); 0-89885-100-9 (v.4); 0-697-11490-2 (v.5). Contact publisher for price information. 0731-8081.

Summarizes tests drawn from relevant professional journals but not yet commercially available. Primary focus is educational tests. Volumes are published periodically and cover earlier years.

696. Educational Measurement. Edited by Linn, Robert L. (The American Council on Education/Macmillan Series on Higher Education). American Council on Education/Macmillan, 1989. 610p. LC: 88-17461. ISBN: 0-02-922400-4. $60.00. 3rd edition. Sponsored jointly by the National Council on Measurement in Education and the American Council on Education.

Contains 18 chapters written by well known authorities in educational measurement. Extensive bibliographies, figures, and tables enhance this key resource in the area of testing.

697. Essentials of Educational Measurement. Ebel, Robert L. and Frisbie, David A. Prentice-Hall, 1986. 360p. LC: 85-12036. ISBN: 0-13-286006-6. $28.95. 4th edition.

Useful for practitioners, teacher education students, and test developers in gaining an understanding of educational measurement. Covers statistical concepts, reliability, validity, use of tests (including essay, true-false, multiple-choice, and standardized tests), test administration, grading, and scoring. Also discusses recent developments in testing such as computerized testing, mandated testing, and item-response theory.

698. ETS Test Collection Catalog. Test Collection, Educational Testing Service. Oryx Press, v. 1, 1986; v. 2, 1988; v.3, 1989; v.4, 1990. 286p. v. 1; 160p., v.2; 202p., v.3; 158p., v.4 LC: 86-678. ISBN: 0-89774-248-6, v.1; 0-89774-439-X, v.2; 0-89774-477-2, v.3; 0-89774-558-2, v.4. Contact publisher for price information.

Describes tests that are available at the Educational Testing Service Test Collection Library. Each volume covers a specific subject area, such as achievement tests (v. 1), vocational tests (v. 2), tests for special populations (v. 3), and cognitive aptitude and intelligence tests (v. 4).

699. The Experiences of Work: A Compendium and Review of 249 Measures and Their Use. Cook, John. Academic Press, 1981. 335p. LC: 81-66680. ISBN: 0-1218-7050-2. $80.00.

Information is provided on 249 measures of work attitudes, values, and perceptions published or referred to in journal articles in 15 principal international journals from 1974 to mid-1980. Includes descriptions of the scales and research applications. Indexes subscales as well as scales.

Group Assessment in Reading: Classroom Teacher's Handbook *See* **CONTENT AREAS (No. 87)**

A Guide to 75 Tests for Special Education *See* **SPECIAL EDUCATION (No. 850)**

700. A Guide to Criterion-Referenced Test Construction. Edited by Berk, Ronald A. Johns Hopkins Univ. Press, 1984. 347p. LC: 84-47955. ISBN: 0-8018-2417-6. $93.40.

Updates and revises *Criterion-Referenced Measurement: The State of the Art,* 1980. Chapters by testing experts thoroughly review past testing practices with recommendations for future actions regarding criterion-referenced testing.

701. Index to Tests Used in Educational Dissertations. Fabiano, Emily. Oryx, 1989. 312p. LC: 89-32021. ISBN: 0-89774-288-5. $84.50.

Serves as a locator to tests in educational dissertations. User is referred to specific entries in *Dissertation Abstracts International.* Covers over 40,000 tests in educational dissertations published from 1938 to 1980. Title, keyword, author, and acronyms can be used to locate tests through the index. Covers achievement, aptitude, personality, vocational ability, and a wide range of other tests. Tests for special populations are also identified.

Intelligence and Exceptionality: New Directions for Theory, Assessment and Instructional Practices *See* **SPECIAL EDUCATION (No. 857)**

702. Introduction to Classical and Modern Test Theory. Crocker, Linda and Algina, James. Holt, Rinehart and Winston, 1986. 527p. LC: 85-17647. ISBN: 0-03-061634-4. Contact publisher for price information.

Presents classical theoretical approaches to testing, recent developments, and how the two are interrelated. Chapters cover an introduction to test theory, reliability, validity, item analysis, and test scoring and interpretation. As a textbook useful to education students, each chapter includes a summary and computational exercises designed to illustrate test theory applications. Designed to be useful to students without strong quantitative backgrounds, verbal explanations accompany quantitative expressions and symbols.

703. Measurement and Assessment in Education and Psychology. Wood, Robert. Falmer Press, 1987. 279p. LC: 87-545. ISBN: 1-85000-161-8. $44.00.

Despite the British slant in this collection of Robert Wood's papers from 1967–1987, there is coverage of the major aspects of assessment and measurement appropriate for college readers.

704. Measurement and Evaluation in Teaching. Gronlund, Norman E. Macmillan, 1985. 540p. LC: 84-866. ISBN: 0-02-348110-2. Contact publisher for price information. 5th edition.

Emphasizes the principles and procedures of testing and evaluation. Standard textbook approach is used to explain testing to undergraduate and graduate students. Covers the role of assessment, preparation of instructional objectives, validity, reliability, test construction, types of tests, utilization of published tests, and test bias issues. Extensive appendixes include basic statistics, a list of test publishers, and a taxonomy of educational objectives.

Measurement for Evaluation in Physical Education and Exercise Science *See* **HEALTH/PHYSICAL EDUCATION (No. 492)**

Measures for Research and Evaluation in the English Language Arts *See* **CONTENT AREAS (No. 89)**

705. Mental Measurement Yearbook. Edited by Conoley, Jane Close and Kramer, Jack J. Univ. of Nebraska Press, 1989. 1014p. LC: 39-3422. ISBN: 0-910674-31-0. $125.00. 10th yearbook. Published since 1938. Recent yearbooks updated by supplements.

Provides descriptive information on tests published in English-speaking countries. Includes references, reviews and information on availability, scoring, and validity. This standard source is indexed by test title, personal name, and subject area.

The Nation's Report Card: Improving the Assessment of Student Achievement *See* **EDUCATIONAL REFORM (No. 259)**

None of the Above: Behind the Myth of Scholastic Aptitude *See* **HIGHER AND CONTINUING EDUCATION (No. 572)**

NTE: National Teacher Examinations *See* **TEACHER EDUCATION (No. 925)**

706. Perspectives on Bias in Mental Testing. Edited by Reynolds, Cecil R. and Brown, Robert T. (Perspectives on Individual Differences). Plenum, 1984. 608p. LC: 84-9800. ISBN: 0-306-41529-1. $55.00.

Addresses the cultural-test-bias hypothesis by presenting the views of prominent test experts concerned with cultural test bias and individual differences. Authors have different academic and cultural backgrounds, as well as employment settings. Different theories regarding cultural test bias are presented by the authors. Background information, ethical considerations, specific tests, racial differences, and experimental research are discussed. In the final chapter Arthur Jensen updates his position in *Bias in Mental Testing* and critiques the other chapters in this volume.

707. Psychoeducational Assessment: Integrating Concepts and Techniques. Helton, George B., Workman, Edward A. and Matuszek, Paula A. Grune & Stratton, 1982. 364p. LC: 82-11775. ISBN: 0-8089-1482-0. $34.50.

Discusses the integration of the many factors involved in assessment. These factors include legal considerations, situational constraints, available assessment models and tools, and ethical considerations. Assessment of different domains such as health factors and intelligence are discussed at length. Particular emphasis is given to legal, ethical, and legislative issues that impact on assessment.

708. Psychoeducational Assessment of Minority Group Children: A Casebook. Edited by Jones, Reginald L. Cobb & Henry, 1988. 429p. LC: 87-20861. ISBN: 0-943539-00-5. $24.95 (pbk.).

Presents procedures for the psychoeducational assessment of children that are thought to be unbiased. Describes and evaluates test instruments and procedures that are useful in assessing minority group children. Alternate methods, case studies, and group methods of unbiased assessment are explored. Emphasis is placed on testing and tests rather than on an integrated assessment approach.

The Psychoeducational Assessment of Preschool Children *See* **EDUCATIONAL PSYCHOLOGY/GUIDANCE/COUNSELING (No. 205)**

709. Psychoeducational Evaluation of Children and Adolescents with Low-Incidence Handicaps. Lazarus, Philip J. and Strickhart, Stephen S. Grune & Stratton, 1986. 317p. LC: 86-14806. ISBN: 0-8089-1779-X. $39.50.

Presents assessment guidelines for low-incidence handicaps that school psychologists must now test for due to recent legislation, litigation, and professional standards. Each contributed chapter has been submitted by a specialist in the area. Handicaps covered include visual impairment, deafness, mental retardation, autism, and cerebral palsy. Additional information is provided on diagnosing handicapped preschool children.

710. Psychological Testing. Anastasi, Anne. Macmillan, 1988. 817p. LC: 86-33227. ISBN: 0-02-303020-8. Contact publisher for price information. 6th edition.

Comprehensive overview of psychological tests and testing that discusses the history and context of testing. Addresses technical and methodological principles of testing, types of tests, and describes individual tests. Excellent introduction to the field of psychological testing. Appendixes include ethical principles of psychologists and a list of test publishers. Extensive list of references and indexes are included.

711. Psychware: A Reference Guide to Computer-Based Products for Behavioral Assessment in Psychology, Education and Business. Krug, Samuel. Test Corporation of America, 1987. 457p. LC: 87-10176. ISBN: 0-933701-11-X. Contact publisher for price information. 2nd edition.

Identifies and describes computer-based products that are applied to assessment and test scoring. Many computerized tests are listed, as are products for computerized test scoring.

Reading: Tests and Assessment Techniques *See* **CONTENT AREAS (No. 91)**

712. The Reign of ETS: The Corporation That Makes Up Minds. Nairn, Allan and Associates. Ralph Nader, 1980. 554p. LC: 80-107761. ISBN: 0-936486-00-7. $30.00 (pbk.). The Ralph Nader Report on the Educational Testing Service.

Explores the structure and role of the Educational Testing Service (ETS) in the realm of standardized testing. Presents ETS as a secretive, bureaucratic, inflexible organization that controls the lives and futures of students through a series of tests that do not allow for human versatility. A lengthy critique of ETS, with over 100 pages of footnotes.

713. Scales, Norms, and Equivalent Scores. Angoff, William H. Educational Testing Service, 1984. 144p. LC: 84-164509. ISBN: 0-317-67895-7. $6.00.

Reprint of Chapter 15 of R.L. Thorndike's *Educational Measurement* published in 1971. Tables and extensive references supplement this useful guide to scaling, norms, equating, and calibration. Comparable scores are discussed in a separate chapter.

714. Standards for Educational and Psychological Testing. American Psychological Association. 1985. 100p. LC: 85-71493. ISBN: 0-9127-0495-0. $23.00.

Well-recognized by professionals as a guide to test development and reporting. Useful in evaluating tests, particularly the technical information.

715. Statistical Models in Psychological and Educational Testing. Gruijter, Dato N.M. de and Kamp, Leo J. Van der. Swets & Zeitlinger, 1984. 294p. ISBN: 90-265-0517-5. $34.00.

Presents an integrated treatment of mental test theory and its applications. Directed to researchers and graduate students, this work focuses on expected true-score theory, linear models and validity, item response theory, and Bayesian estimation. Numerous figures and equations help to illustrate the textual content. Explains statistical models in testing in a straightforward manner.

716. Test Critiques. Edited by Keyser, Daniel J. and Sweetland, Richard C. Test Corporation of America, 1984, v.1 - v.6, 1988. LC: 84-26895. ISBN: 0-9611286-6-6; 0-9611286-7-4; 0-9611286-8-2; 0-933701-02-0; 0-933701-04-7; 0-933701-10-1; 0-933701-20-9. $85.00 per volume.

Published since 1984, there are currently six volumes in this series. Each volume provides descriptive reviews of the most frequently used educational, business, and psychological tests available. Technical aspects as well as practical applications are considered.

717. Test Policy and Test Performance: Education, Language, and Culture. Gifford, Bernard R. (Evaluation in Education and Human Services). Kluwer Academic, 1989. 306p. LC: 89-2382. ISBN: 0-7923-9014-8. $47.50.

Sponsored by the National Commission on Testing and Public Policy, these papers were originally presented at a conference in 1986. Testing experts address public policy, educational decision making, and cultural differences as they affect or are affected by tests. In addition to formal papers, several sections contain written versions of informal remarks presented at the conference.

718. Testers and Testing: The Sociology of School Psychology. Milofsky, Carl. Rutgers Univ. Press, 1989. 266p. LC: 88-28293. ISBN: 0-8135-1407-X. $30.00.

An empirical study of public school psychologists in Illinois that addresses the issue of administering intelligence tests and subsequent placement in special education classes. The methods and bias of test administrators are examined in-depth, particularly as it relates to race.

719. Testing Children: A Reference Guide for Effective Clinical and Psychoeducational Assessments. Edited by Weaver, S. Joseph. Test Corporation of America, 1984. 304p. LC: 84-8882. ISBN: 0-9611286-2-3. $40.00.

Useful handbook for practitioners engaged in clinical, educational, and psychological assessment of children. Fifteen chapters by assessment experts are followed by bibliographical data. An appendix of tests referred to in preceding chapters provides descriptive and publication information.

Testing in Counseling; Uses and Misuses *See* **EDUCATIONAL PSYCHOLOGY/GUIDANCE/COUNSELING (No. 211)**

720. Testing Information Sources for Educators. Fabiano, Emily and O'Brien, Nancy. (ERIC/TME Report, no. 94). ERIC Clearinghouse on Tests, Measurement, and Evaluation, Educational Testing Service, 1987. 61p. Contact publisher for price information.

Provides a listing of the major sources of testing literature for educators and practitioners. Includes books, newsletters and journals, computer-based services, lists of organizations and agencies, and indexes. Also supplies a list of test publishers and a regional listing of test collections available to the education community.

721. Tests: A Comprehensive Reference for Assessments in Psychology, Education and Business. Sweetland, Richard C. and Keyser, Daniel J. Test Corporation of America, 1986. 1122p. LC: 86-14416. ISBN: 0-933701-05-5. $49.00. 2nd edition. Future updates are planned.

Revises, updates, and adds to information found in earlier editions. Provides ready reference information for test that may be reviewed in-depth in *Test Critique*.

722. Tests and Assessment. Walsh, W. Bruce and Betz, Nancy E. Prentice-Hall, 1985. 427p. LC: 84-17810. ISBN: 0-13-911769-5. Contact publisher for price information.

Basic text offers a history of assessment, basic statistical concepts in testing, a review of reliability and validity, ethical standards and issues related to testing, and discussions of specific tests. Assessment of specific characteristics, abilities, aptitudes, and situations is also discussed. Figures and tables serve to highlight and clarify the text.

723. Tests in Education: A Book of Critical Reviews. Levy, Philip and Goldstein, Harvey. Academic Press, 1984. 718p. LC: 83-73142. ISBN: 0-12-445880-7. $49.00.

Provides reviews of a variety of tests in education. Focuses on British tests, although several U.S. tests are included. Complements and is similar to the *Mental Measurement Yearbooks*.

724. Tests in Microfiche. Educational Testing Service, 1975–. No. of fiche varies $150.00 (set "O" published 1990). Regularly updated. Accompanied by paper indexes.

Consists of unpublished tests reproduced on microfiche and an annotated paper index that provides author, title, and subject access. Serves as a source for tests that may not have been copyrighted.

725. Tests in Print III: An Index to Tests, Test Reviews, and the Literature on Specific tests. Edited by Mitchell, James V. Jr. Univ. of Nebraska Press, 1983. 714p. LC: 83-18866. ISBN: 0-910674-52-3. $85.00. Earlier editions published in 1961 and 1974 may still contain pertinent data.

Serves as a master index to the contents of the *Mental Measurement Yearbooks* and provides an updated list of available published tests. Includes comprehensive bibliographies leading to references on construction, validity and use of tests, and a directory of commercial test publishers.

726. Using Standardized Tests in Education. Mehrens, William A. and Lehmann, Irvin J. Longman, 1987. 529p. LC: 85-23148. ISBN: 0-582-29022-8. $25.95. 4th edition.
   Provides a general overview of standardized tests in education. Coverage includes norm and criterion-referenced tests, reliability and validity, test anxiety, coaching, test selection, accountability, and the future of testing. Brief evaluations of selected tests are included in this introductory text.

What's Happening in Teacher Testing: An Analysis of State Teacher Testing Practices *See* **TEACHER EDUCATION (No. 940)**

Journals

727. Educational and Psychological Measurement. Educational and Psychological Measurement, Box 6856, College Station, Durham, NC 27708. Quarterly. $55.00. ISSN: 0013-1644. 1941. Subtitle: *A Quarterly Journal Devoted to the Development and Application of Measures of Individual Differences.*

728. Educational Measurement: Issues and Practice. National Council on Measurement in Education, 1230 17th St., NW, Washington, DC 20036. Quarterly. $14.00. ISSN: 0731-1745. 1982.

729. FairTest Examiner. National Center for Fair & Open Testing, P.O. Box 1272, Harvard Square Station, Cambridge, MA 02238. Quarterly. Contact publisher for price information. 1987.

JEM *See* **Journal of Educational Measurement MEASUREMENT (No. 730)**

730. Journal of Educational Measurement. National Council on Measurement in Education, 1230 17th St., NW, Washington, DC 20036. Quarterly. $20.00. ISSN: 0022-0655. 1964.

731. Measurement and Evaluation in Counseling and Development. American Assn. for Counseling and Development, 5999 Stevenson Ave., Alexandria, VA 22304. Quarterly. $12.00. ISSN: 0748-1756. 1988. Former title: *Measurement and Evaluation in Guidance.*

Measurement and Evaluation in Guidance *See* **Measurement and Evaluation in Counseling and Development MEASUREMENT (No. 731)**

732. News on Tests. Educational Testing Service, Test Collection, Princeton, NJ 08541. 10/year. $45.00. ISSN: 0271-8472. 1979. Supersedes: *Test Collection Bulletin,* 1967–1978.

733. Studies in Educational Evaluation. Pergamon, Maxwell House, Fairview Park, Elmsford, NY 10523. 3/year. $110.00. ISSN: 0191-491X. 1974.

Test Collection Bulletin *See* **News on Tests MEASUREMENT (No. 732)**

Multicultural Education

Bilingual education, multicultural education, racism in schools, and minorities in education are included in this section. A significant number of related materials appear in the section on **Comparative Education.** Many of the books were published in the United Kingdom or have a British perspective. In general, the approach is liberal or is a criticism of the social structure that encourages racism and separate tracks for minorities in education. Some ethnographic research materials are included. Several items, such as the *Interracial Books for Children Bulletin,* have reviews or papers on topics written by a member of the minority group under discussion.

Books

734. The Best of Two Worlds: Bilingual-Bicultural Education in the U.S. Castellanos, Diego with Leggio-Castellanos, Pamela. New Jersey State Department of Education, 1985. 293p. LC: 83-50825. Contact publisher for price information. 2nd printing. PTM No. 200.19.

Provides a historical perspective of bilingual education in the United States. Chronicles the most significant events and forces leading to the bilingual controversy of the 1970s and consequently shaping the current bilingual philosophy. Discusses legislation, accountability, and rights of the student. Includes extensive references.

735. Bilingual Education: A Sourcebook. Ambert, Alba N. and Melendez, Sarah E. (Garland Reference Library of Social Science, vol. 197). Garland, 1985. 340p. LC: 83-48211. ISBN: 0-8240-9055-1. $17.95 (pbk.).

Argues for bilingual education programs for children with limited English proficiency. Written for teachers, administrators, teacher educators, and parents, this comprehensive work discusses legal issues, antibilingualism, program models, and assessment. Each chapter analyzes a specific aspect of bilingual education and contains a lengthy annotated bibliography. A key resource in the field of bilingual education.

736. Bilingual Education: History, Politics, Theory and Practice. Crawford, James. Crane, 1989. 204p. LC: 89-60152. ISBN: 0-89075-556-6. $16.98 (pbk.).

As the subtitle suggests, this is an overview of the history, politics, theory, and practice of bilingual education. Argues for the need to educate bilingually in our multifaceted, pluralist society. Suggests that opposition to bilingual education for segments of the population is a form of racism. Several strategies for implementing bilingual education programs and variations of programs are presented.

The Bilingual Special Education Interface *See* SPECIAL EDUCATION (No. 828)

Bilingual Special Education Resource Guide *See* RESOURCES FOR TEACHING (No. 777)

737. Bilingualism in Education: Aspects of Theory, Research and Practice. Cummins, Jim and Swain, Merrill. (Applied Linguistics and Language Study). Longman, 1986. 235p. LC: 85-23149. ISBN: 0-582-55380-6. Contact publisher for price information.

Offers a synthesis of recent theoretical and empirical work relating to the educational development of bilingual children from both majority and minority language backgrounds. Defines and reconciles two concepts of bilingual proficiency that have direct impact on the schooling of the bilingual child. Proposes several methods for developing plans for bilingual education.

738. Central American Refugees and U.S. High Schools: A PsychoSocial Study of Motivation and Achievement. Suarez-Orozco, Marcelo M. Stanford Univ. Press, 1989. 182p. LC: 88-29315. ISBN: 0-8047-1498-3. $32.50.

Reports an ethnographic study of new immigrants from Central America within the context of minority status and schooling issues in a pluralistic society. Explores the influence of language and cultural differences on school performance, external influence, internal motivation, and perceptions about career opportunities in regard to academic performance and achievement.

739. Comprehensive Multicultural Education: Theory and Practice. Bennett, Christine I. Allyn and Bacon, 1986. 339p. LC: 85-26796. ISBN: 0-205-08587-3. Contact publisher for price information.

Demonstrates how multicultural education can help teachers better prepare and develop students' intellectual, social, and personal skills and abilities. Explores basic concepts in the related disciplines of sociology, psychology, and anthropology to aid the reader in understanding the information presented. Uses a mixture of research, case studies, and examples to present the reasons and methods for incorporating multicultural instruction in the classroom.

740. Crosscultural Understanding: Processes and Approaches for Foreign Language, English as a Second Language and Bilingual Educators. Robinson, Gail L. Nemetz. (Language Teaching Methodology Series). Pergamon, 1985. 133p. LC: 85-558. ISBN: 0-08-031059-1. Contact publisher for price information.

Explores culture learning and its application to bilingual education and ESL. Utilizes psychological and anthropological perspectives to analyze how first cultures (similarly to first languages) are acquired and how this knowledge may be used to aid in the learning of second cultures. Addressed to practitioners and teachers-in-training in the areas of crosscultural teaching, ESL, bilingual and foreign language teaching.

741. The Culture Concept in Educational Studies. Burtonwood, Neil. NFER-Nelson, 1986. 182p. LC: 86-5215. ISBN: 0-7005-1016-8. Contact publisher for price information.

Argues that exposure to multicultural education offers a stimulating challenge to students that will enhance their academic achievement. Using the concept of culture to explain lack of achievement for minority groups and as a form of justification for a multicultural curriculum is explored in this work. The philosophy and related research of culture concept is explained within the context of education studies.

Defensible Programs for Cultural and Ethnic Minorities *See* RESOURCES FOR TEACHING (No. 789)

742. Disruptive School Behavior: Class, Race and Culture. Hanna, Judith L. Holmes & Meier, 1988. 246p. LC: 87-11947. ISBN: 0-8419-1134-7; 0-8419-1164-9 (pbk.). $39.50; $22.50 (pbk.).

The core of this book is a case study of life in a desegregated school in Dallas, Texas told from students' reports and experiences over a period of a year. A central theme emerged from the students' concerns—a counterculture of disruptive behavior exists; the author deals with possible causes and proposes long-range solutions.

743. Education and Cultural Pluralism. Edited by Craft, Maurice. (Contemporary Analysis in Education Series, no. 6). Falmer, 1984. 199p. LC: 84-1673. ISBN: 1-85000-000-X. $17.00 (pbk.).

Separately authored chapters address issues in multicultural education, particularly the relationship of home and school. Considers the policy implications of cultural diversity as a societal objective and attempts to provide an open forum for differing views and approaches. Bilingual education and minorities in the classroom are two of several topics covered in this British publication.

744. Education in Multicultural Societies. Corner, Trevor. Croom Helm/St. Martin, 1984. 288p. LC: 84-40038. ISBN: 0-312-23726-X. $25.00.

Separately authored chapters, many previously presented as papers, discuss multicultural education in a variety of countries. These include the United Kingdom, the United States, Canada, Yugoslavia, Australia, Nigeria, the Caribbean, and several southeast Asian countries. A bibliography and a discussion of the comparative analysis

method applied to multicultural education enhance this research-based volume.

745. The Education of Poor and Minority Children: A World Bibliography. Weinberg, Meyer. Greenwood Press, 1981; Supplement: 1979–1985, 1986. 2 vols. (1986) LC: 86-12161; 80-29441 (1981). ISBN: 0-313-24880-X; 0-313-21996-6 (1981). $76.95 (1986 sup.).

Original two-volume set of over 40,000 entries is supplemented by a volume covering 1979–1985. Sources cover history, law, social sciences, education and related areas. Resources include books, journal articles, dissertations, government documents, and newspaper articles. Emphasis is on U.S. minorities, with nearly a quarter of the entries covering areas outside the United States. Resources are divided by subject, minority group, and geographic area.

746. Global Guide to International Education. Edited by Hoopes, David S. Facts on File, 1984. 704p. LC: 82-1545. ISBN: 0-87196-437-6. $95.00.

Sourcebook of information on international education organizations, academic programs, and other published resources. Also serves as a directory of organizations and institutions involved in international education. Comprehensive compilation of information about international education and resources to assist Americans in participating in international education at the elementary, secondary, and postsecondary level. Geographical arrangement of academic programs in specified area studies is a valuable aid.

747. Guide to Resource Organizations Serving Minority Language Groups. Torres Reilly, Marta, Libby, Michael and Sauve, Deborah. (Resources in Bilingual Education). National Clearinghouse for Bilingual Education, 1981. 186p. ISBN: 0-89763-053-X. Contact publisher for price information.

A collection of profiles of 242 organizations serving as resources to the bilingual community. Each entry includes the organization's name, address, telephone number, and contact person. As available, information about purpose, founding date, target languages, and cultural groups is included. Indexes to languages, locations, subjects, and cultural audience enhance guide's usefulness. Appendixes include listings of Title VII Centers and National Origin Desegregation Assistance Centers.

748. International Handbook of Bilingualism and Bilingual Education. Edited by Paulston, Christina B. Greenwood, 1988. 603p. LC: 87-263. ISBN: 0-313-24484-7. $85.00.

Presents a theoretical framework of the contextual situations of language maintenance and shift in bilingual education. Information about languages and language families in the world and where they are located is presented also. The main substance of this book consists of 25 case studies of bilingualism and multilingualism in various countries around the world. Excluding Australia and Antarctica, the major continents of the world are covered in the case studies.

749. Interpretive Ethnography of Education: At Home and Abroad. Edited by Spindler, George and Spindler, Louise. Erlbaum, 1987. 505p. LC: 87-577. ISBN: 0-89859-924-5. $69.95.

Contains contributed chapters that discuss ethnographic methods, cross-cultural studies, and multicultural education. Addresses issues within the United States and abroad. Immigrant minority and native populations are considered.

750. Literacy in School and Society: Multidisciplinary Perspectives. Edited by Zuanelli Sonino, Elisabetta. (Topics in Language and Linguistics). Plenum, 1989. 291p. LC: 89-35803. ISBN: 0-306-43166-1. Contact publisher for price information.

Discusses the concept of literacy in monolingual and plurilingual societies. Research from international perspectives is presented by scholars from around the world. Provides sociolinguistic, psycholinguistic, and educational perspectives on the relationship between literacy and language.

751. Many Voices: Bilingualism, Culture and Education. Miller, Jane. Routledge & Kegan Paul, 1983. 212p. LC: 82-20433. ISBN: 0-7100-9331-4. Contact publisher for price information.

Argues that confidently bilingual children perform well in school. Supports this hypothesis with examples and research. Advocates utilizing language diversity in the classroom to enrich the curriculum for all students. An examination of the work of writers who have used a second language is used to support the theory that multilingual and multicultural approaches enhance and develop individuals and their work.

Methods and Perspectives in Urban Music Education *See* CONTENT AREAS (No. 54)

752. Minority Education: From Shame to Struggle. Edited by Skutnabb-Kangas, T. and Cummins, J. (Multilingual Matters, vol. 40). Multilingual Matters, Ltd., 1988. 410p. ISBN: 1-85359-004-5. $89.00.

Analyzes the educational problems of minority students as manifestations of institutionalized problems in society such as racism and classism. Contributors describe programs and strategies to improve minority education based on research undertaken in a number of different countries. Most of the contributors are members of minority groups and offer their unique perspectives to the issues of minority education.

753. Multicultural Education: A Sourcebook for Teachers. Cohen, Louis and Cohen, Alan. Harper & Row, 1986. 316p. ISBN: 0-06-318352-8. Contact publisher for price information.

Designed for practitioners and teacher trainees, this selection of readings provides both liberal and right-wing perspectives on multicultural education. Focuses on issues in British education and society, yet has applications in other countries. The honest recognition of the negative impact of stereotyping, racism, and bias on the student is a step toward improving education for all.

754. Multicultural Education in Western Societies. Edited by Banks, James A. and Lynch, James. Holt, Rinehart & Winston, 1986. 209p. ISBN: 0-03-910676-4. Contact publisher for price information.

Examines the various ideological positions, concepts, and paradigms that have emerged in a selected group of Western nations in which multicultural education has developed. Proposes guidelines for developing curricula and programs related to ethnic and cultural diversity. Focuses on developing policies and programs that will increase the achievement of ethnic minority students.

755. Multicultural Teacher Education. Commission on Multicultural Education, American Assn. of Colleges for Teacher Education. American Assn. of Colleges for Teacher Education, 1980. 4 vols. LC: 80-80105. ISBN: 0-89333-017-5. $4.00 (pbk.), v. 1. Each volume has a separate subtitle: Vol. 1, *Preparing Educators to Provide Educational Equity*; Vol. 2, *Case Studies of Thirteen Programs*; Vol. 3, *An Annotated Bibliography of Selected Resources*; and Vol. 4, *Guidelines for Implementation.*

Four volumes were developed to assist teacher education institutions in the design or restructuring of multicultural education programs. Includes case studies, strategies, guidelines, and resources to aid in improving multicultural instruction.

756. Multiethnic Education; Theory and Practice. Banks, James A. Allyn and Bacon, 1988. 312p. LC: 87-17573. ISBN: 0-205-11169-6. Contact publisher for price information. 2nd edition.

Designed to assist practitioners in clarifying the philosophical and definitional issues related to multiethnic education and to utilize effective teaching methods that reflect ethnic diversity. Discusses history, goals, and practices in multiethnic education; defines major concepts; covers philosophical issues; explores curriculum reform; and provides strategies, guidelines, and procedures to assist the instructor of multiethnic education. Appendix contains a Multiethnic Education Inventory.

Outside In: Minorities and the Transformation of American Education *See* HISTORY AND PHILOSOPHY OF EDUCATION (No. 656)

757. Placement Procedures in Bilingual Education: Educational and Policy Issues. Edited by Rivera, Charlene. (Multilingual Matters, vol. 12). Multilingual Matters, Ltd., 1984. 168p. ISBN: 0-905028-32-5. Contact publisher for price information.

Explores the issues surrounding language proficiency assessment in the context of bilingual education. Charts the evolution of language proficiency assessment and its continued development. Covers both theoretical and practical issues related to policy, literacy, and educational concerns in language proficiency. Critiques the measurement instruments currently in use.

758. The Politics of Multiracial Education. Sarup, Madan. (Routledge Education Books). Routledge & Kegan Paul, 1986. 140p. LC: 85-8297. ISBN: 0-7102-0570-8. $18.95.

Examines current development and controversies in multicultural education. Discusses children and racial attitudes, minority education, racism, feminism and black women, and youth unemployment. Despite its British orientation, many of the arguments are universally applicable. Political and educational recommendations are included in final chapters.

Psychoeducational Assessment of Minority Group Children: A Casebook *See* MEASUREMENT (No. 708)

759. Race and Culture in Education: Arising from the Swann Committee Report. NFER-Nelson, 1987. 147p. ISBN: 0-7005-1152-0. Contact publisher for price information.

Discusses multicultural education in British schools particularly as affected by the 1985 Swann Committee's report on the education of ethnic minorities. Critically examines the Swann report in its political and ideological contexts. Practical strategies to combat racism and to encourage cultural diversity in the classroom are presented. Advocates the development of a research-based multicultural curriculum.

760. Racism, Diversity and Education. Edited by Gundora, Jagdish, Jones, Crispin and Kimberly, Keith. (Studies in Teaching and Learning). Hodder & Stoughton, 1986. 192p. ISBN: 0-340-34192-0. Contact publisher for price information.

Examines the educational system to determine how best to combat racism, particularly in British society. Ten contributors examine practices, procedures, and policies that can be implemented to improve multicultural education. Addresses sexism, racism, science instruction, library materials, Black perspectives, and socialization among other topics, all within the context of multicultural education.

Raising Silent Voices: Educating the Linguistic Minorities for the 21st Century *See* SPECIAL EDUCATION (No. 873)

761. The School Achievement of Minority Children: New Perspectives. Edited by Neisser, Ulric. L. Erlbaum, 1986. 198p. LC: 85-25339. ISBN: 0-89859-685-8. $19.95.

Departing from the traditional theories of cultural deprivation or genetic inferiority to explain the often poor performance of minority students, several alternative theories are offered. These hypotheses include the effect of caste, white hegemony, ineffective schools, differential treatment, and the effects of prejudice and stress. Each hypothesis is explored in detail by the authors of each chapter. Positive interventions and trends are also presented.

762. A Teacher's Guide to Multicultural Education. Nixon, Jon. Blackwell, 1985. 183p. LC: 84-19136. ISBN: 0-631-13561-8. $39.95.

Focuses on intercultural relationships in education, particularly on racism. Discusses how teachers can counteract racism within schools with institutional support and through research and development. Addresses broad, theoretical issues as well as some classroom activities.

Teaching the Moderately and Severely Handicapped Student and Autistic Adolescent: With Particular Attention to Bilingual Special Education *See* SPECIAL EDUCATION (No. 888)

Journals

763. Anthropology & Education Quarterly. American Anthropological Association, Council on Anthropology and Education, 1703 New Hampshire Ave., NW, Washington, DC 20009. Quarterly. $30.00. ISSN: 0161-7761. 1970. Former titles: *Council on Anthropology and Education Quarterly* and *CAE Newsletter*.

CAE Newsletter *See* Anthropology & Education Quarterly MULTICULTURAL EDUCATION (No. 763)

Council on Anthropology and Education Quarterly *See* Anthropology & Education Quarterly MULTICULTURAL EDUCATION (No. 763)

Educating the Disadvantaged *See* Readings on Equal Education MULTICULTURAL EDUCATION (No. 772)

764. Equity and Excellence. School of Education,, 130 Furcolo, Univ. of Massachusetts, Amherst, MA 01003. Quarterly. $40.00. ISSN: 0894-0681. 1963. Former title: *Integrateducation.*

Integrateducation *See* Equity and Excellence MULTICULTURAL EDUCATION (No. 764)

Interracial Books for Children *See* Interracial Books for Children Bulletin MULTICULTURAL EDUCATION (No. 765)

765. Interracial Books for Children Bulletin. Council on Interracial Books for Children, 1841 Broadway, New York, NY 10023. Irregular. $24.00. ISSN: 0146-5562. 1967. Former title: *Interracial Books for Children.*

766. Journal of American Indian Education. Arizona State Univ., Center for Indian Education, College of Education, Farmer 302, Tempe, AZ 85287. 3/year. $14.00. ISSN: 0021-8731.

767. Journal of Cross-Cultural Psychology. Sage Publications, 211 W. Hillcrest Dr., Newbury Park, CA 91320. Quarterly. $85.00. ISSN: 0022-0221. 1970.

768. Journal of Multicultural Counseling and Development. American Assn. for Counseling and Development, 5999 Stevenson Ave., Alexandria, VA 22304. 4/year. $10.00. ISSN: 0883-8534. 1972. Former title: *Journal of Non-White Concerns in Personnel and Guidance.*

769. Journal of Negro Education. Howard Univ., Bureau of Educational Research, 2400 Sixth St., NW, Washington, DC 20059. Quarterly. $12.50. ISSN: 0022-2984. 1932.

Journal of Non-White Concerns in Personnel and Guidance *See* Journal of Multicultural Counseling and Development MULTICULTURAL EDUCATION (No. 768)

770. Multicultural Education Journal. Alberta Teachers' Assn., Multicultural Education Council, 11010 142nd St., Edmonton, Alberta T5N 2R1, Canada. 2/year. $15.00 Canadian. ISSN: 0823-6283. 1983.

771. Negro Educational Review. Negro Educational Review, Inc., P.O. Box 2895, West Bay Annex, Jacksonville, FL 32203. Quarterly. $15.00. 1950.

772. Readings on Equal Education. AMS Press, 56 E. 13th St., New York, NY 10003. Annual. $47.50. ISSN: 0270-1448. 1968. Former title: *Educating the Disadvantaged.*

Resources for Teaching

Materials appropriate to the daily practice of teaching in schools have been gathered in this section. Topics covered range from classroom discipline to the teaching of specific content areas in the curriculum. Due to the interdisciplinary nature of these materials, cross-references are used extensively to other categories. Journals have not been included, but will be found in the appropriate sections such as **Content Areas—Science**. Materials with practical, classroom-oriented applications have been identified for inclusion.

Books

773. Adaptive Mainstreaming: A Primer for Teachers and Principals. Reynolds, Maynard C. and Birch, Jack W. Longman, 1988. 396p. LC: 87-17081. ISBN: 0-317-67988-0. $21.85. 3rd edition.

An introduction to teaching exceptional children through adaptive mainstreaming, i.e., regular schools becoming more adaptive with a "least restrictive" environment, referring fewer children to special education. The change in title from the previous edition reflects this theme. Provides historical perspectives, state-of-the-art practices on mainstreaming, methods for dealing with categorical and non-categorical exceptional students, and reviews trends and new directions in the field.

774. Applying Educational Psychology in the Classroom. Dembo, Myron H. Longman, 1988. 571p. LC: 87-3437. ISBN: 0-582-29038-4. $26.95. 3rd edition.

Textbook presentation of educational psychology and decision making, cognitive factors, personal and social factors, exceptional students, classroom dynamics, instructional planning, classroom management, measurement, and different theories of psychology. Includes student activities and references to research and related literature.

775. Becoming an Effective Classroom Manager: A Resource for Teachers. Steere, Bob F. State Univ. of New York Press, 1988. 215p. LC: 87-9907. ISBN: 0-88706-620-8. $39.50.

Advocates a multifaceted approach to classroom management techniques. Argues that effective teachers must have instructional, managerial, and problem-solving skills. Presents a variety of management models designed to prevent or resolve classroom disruptions, including crying, fighting, tattling, cheating, and stealing.

776. Behavior Management Handbook: Setting Up Effective Behavior Management Systems. McIntyre, Thomas. Allyn & Bacon, 1989. 318p. LC: 88-15526. ISBN: 0-205-11709-0. Contact publisher for price information.

A practical handbook for in-service and pre-service teachers to help make them better classroom behavior managers. Sections provide an overview of students who experience emotional/behavioral difficulties and issues related to their education; procedures for the identification of students with inappropriate behaviors; numerous behavior management approaches and how to implement them. Companion volume to *A Resource Book for Remediating Common Behavior and Learning Problems.*

777. Bilingual Special Education Resource Guide. Edited by Thomas, Carol H. and Thomas, James L. Oryx Press, 1982. 189p. LC: 82-8149. ISBN: 0-89774-008-4. $36.00.

Serves as a resource guide for teachers and other practitioners concerned with education of the bilingual exceptional child. Several chapters address issues such as assessment, curriculum, social and emotional needs, and parent involvement. The second part of the book provides information about resources, including agencies, teacher training programs, databases, journals, indexes, a directory of specialists, and an appendix of producers and distributors of bilingual special education materials.

778. Building Classroom Discipline. Charles, C.M. Longman, 1989. 202p. LC: 88-6777. ISBN: 0-8013-0230-7. $13.55 (pbk.). 3rd edition.

Presents three aspects of classroom discipline: preventive, supportive, and corrective. Recommends ways to organize and implement an effective discipline system that is tailored to individual teaching styles. Reviews eight models of discipline, provides guidelines for developing a personal system of discipline, and presents examples of discipline systems at various grade levels.

779. Children and Computers Together in the Early Childhood Classroom. Davidson, Jane Ilene. Delman, 1989. 274p. LC: 88-25750. ISBN: 0-8273-3341-2. $19.95.

A readable text with practical information for teachers interested in using computers with youngsters in early childhood education. There are clear directions for setting up computers in the classroom, guidelines for selecting software, suggestions for teaching strategies, and activities for teaching resources.

780. Children in Conflict: Educational Strategies for the Emotionally Disturbed. Reinert, Henry R. and Huang, Allen. Merrill, 1987. 261p. LC: 87-60451. ISBN: 0-675-20740-1. $26.95. 3rd edition.

First develops a rationale for use of the "children in conflict" concept. Reviews the major educational interventions/approaches for the emotionally disturbed, identifying their strengths and weaknesses—biophysical, psychodynamic, behavioral, counter theory, sociological, and ecological approaches. These approaches are merged into an effective program to apply in the classroom.

781. Children with Speech and Language Difficulties. Webster, Alec and McConnell, Christine. (Special Needs in Ordinary Schools). Cassell Educational, 1987. 239p. LC: 86-32668. ISBN: 0-30431-378-5. Contact publisher for price information.

Designed to help teachers who want to know more about the special needs of children with speech and language difficulties. After providing a conceptual model of normal speech and language development, explains how language development goes astray, how to identify potential problems, how to intervene, and gives some practical advice for teachers about strategies for working with children with speech and language difficulties.

782. Chronic Acting Out Students and Child Abuse: A Handbook for Intervention. Sandberg, David N. Lexington Books, 1987. 198p. LC: 86-27403. ISBN: 0-669-14736-2. $24.95.

Aside from the practical information provided, the purpose here is advocacy and calling for educators to recognize the link between child maltreatment and chronic acting-out children (CAC) in schools. Practical information includes description of CAC and the effects of their abuse and neglect, effective interventions for CACs and others. Includes case-study examples.

783. Classroom Discipline: Case Studies and Viewpoints. Kohut, Sylvester and Range, Dale G. Natl. Education Assn., 1986. 112p. ISBN: 0-8106-1486-3. $9.95. 2nd edition.

Designed to aid the practitioner or student teacher concerned with classroom management and discipline. Utilizes case studies to present possible situations confronting an instructor and offers discussion questions and possible solutions. Theory, research, and practice in the area of discipline are presented prior to the case studies in order to provide a background and overview.

784. Classroom Encounters: Problems, Case Studies, Solutions. Shuman, R. Baird. (NEA Aspects of Learning). Natl. Education Assn. of the U.S., 1989. 256p. LC: 89-12381. ISBN: 0-8106-3001-X. Contact publisher for price information. Stock no. 3001-X.

Addresses the problems confronting first-year teachers through the case study method. Provocative, even extreme, case studies, all based on real situations, provide all levels of practitioners with the opportunity to consider alternate ways of coping with difficult situations. Ranging from irate parents to murder in the classroom, each case study offers several coping mechanisms and points for further consideration.

785. Classroom Management for Elementary Teachers. Evertson, Carolyn M. et al. Prentice-Hall, 1984. 191p. LC: 83-13844. ISBN: 0-13-136127-9 (pbk.). $20.00 (pbk.).

Practical guide to creating a well-managed classroom. Includes case studies, recommendations regarding classroom arrangement and procedures, reward systems, and ongoing practices to maintain an effective learning environment. Management of special populations and evaluation for the program's success are also discussed. Additional readings and activities are provided.

786. Classroom Measurement and Evaluation. Hopkins, Charles D. and Antes, Richard L. F. E. Peacock, 1985. 527p. LC: 83-61761. ISBN: 0-87581-297-X. $32.95. 2nd ed.

Basic text offers directions on construction and design of educational tests. Psychological tests are discussed briefly. Covers test design, selection of tests, interpreting results, standardized tests, validity, reliability, and test administration. Supported by a glossary, code of ethics, and several pertinent appendixes and tables.

787. Computers, Curriculum and Whole-Class Instruction: Issues and Ideas. Collis, Betty. (Wadsworth Series in Computer Education). Wadsworth, 1988. 412p. LC: 87-27917. ISBN: 0-534-08460-5. Contact publisher for price information.

Synthesizes many practical ideas and strategies for use in the classroom with research findings and theoretical perspectives on using computers for whole-class instruction. The core of the book concerns the use of computers in each of the four major curriculum areas—language arts, science, social studies, mathematics. Contains many useful computer application lesson ideas and software references.

788. Creative Classroom Testing. Carlson, Sybil. Educational Testing Service, 1988. 192p. ISBN: 0-317-67890-6. $14.95.

Handbook on test construction for classroom tests provides examples of items for ten different types of questions. Invaluable tool for a classroom teacher wishing to construct tests.

789. Defensible Programs for Cultural and Ethnic Minorities. Edited by Maker, C. June and Schiever, Shirley W. (Critical Issues in Gifted Education, v.2). Pro-Ed, 1989. 347p. LC: 88-992. ISBN: 0-89079-184-8. Contact publisher for price information.

Examines critical issues related to providing special services to gifted students from cultural and ethnic minorities—Hispanic, American Indian, Asian, and black populations are covered in four sections. Each section addresses information on screening and selection, curriculum strategies, and administrative implications.

790. Developmental/Adapted Physical Education: Making Ability Count. Eichstaedt, Carl B. and Kalakian, Leonard H. Macmillan, 1987. 658p. LC: 86-28449. ISBN: 0-02-331710-8. 2nd edition.

An important text for all who work with handicapped or learning disabled children. Methodology and teaching techniques using the developmental approach to physical education for individuals with handicapping conditions are presented within the guiding principle of "making ability count" by placing the person before the disability and focusing on what the handicapped person can do.

791. Discipline in the Secondary Classroom: A Problem-by-Problem Survival Guide. Sprick, Randall S. Center for Applied Research in Education, 238p. LC: 85-12794. ISBN: 0-87628-248-6. $22.95.

Written for practicing teachers, this book offers techniques for dealing with behavior problems and for motivating secondary level students. A guide to specific problems is reinforced with solutions and long-term suggestions for improving the climate of discipline and respect.

792. Drug Education: Content and Methods. Girdano, Daniel A. and Dusek, Dorothy E. Random House, 1988. 334p. LC: 88-104184. ISBN: 0-394-35640-3. $15.95. 4th edition; Educational materials revised by Philip A. Gapinski.

Updates the multidimensional (social, psychological, physiological) scientific knowledge that serves as content for a drug education course providing information, teaching methods, activities, and discussion topics. The format for each topic/chapter is consistent: information content, references, methods for teaching, activities and discussion topics, and some sample lesson plans. The pages of the text are perforated for pull-out.

793. Dynamic Physical Education for Elementary School Children. Dauer, Victor Paul and Pangrazi, Robert P. Collier Macmillan, 1989. 694p. LC: 88-5315. ISBN: 0-02-327730-0. Contact publisher for price information.

This ninth edition remains as a guide to instruction and program development in physical education at the elementary level. Major changes include sections on planning for teaching of children with disabilities, greater emphasis on fitness and wellness, and expansion of information on areas such as microcomputer applications. Includes an abundance of activities and skill development techniques. An accompanying volume, *Lesson Plans for Dynamic. . .Children* is available.

794. Dynamics of Effective Teaching. Kindsvatter, Richard, Wilen, William and Ishler, Margaret. Longman, 1988. 340p. LC: 87-4007. ISBN: 0-582-28613-1. $19.95 (pbk.).

Addressed to teachers-in-training and teachers, this book discusses effective teaching at the secondary level. Presents relevant research and theory in conjunction with developing patterns of effective teacher behavior. Incorporates information about several assessment instruments useful in evaluating teacher performance. Covers classroom discipline, pupil evaluation, instructional techniques, and classroom climate.

795. Educating the Young Thinker: Classroom Strategies for Cognitive Growth. Copple, Carol, Sigel, Irving E. and Saunders, Ruth. L. Erlbaum, 1984. 266p. LC: 79-89436. ISBN: 0-89859-523-1. $19.95 (pbk.). Originally published in 1979.

Advocates teaching based on inquiry and discovery methods. Utilizes Piagetian concepts to develop teaching models and strategies. Makes a case for representational processes in learning, using "representational competence" as a major theme. Blends cognition and learning style in creating strategies to aid classroom teachers in preschool and primary grades.

796. Emotional Problems of Childhood and Adolescence: A Multidisciplinary Perspective. Edited by Epanchin, Betty C. and Paul, James L. Merrill, 1987. 376p. LC: 86-63012. ISBN: 0-675-20566-2. $30.95.

Presents current research and state-of-the-art practice used in the treatment and education of children with behavior disorders from a human ecological point of view. Types of behavior disorders considered are children with hyperactivity and hyperaggressiveness, overcontrolled anxiety and stress-related disorders, and children with social problems.

797. Foundations of Early Childhood Education: Teaching Three, Four and Five-Year-Old Children. Spodek, Bernard, Saracho, Olivia V. and Davis, Michael D. Prentice-Hall, 1987. 334p. LC: 86-12249. ISBN: 0-13-329822-1. Contact publisher for price information.

Introductory text for students planning to teach three to five year olds. Integrates theory with practice and provides examples and illustrations to highlight each chapter. Provides a historical overview and discusses types of programs, teacher preparation, young students, planning, evaluation, play, and other curriculum areas.

798. A Handbook for Substitute Teachers. Dodd, Anne Wescott. C.C. Thomas, 1989. 140p. LC: 88-24905. ISBN: 0-398-05539-4. $29.75.

Written with a positive tone, this handbook provides very basic information about substitute teaching. Includes information on qualifications, pay, finding work, classroom activities, and classroom management. The data on state requirements for substitute teachers (high school diploma in several states) may surprise and shock the reader.

799. Instructional Media and the New Technologies of Instruction. Heinich, Robert, Molenda, Michael and Russell, James D. Macmillan, 1989. 456p. LC: 88-12921. ISBN: 0-02-353020-0. Contact publisher for price information. 3rd edition.

Although this text has undergone major revisions, the attractive format has been kept along with the interesting special features: close-ups (mini-case studies of "how-to" media applications), flashbacks (brief historical developments of media), AV showmanship (tips on delivering media presentations), and others. Instructors and adopters of this textbook are offered special services in developing a course: telelecture by phone, a newsletter, workshops.

800. Instructional Strategies for Secondary School Physical Education. Harrison, Joyce M. and Blakesmore, Connie L. William C. Brown, 1989. 596p. LC: 87-072271. ISBN: 0-697-07285-1. Contact publisher for price information. 2nd edition.

Provides the prospective and in-service teacher with skills needed to design and implement effective instructional programs in secondary physical education beginning with middle schools. Combines the theoretical and practical with discussion on curriculum theory and design and many examples and suggestions for lessons and units.

801. Integration Strategies for Students with Handicaps. Edited by Ross, Robert G. P.H. Brookes, 1989. 360p. LC: 88-35365. ISBN: 1-55766-010-7. $35.00.

Instructional techniques are the emphasis in this textbook on integrating/mainstreaming students with disabilities in the regular classroom. For each type of disability addressed, information includes research findings, an educational model for service delivery, and several instructional activities. Also discusses innovative techniques that cut across several types of disabilities, e.g., microcomputers.

802. The Invitational Elementary Classroom. Wilson, John H. C.C. Thomas, 1986. 156p. LC: 86-14414. ISBN: 0-398-05274-3. $20.50.

Introduces the concepts and process of invitational teaching to elementary teachers. Argues that basic skills can be best learned when children's affective development is an equal part of the curriculum. Advocates the importance of student self-esteem in successful learning.

803. Modern Technology in Foreign Language Education: Applications and Projects. Edited by Smith, William Flint. National Textbook, 1989. 368p. LC: 89-141682. ISBN: 0-8442-9387-3. Contact publisher for price information. Prepared in conjunction with the American Council on the Teaching of Foreign Languages.

Each of the writings in this collection examines or demonstrates how the creative combination of media and materials can be used in the teaching of foreign languages. Eighteen reports describe projects, products, and courseware developed for language teaching and learning with media applications. There is a companion volume: *Modern Media in Foreign Language Education: Theory and Implementations.*

804. The Piaget Handbook for Teachers and Parents: Children in the Age of Discovery, Preschool-Third Grade. Peterson, Rosemary and Felton-Collins, Victoria. (Early Childhood Education Series). Teachers College Press, 1986. 72p. LC: 86-23054. ISBN: 0-8077-2841-1. $8.95 (pbk.).

Written primarily for parents and teachers of preschool through third grade children, this handbook provides an introduction to Piagetian theory and activities. Basic, simple language and activities are presented to the reader for consideration. Activities may be used in either home or school to provide an enriched environment. A glossary and resource list supplement the text.

805. Principles of Safety in Physical Education and Sport. Edited by Dougherty, Neil J. American Alliance for Health, Physical Education, 1987. 189p. LC: 87-141286. ISBN: 0-88314-345-3. $12.95. Sponsored by the National Association for Sport and Physical Education.

A resource providing the professional in physical education and sport with information on safe units of instruction in 15 commonly taught sports and activities. The narrative discussions are brief checklists; outlines are heavily used so that efficient use of the material is facilitated for developing teaching plans and quick pre-class safety checks.

806. The Professional Teacher's Handbook: A Guide for Improving Instruction in Today's Middle and Secondary Schools. Hoover, Kenneth H. Allyn and Bacon, 1982. 672p. LC: 81-19093. ISBN: 0-205-07724-2. Contact publisher for price information. 3rd edition.

Standard textbook approach to educational strategies, methods, problems, and assessment. Useful to pre-service and in-service instructors.

807. Progress Without Punishment: Effective Approaches for Learners with Behavior Problems. Donnellan, Anne M. et al. (Special Education Series). Teachers College Press, 1988. 168p. LC: 88-14103. ISBN: 0-8077-2911-6. $15.95.

An attempt to debunk the myth that punishment is necessary for behavior change by advocating and exploring the use of alternative, nonaversive intervention procedures to challenge behavioral problems. Following some basic information on positive programming and nonaversive behavioral technology, teaching techniques and behavioral management strategies as reasonable alternatives to punishment are presented.

808. Reading Instruction for the Gifted. Cushenbery, Donald C. C.C. Thomas, 1987. 167p. LC: 87-1897. ISBN: 0-398-05332-4. $29.50.

Practical sources of information and teaching suggestions for teachers of gifted learners. Begins with definition, identification, and historical overview of gifted education followed by chapters covering teaching methods to help gifted readers. Many sources of reading and instructional materials are provided in the appendixes.

809. Recommended English Language Arts Curriculum Guides, K-12. ERIC Clearinghouse on Reading Communications Skills/NCTE, 1986. 26p. ISBN: 0-8141-3951-5. $4.75.

Annotated list of recommended curriculum guides in the English language arts. Viewed as an extremely crucial service to the teaching profession, the evaluation of curriculum guides is undertaken on a regular basis and the results published. In addition to listing and evaluating guides, the National Council of Teachers of English includes its criteria for planning and evaluating English language arts curriculum guides as a regular feature of this publication.

810. A Resource Book for Remediating Common Behavior and Learning Problems. McIntyre, Thomas. Allyn & Bacon, 1989. 465p. LC: 88-15527. ISBN: 0-205-11707-4. Contact publisher for price information.

A practical resource guide to strategies and interventions for dealing with over 350 different behaviors. Between 10 and 100 effective interventions are listed for each behavior. A companion book, *The Behavior Management Handbook*, provides additional guidance.

811. Secondary School Reading: What Research Reveals for Classroom Practice. Edited by Berger, Allen and Robinson, H. Alan. ERIC Clearinghouse on Reading and Communication Skills, National Institute of Education, 1982. 206p. LC: 82-61719. ISBN: 0-8141-4295-8. $12.95 (pbk.). NCTE Stock no. 42958.

Updated version of *What We Know About High School Reading.* Cooperative venture between National Conference on Research in English, the National Council of Teachers of English and its Commission on Reading, and the ERIC Clearinghouse on Reading and Communication Skills. Separately authored chapters present current research related to reading instruction that may be useful to secondary school classroom teachers.

812. Skill Streaming the Elementary School Child: A Guide for Teaching Prosocial Skills. McGinnis, Ellen and Goldstein, Arnold P. with Sprafkin, Robert P. and Gershaw, N. Jane. Research Press, 1984. 246p. LC: 84-61282. ISBN: 0-87822-235-9. $13.95 (pbk.).

Designed for use with elementary handicapped and non-handicapped students, this book offers a prosocial skills approach designed to teach positive, productive social behaviors. Such skills may increase the chance for successful mainstreaming of exceptional students. Offers screening procedures to identify students lacking in prosocial skills, and a step-by-step curriculum for implementing structured learning of prosocial skills in the classroom.

813. Smart Kids with School Problems: Things to Know and Ways to Help. Vail, Priscilla L. Dutton, 1987. 256p. LC: 87-502. ISBN: 0-525-24557-X. $18.95.

Smart kids with school problems are referred to by the author as "conundrum kids," challenging puzzles. These students are described, exploring strengths and weaknesses in currently operating learning systems—visual, motor, auditory, language, and psychological; suggests how to match developmental levels with academic needs. Reports three case studies of gifted students who survived schooling.

814. The Special Educator's Handbook. Westling, David L. and Koorland, Mark A. Allyn & Bacon, 1988. 255p. LC: 87-14384. ISBN: 0-205-11137-8. $31.95.

A practical guide primarily for first year teachers of students with special needs but for anyone working with that special student population. The bulk of the text is devoted to helping the teacher operate within and outside the special education environment but also provides instructions for the new teacher in beginning and maintaining a successful career. A useful "Suggestion Box" section provides excellent ideas and activities.

815. Strategies for Classroom Discipline. Englander, Meryl E. Praeger, 1986. 359p. LC: 85-28287. ISBN: 0-275-92093-3. $15.95 (pbk.).

Advocates a multifaceted approach to classroom discipline that is goal directed within a unified framework having a research base. Nine alternatives to punishment that fit within these requirements are presented. Discusses the issue of punishment; presents strategies for intervention, and identifies, describes, and illustrates additional strategies that have proven effective. Bibliography and tables enhance the usefulness of this book.

816. Student Stress: A Classroom Management System. Swick, Kevin J. NEA Professional Library, Natl. Education Assn., 1987. 96p. LC: 87-7051. ISBN: 0-8106-1696-3. $8.95. Stock no. 1696-3.

States that children under stress perform poorly in academics and develop behaviors that may make them susceptible to serious social problems. Advocates a systematic approach to coping with stress. Classroom management techniques that focus on positive relationships and concepts will aid greatly in stress reduction, according to the information presented in this timely text.

817. Successful Student Teaching: A Handbook for Elementary and Secondary Student Teachers. Hevener, Fillmer, Jr. Century Twenty One, 1981. 133p. LC: 80-69332. ISBN: 0-86548-040-0. $9.95.

Very practical handbook designed to aid the college student in the student teaching experience. Discusses how to become a candidate for student teaching, learning the community and school, organizing oneself, relating to the supervising teacher and counselor, working with students and parents, classroom management, instructional issues, and professionalism. Includes a model lesson plan, glossary, and a succinct list of advice from successful student teachers.

818. Teaching Science to Children: A Resourcebook. Iatridis, Mary D. (Garland Reference Library of Social Science, v. 304). Garland, 1986. 110p. LC: 84-48879. ISBN: 0-8240-8747-X. $28.00.

Annotated bibliography of resources related to science instruction. Resources are divided into four categories: textbooks, science activities books, books for children, and science education for handicapped children. Each chapter is introduced with an overview of the resources and instructional approaches.

819. Teaching Students with Behavior Disorders: Techniques and Activities for Classroom Instruction. Gallagher, Patricia A. Love, 1988. 406p. LC: 87-83465. ISBN: 0-89108-200-X. $31.95. 2nd edition.

A comprehensive text for pre-service and in-service teachers who (will) have troubled youth in their classroom; troubled youth here is synonymous with children with atypical behavior, behavior disorders, or emotional handicaps. Provides a definition of the student population, strategies for planning, assessment, curriculum, instructional management, and communication with significant adults. Many classroom techniques are illustrated.

820. Teaching Thinking Skills: English/Language Arts. Jones, Beau Fly et al. (Building Students' Thinking Skills). National Education Assn., 1987. 104p. LC: 86-21809. ISBN: 0-8106-0204-0. $6.95. Stock no. 0204-0.

Produced in cooperation with the NEA Mastery in Learning Project, this volume and its counterpart *Teaching Thinking Skills: Mathematics* offer a framework for content area teachers to use in the classroom to teach thinking skills. Recent research is considered and instructional applications are presented. Readable text includes helpful glossary and bibliography.

821. Using Computers in the Teaching of Reading. Strickland, Dorothy S., Feeley, John T. and Wepner, Shelley. (Computers in the Curriculum Series). Teachers College Press, 1987. 240p. LC: 86-14567. ISBN: 0-8077-2823-3. $16.95.

A practical guide to the ways in which computers can be used to teach reading with a minimal knowledge of programming language. The teaching ideas and strategies are described using Robert Taylor's *Computers in the School* framework for the three major functions of the computer as tutor (instruction), as tool (assistance), and as tutee (creative problem solving). Includes an extensive guide to resources, many described throughout the book.

822. What, When & How to Talk to Students About Alcohol & Other Drugs: A Guide for Teachers. Milgram, Gail Gleason and Griffin, Thomas. Hazelden, 1986. 86p. LC: 86-128351. ISBN: 0-89486-336-3. $4.95.

A practical, brief guide for teachers to help them talk more clearly and effectively with students about decisions regarding alcohol and other drug use. Provides information students need to know about chemical use; communication techniques and strategies; framework for program design and implementation to incorporate drug education into the curriculum; planned activities and discussion exercises by grade level.

823. Writing with Computers in the Early Grades. Edited by Hoot, James L. and Silvern, Steven B. Teachers College Press, 1988. 228p. LC: 88-18477. ISBN: 0-8077-2920-5; 0-8077-2919-1 (pbk.). $27.95; $15.95 (pbk.).

Explores the potential use of the microcomputer for improving writing in grades K-4 through word processing. Covers these areas regarding word processing: as a writing tool, how to maximize use in the classroom, support programs to use in conjunction with, and some issues regarding use with young children, such as keyboarding and those with special needs.

Special Education

"Special Education," rather than "Exceptional Children" or "Handicapped," has been used in a broad sense to cover a wide range of subtopics or subpopulations, such as learning disabilities, behavior disorders, and visual and hearing impairments. Journal selections also reflect this coverage. The focus is not only on children; all age and ability levels, including gifted, are covered. If a book title covered several (or all) aspects of special education a subject index heading was not created; if one or two specific subtopics were the focus, subject headings were employed for each as access points. Titles devoted to medical or very technical aspects of special education, or those intended only for parents of special education children, were included on a selective basis.

Books

Adaptive Mainstreaming: A Primer for Teachers and Principals *See* RESOURCES FOR TEACHING (No. 773)

824. **Assessment in Special and Remedial Education.** Salvia, John and Ysseldyke, James E. Houghton Mifflin, 1988. 575p. LC: 87-80617. ISBN: 0-395-44725-9. $38.36. 4th edition.

A first course in assessment for educators or students involved with special education. Aims to provide knowledge of the basic uses of tests, important attributes of good tests, and the kinds of behaviors sampled by particular tests. Many test samples are included for domains under discussion and subsequently reviewed. Instructor's manual available.

825. **Auditory Disorders in School Children: Identification, Remediation.** Edited by Roeser, Ross J. and Downs, Marion P. Thieme Medical Publishers, 1988. 371p. LC: 87-27809. ISBN: 0-86577-270-3. $31.00. 2nd edition.

Concentrates on two major areas: identification—assessing school children with auditory impairment and developing and carrying out an effective hearing conservation program; remediation—state and federal guidelines, mainstreaming, and other remedial processes that vary depending on the severity of the disorder, materials available, and family counseling techniques.

826. **Autism: Strategies for Change: A Comprehensive Approach to the Education and Treatment of Children with Autism and Related Disorders.** Edited by Groden, Gerald and Baron, Grace. Gardner, 1988. 244p. LC: 87-8682. ISBN: 0-89876-135-2. $29.95.

The Groden Center in Providence, Rhode Island provides the setting for this book written by professionals actively engaged in providing treatment and educational services for children and young adults with autism and related disorders. Dedicated to the whole-child model, the Center's approach is characterized by three major perspectives: developmental, behavioral, and ecological; program components are covered in the text.

Behavior Management Handbook: Setting Up Effective Behavior Management Systems *See* RESOURCES FOR TEACHING (No. 776)

827. **Beyond Separate Education: Quality Education for All.** Edited by Lipsky, Dorothy K. and Gartner, Alan. Paul H. Brookes, 1989. 302p. LC: 88-30495. ISBN: 1-55766-017-4. $32.00.

A compilation of essays by several authors with a clear theme in mind—the entitlement of all children to effective education in integrated settings. Begins and ends by examining PL94-142—what has been achieved under current implementation and the need to reshape the law for the future, to challenge a dual system approach to education. Includes recent research on students labeled handicapped; how "regular" education can be adapted to serve a wider range of students.

828. **The Bilingual Special Education Interface.** Baca, Leonard M. and Cervantes, Hermes T. C. E. Merrill, 1989. 382p. LC: 88-62585. ISBN: 0-675-20833-5. $26.95. 2nd edition.

Designed to familiarize educators with the major needs of the limited English-proficient exceptional child and emphasizing the interface between bilingual and special education. Deals with language acquisition and assessment of the bilingual exceptional child, curriculum development, and developing individualized educational programs for this population.

Bilingual Special Education Resource Guide *See* RESOURCES FOR TEACHING (No. 777)

829. Child Abuse: The Educational Perspective. Edited by Maher, Peter. B. Blackwell, 1987. 287p. ISBN: 0-63115-071-4. Contact publisher for price information.

A study of the educational perspective of child abuse to make educators aware of the issue and its importance. Essays cover the historical and cultural setting within which child abuse takes place; extent of the problem; ways in which abusing families operate; different forms of maltreatment; and interdisciplinary approach for professionals.

Children in Conflict: Educational Strategies for the Emotionally Disturbed *See* **RESOURCES FOR TEACHING (No. 780)**

Children with Speech and Language Difficulties *See* **RESOURCES FOR TEACHING (No. 781)**

Chronic Acting Out Students and Child Abuse: A Handbook for Intervention *See* **RESOURCES FOR TEACHING (No. 782)**

830. College and the Learning Disabled Student: Program Development, Implementation, and Selection. Mangrum, Charles T. and Strichart, Stephen. Grune & Stratton, 1988. 304p. LC: 87-35268. ISBN: 0-8089-1900-8. $29.50. 2nd edition.

Intended for anyone concerned with college opportunities for learning disabled students. Provides information on college programs and admission policies; state and federal laws regarding the programs; components of college learning disabilities programs—testing, advisement, individualization; three college program models—two-year, four-year and special college settings. Another series by Academic Press offers *A Guide to Colleges for Learning Disabled Students; . . .Mobility Impaired Students;* and *. . .Hearing Impaired and Visually Impaired.*

831. Complete Legal Guide to Special Education Services: A Handbook for Administrators, Counselors and Supervisors. Osborne, Allan G. Parker Publishing, 1988. 224p. LC: 88-17579. ISBN: 0-13-162025-8. $34.95.

Designed to provide the educational administrator with detailed information and guidelines for a better understanding of the legal issues involved in the provision of special education services in the school. The focus is on the "Education for all Handicapped Children Act": a historical perspective, how the courts have interpreted the act; and how the law is to be implemented. Dotted with samples of ready-to-use work forms and checklists in application of the law.

832. Computers and Exceptional Individuals. Edited by Lindsey, Jimmy D. Merrill, 1987. 381p. LC: 86-62349. ISBN: 0-675-20625-1. $19.95.

A practical approach to computer technology and the exceptional person, with a limited use of computer jargon. Provides information on the use of computers at home, school, and community and the interaction of computers with individuals with different levels of disability and other topics.

833. Coping with the Multi-Handicapped Hearing Impaired: A Practical Approach. Edited by Prickett, Hugh T. and Duncan, Earlene. C.C. Thomas, 1988. 80p. LC: 87-18084. ISBN: 0-398-05412-6. $19.75.

Offers some practical techniques and strategies for practicing teachers and school-based administrators of the multi-handicapped hearing impaired (MHHI) to apply in school situations. Also useful for educators without any knowledge of education for the MHHI student.

834. Counseling Exceptional Students. Edited by Rotatori, Anthony F. et al. Human Sciences, 1986. 334p. LC: 85-19724. ISBN: 0-89885-274-9; 0-89885-275-7 (pbk.). $39.95; $16.95 (pbk.).

The recent public laws in special education have placed many children with exceptionalities in the mainstream; this book was designed to provide the disability-specific information necessary to counsel the mainstreamed exceptional child. Exceptionalities covered include learning disabled, mildly behaviorally disordered, hearing-impaired, health impaired, etc.

Defensible Programs for Cultural and Ethnic Minorities *See* **RESOURCES FOR TEACHING (No. 789)**

835. Diagnosis and Management of Learning Disabilities: An Interdisciplinary Approach. Brown, Frank R. and Aylward, Elizabeth H. College Hill, 1987. 212p. LC: 87-3133. ISBN: 0-316-11189-9. $24.50.

Proposes an interdisciplinary approach to the diagnosis and treatment of learning disabilities. The authors, a pediatrician and a psychologist, describe what is done when evaluating and planning treatment for a child with learning disabilities from the first suspicion. They present methods used to integrate data from various disciplines to arrive at a diagnosis; types of treatment plans available; ways to convey information to parents; and planning for a follow-up.

836. Disputable Decisions in Special Education. Cruikshank, William M. Univ. of Michigan Press, 1986. 267p. LC: 86-4371. ISBN: 0-472-10077-7. $37.50.

The author, well-known in the field of special education, has "come down hard" on some matters and issues in the field in this collection of essays. These include such topics as true attention to individual differences, factors of fear, guilt and rejection in the handicapped, the exceptional child as a minority representative, and the issue of noncategorical education.

Disruptive School Behavior: Class, Race and Culture *See* **MULTICULTURAL EDUCATION (No. 742)**

837. Early Childhood Special Education: Birth to Three. Jordan, June B. et al. Council for Exceptional Children, 1988. 257p. LC: 87-36529. ISBN: 0-86586-179-X. $25.50.

PL 99-457 mandates service and programs for handicapped infants and toddlers. This text is designed to deal with the issues arising from implementation of that legislation. Each chapter addresses a question posed on issues, including: leadership, identifying the population, effective program models, and maximizing parent involvement.

838. Educating Disabled People for the 21st Century. Cain, Edward J. and Taber, Florence M. College-Hill Press, 1987. 230p. LC: 87-13776. ISBN: 0-316-12381-1. $24.00.

A comprehensive analysis of the impact of current and future electronic technologies on disabled students in special education programs. To prepare them for the new "Information Age," the text considers projections about life in the new age, the potential impact of four advanced technologies on individuals with handicaps, and curriculum implications of the futurist projections for today's special education programs.

839. Educating the Gifted: A Sourcebook. Greenlaw, M. Jean and McIntosh, Margaret E. American Library Assn., 1988. 468p. LC: 87-26915. ISBN: 0-8389-0483-1. $45.00.

A combination of text and bibliographies providing a comprehensive resource on educating the gifted. Each chapter begins with an overview of a major aspect of gifted education—history, identification, programming, curriculum, teacher education, parent education—culminating with an annotated bibliography of articles, books and other materials on that aspect. Useful appendix evaluates and recommends curriculum materials.

840. The Education of Children with Motor and Neurological Disabilities. Haskell, Simon H. and Barrett, Elisabeth K. Nichols, 1989. 255p. LC: GB88-55792. ISBN: 0-41231-620-X. $19.95. 2nd edition.

An introduction to the education of children with motor or neurological disabilities through discussion on four main aspects: medical, psychological research, pedagogical, and educational theories. Describes teaching practices, particularly for reading, spelling, handwriting, and arithmetic, and educational provisions for this population in the United States, the United Kingdom, Australia, Sweden, and Hungary.

Emotional Problems of Childhood and Adolescence: A Multidisciplinary Perspective *See* **RESOURCES FOR TEACHING (No. 796)**

841. Encyclopedia of Special Education: A Reference for the Education of the Handicapped and Other Exceptional Children and Adults. Edited by Reynolds, Cecil R. and Mann, Lester. Wiley, 1987. 1793p. LC: 86-33975. ISBN: 0-471-82858-0 set. $250.00 set. 3 Volumes.

A reference source concerning the education of exceptional children for the professional as well as lay person; written with a readable style. Broad in scope, the content extends into psychology, medicine, politics, and other fields relevant to an understanding of special education. Developments in special education worldwide are covered as are the historical roots of special education. Material in the three volumes is organized alphabetically in seven areas: biographies, tests, service delivery, interventions, handicapping conditions, legal aspects, and support services.

842. Excellence and Equality: A Qualitatively Different Perspective on Gifted and Talented Education. Fetterman, David M. (SUNY Series, Frontiers in Education). State Univ. of New York Press, 1988. 189p. LC: 87-10078. ISBN: 0-88706-640-2; 0-88706-641-0 (pbk.). $34.50; $10.95 (pbk.).

This is a qualitatively different perspective on gifted and talented education (GATE) in two respects: by focusing on GATE programs that are actually working, and in the use of research conducted from an anthropological approach using interviews, observations, and discussion. An intense empirical study was made of 433 programs in California, a case study of a program in Illinois, and a review of programs throughout the world. Concludes with a model of academic and administrative excellence.

843. Exceptional Child Education Resources (ECER). Council for Exceptional Children, 1969–. $75.00/yr., institutions. 0160-4309; quarterly.

A quarterly publication providing abstract coverage of publications in all aspects of special education: research reports, journals, curriculum guides, dissertations, professional texts, current nonprint media, ERIC documents, and other types. Many of the publications are available from the ERIC Document Reproduction Service. Author, subject, and title indexes are available quarterly and cumulated annually.

844. The FCLD Learning Disabilities Resource Guide: A State-by-State Directory of Special Programs, Schools, and Services. Columbia Univ. Press, 1985. 409p. LC: 85-13874. ISBN: 0-8147-2579-1. $40.00. Created and published for the Foundation for Children with Learning Disabilities by Education Systems, Inc. Includes 1986 supplement at back of volume.

Extensive resource guide to services, schools, special programs, summer camps, and college programs for the learning disabled child or adult. Introductory chapter provides an overview and related terminology.

845. Financial Aid for the Disabled and Their Families, 1988–1989. Edited by Schlachter, Gail A. and Weber, R. David. Reference Service Press, 1988. 269p. LC: 87-063263. ISBN: 0-918276-04-7. $32.50.

A single source with up-to-date information about the hundreds of programs that have been established for the disabled or members of their family. Covers scholarships, fellowships, loans, grants, awards, and internships grouped by specific population groups. State source of benefits and reference sources on financial aid are also included. Includes program title, sponsoring organization, geographic subject, and calendar indexes.

846. Fostering Academic Excellence. McLeod, John and Cropley, Arthur. Pergamon, 1989. 289p. LC: 88-19582. ISBN: 0-08-036460-8; 0-08-036459-4 (pbk.). $45.00; $22.50 (pbk.).

An introductory text on the study of the education of academically able students for those educators who would foster the development of those who are gifted with "academic excellence." Provides basic background of giftedness—definition, nature, and relationship of intelligence and creativity; research and theory that have characterized work with children; testing, identifying, and mainstreaming the academically able.

847. Gallaudet Encyclopedia of Deaf People and Deafness. Edited by Van Cleve, John V. McGraw-Hill, 1987. LC: 86-15396. ISBN: 0-07-079229-1. $300.00 set. 3 volumes.

Presents 273 entries covering information from studies in the varied disciplines of the sciences, social sciences and humanities, and a considerable number of biographies. Entries are divided into sections and subsections that are listed in an index. Many cross-references are provided.

848. Gifted, Talented, and Creative Young People: A Guide to Theory, Teaching, and Research. Stein, Morris I. (Garland Reference Library of Social Science, v.120). Garland, 1986. 465p. LC: 81-48419. ISBN: 0-8240-9392-5. $80.00.

The books and articles annotated and summarized in this volume were selected to meet the needs of teachers, counselors, students, and professional researchers needing a rapid survey and introduction to gifted education. Incorporates key works in the field with overviews of the status and history of gifted education focusing on the 1970–1980 decade. Indexes and addresses for key agencies and associations are provided.

849. A Greenhouse for the Mind. Sanders, Jacquelyn S. Univ. of Chicago Press, 1989. 156p. LC: 88-23346. ISBN: 0-226-73464-1. $19.95.

A twofold purpose has been set for this book: to present the approach and rationale regarding the education of disturbed youngsters at the Sonia Shankman Orthogenic School of the University of Chicago; to present the author's ideas regarding the application of principles evolved from work at the School to other areas of education, such as regular classrooms.

850. A Guide to 75 Tests for Special Education. Compton, Carolyn. D.S. Lake, 1984. 341p. LC: 83-62086. ISBN: 0-822-43583-7. $22.95.

A selective guide to reviews of widely used tests in special education, for anyone who needs to interpret reports with test information on children or select a test. Each review includes characteristics of the test and discussions of the format, strengths, and limited factors of the test. Following an overview of assessment procedures, reviews are grouped into three areas: skill area tests; pre-school and kindergarten tests; and intelligence tests and developmental scales.

851. Handbook of Learning Disabilities. Edited by Kavale, Kenneth A., Forness, Steven R. and Bender, Michael. College-Hill, 1987–. LC: 86-26396. ISBN: 0-316-48368-0; 0-316-48370-2; 0-316-48374-5. $29.50 Volume I; $24.50 Volume II; $22.50 Volume III.

The *Handbook* presents comprehensive coverage about learning disabilities (LD) and provides basic information as well as in-depth critical evaluation. The focus of Volume I, "Dimensions and Diagnosis," is on the current primary issues and major characteristics of LD and on diagnosis and assessment of LD as a multidisciplinary process. In Volume II "Methods and Interventions," the focus shifts to the treatment process of LD, the approaches used in academic instruction, and planning remedial programs. Volume III addresses "Programs and Practices" available to deliver the methods and interventions described in Volume II; suggests service arrangements and the role of technology in service delivery.

852. Handbook of Special Education: Research and Practice. Edited by Wang, Margaret, Reynolds, Maynard C. and Walberg, Herbert J. Pergamon, 1987–. LC: 87-18965. ISBN: 0-08-033396-6. $250.00 set. 3 Volumes.

This *Handbook* is a collection of "research syntheses" summarizing the research knowledge in nine topic areas: learning characteristics of handicapped students, effectiveness of differential programming, noncategorical programming for mildly handicapped students, mild mental retardation, behavioral disorders, learning disability, deaf children, visually handicapped, and handicapped infants. A review of the research literature and the state of the art are given for each area, as well as the state of practice and recommendations for improvements.

853. Handicapped Students and Special Education. Data Research, Inc., 1988. 521p. LC: 88-20267. ISBN: 0-939675-07-2. $40.00. 5th edition.

A reference for educators to important case, statutory, and regulatory law in the field of special education and handicapped student rights. Contains full text of the Education for All Handicapped Children Act as amended through 1988, the major federal regulations governing the education of the handicapped, and the five landmark U.S. Supreme Court decisions dealing with special education.

854. Helping Students Succeed in the Regular Classroom: A Guide for Developing Intervention Assistance Programs. Zins, Joseph E. et al. (Jossey-Bass Social and Behavioral Science Series/Jossey-Bass Education Series). Jossey-Bass, 1988. 254p. LC: 87-46350. ISBN: 1-55542-096-6. $24.95.

Explains the rationale for providing intervention assistance programs and discusses the practical issues involved in planning, developing, implementing, and evaluating such programs. Consultation as a services delivery system is highlighted with detailed discussion of how to implement and operate the approach on a systematic basis; affective and socialization interventions are covered.

855. Instructional Strategies for Teaching the Gifted. Parker, Jeannette P. Allyn & Bacon, 1989. 341p. LC: 88-14436. ISBN: 0-205-11676-0. Contact publisher for price information.

Presents a model, the Leadership Training Model, for curriculum development based on the philosophy that leadership training should be the primary goal of special programs for the gifted. Strategies recommended for leadership training are presented—cognitive, affective, and creative strategies—with instructions for their use in the regular classroom or in gifted programs that do not espouse the leadership perspective.

856. Integrating Computers into the Curriculum: A Handbook for Special Educators. Edited by Behrmann, Michael M. College-Hill Press, 1988. 291p. LC: 88-9244. ISBN: 0-316-08755-6. $26.50.

Provides fundamental knowledge on the computer as a tool for teachers, administrators, other school personnel, and children. Following some basic information on computers and technology, the text covers current applications that benefit children and school personnel—testing, instruction, telecommunications, and therapeutic applications.

Integration Strategies for Students with Handicaps *See* RESOURCES FOR TEACHING (No. 801)

857. Intelligence and Exceptionality: New Directions for Theory, Assessment and Instructional Practices. Day, Jeanne D. and Borkowski, John. Ablex, 1987. 262p. LC: 87-11405. ISBN: 089-391-3944. $34.50.

Encourages greater understanding of what intellectual and motivational processes best explain the delayed or accelerated performance of exceptional children. Exceptionality and intelligence are examined from three perspectives: role of intelligence theories and tests in the diagnosis of exceptionality; use of intelligence in designing education programs; and the importance of exceptional populations on developing new models of intelligence.

858. Learning Disabilities, Medicine and Myth: A Guide to Understanding the Child and the Physician. Johnston, Robert B. College-Hill Press, 1987. 141p. LC: 86-26836. ISBN: 0-316-46987-4. $19.50.

A light "expose" of the myths regarding the nature of learning and attention disabilities and the interaction of professionals working in this field. Covers the practical aspects of identifying learning and attention disabilities, moves to the demystification of what physicians do, the dynamics of a team approach, and the need to "demedicalize" these disabilities and to promote more empathy for parents.

859. Learning Disabilities: State of the Art and Practice. Edited by Kavale, Kenneth A. College-Hill Press, 1988. 236p. LC: 88-14115. ISBN: 0-316-48378-8. $25.00.

The primary aim of this volume is to complement the information found in introductory textbooks by reviewing the most recent literature in the learning disabilities

(LD) field; intended as a continuing series. Topics chosen for discussion are those likely to be in a state of flux: definition and nature of LD; classification and assessment; academic, social, and cognitive interventions; and future prospects.

860. Learning Disabled Children Growing Up: A Follow-Up into Adulthood. Spreen, Otfried. Oxford Univ. Press, 1988. 167p. LC: 87-28171. ISBN: 0-19-520641-X. $29.95.

A study of the long-term adjustment of groups of learning disabled (LD) children as they grow into adulthood compared with "average" learners. In the first phase, 203 LD children were followed up to 18 years, to 25 years in Phase II, and compared to a control group of 52 average learners. The initial database of information consisted of structured interviews, questionnaires, and school record data; normative data for the average learners was also provided.

861. Litigating Intelligence: IQ Tests, Special Education and Social Science in the Courtroom. Elliott, Rogers. Auburn House, 1987. 226p. LC: 86-32068. ISBN: 0-86569-156-8. $26.00.

Each chapter focuses on two lawsuits/trials that raised many wide-ranging issues under discussion here—the nature of intelligence, IQ testing, meaning of culture, and mental retardation. The legal issue in each case surveyed concerned the role of intelligence testing in assigning black children to special education classes. Conveys what happens to social science data in the adversary system.

862. Lives on the Boundary: The Struggles and Achievement of America's Underprepared. Rose, Mike. Free Press, 1989. 255p. LC: 88-21469. ISBN: 0-02-926821-4. $22.00.

A very personal book offering a glimpse of the author's childhood experiences with a remedial label and how his work with literacy for the past two decades has focused on stimulating the underprepared, those who have trouble reading and writing in the schools and workplace. Their stories are told here as is his.

863. The Magic Feather: The Truth About "Special Education". Granger, Lori and Granger, Bill. Doubleday, 1986. 259p. LC: 86-8973. ISBN: 0-385-29831-5. $9.95.

The parents of a child who was diagnosed as handicapped upon entering school have developed this parent's guide to special education. They share their own experiences upon entering the world of special education; provide some historical background for and explanation of the "nightmares" in the special education "jungle"; and explain how parents can overcome their own "nightmares" with special education.

864. Mainstreaming the Exceptional Child: A Bibliography. Clarkson, Mary Cervantes. (Checklists in the Humanities and Education: A Series, no. 6). Trinity Univ. Press, 1982. 240p. LC: 81-84656. ISBN: 9-11536-92-2. $25.00.

A bibliography of books, journal articles, ERIC documents, theses, government publications, proceedings, and pamphlets published from 1964 to 1981. Entries are divided into eight categories, including gifted; no annotations provided. Subject index for additional access.

865. Medical Problems of Students with Special Needs: A Guide for Educators. Holvoet, Jennifer F. and Helmstetter, Edwin A. College-Hill Press, 1989. 373p. LC: 88-13230. ISBN: 0-316-37180-7. $29.50.

Focuses on the types of medical information important to special education personnel and how to use the information to provide better educational services. Using medical records, evaluation reports, and common medical terminology are covered in the first section. Other topics covered are how to integrate human resources into teams to develop educational approaches; how to handle illness and medical emergencies; and determining whether a child is abused or neglected and how to handle such a child.

866. The Milwaukee Project: Preventing Mental Retardation in Children at Risk. Garber, Howard L. American Assn. of Mental Retardation, 1988. 434p. LC: 87-26970. ISBN: 0-940898-16-0. $40.00.

The Milwaukee Project, spanning two decades, provides a longitudinal empirical base on a form of mental retardation called "cultural-familial mental retardation." The study focuses on manipulations of rearing conditions—at home and school—and manipulating those conditions known to put children at risk. The research clearly indicates that early intellectual development is not fixed and can be modified by manipulating experience and early interventions.

867. Outside the Mainstream: A History of Special Education. Hurt, John S. Batsford Ltd., 1988. 222p. LC: GB87-34397. ISBN: 0-71345-291-9. 17.95 pounds.

The scope of British special education goes beyond that normally included as "special." As the title implies, those children whose schooling took place outside the ordinary school system—orphans, paupers, social deviants—are considered in this historical study as is the education of the physically or mentally handicapped child.

868. Persons with Profound Disabilities: Issues and Practices. Edited by Brown, Fredda and Lehr, Donna H. Paul H. Brookes, 1989. 343p. LC: 88-30468. ISBN: 1-55766-015-8. $30.00.

The literature often places the profoundly disabled under the label of "those with severe handicaps"; while there is some commonality, certain concepts and practices need to be further developed for the profoundly handicapped. Those are dealt with in this book: teaching issues facing professionals, the integration of profoundly disabled into the regular classroom, legal issues, and practices appropriate for these individuals, such as their motor and communication development and educational programming.

869. Policy Implementation and PL 99-457: Planning for Young Children with Special Needs. Edited by Gallagher, James J., Trohanis, Pascal L. and Clifford, Richard M. Paul H. Brookes, 1989. 223p. LC: 88-30324. ISBN: 1-55766-013-1. $28.00.

Through a series of papers this text presents the wide range of issues confronting practitioners and administrators attempting to implement Public Law 99-457, which addresses the needs of infants, toddlers, and preschoolers who are developmentally delayed. Guidelines and action plans are offered to meet the planning needs of the states, which are responsible for organizing programs. The topics include overview of the law, financial issues, and effectiveness of policy implementation.

870. The Politics of Reading: Power, Opportunity and Prospects for Change in America's Public Schools. Fraats, JoMichelle B. Teachers College Press, 1987. 237p. LC: 87-9937. ISBN: 0-8077-2858-6; 0-8077-8578-3 (pbk.). $29.95; $17.85 (pbk.).

Research focusing on an examination of equal opportunity in reading programs and the delivery of services in reading instruction to assess the relationship between power and opportunity in American elementary education. Fieldwork included data gathered from interviews with 103 school personnel and class observations. Strategies for improvement are suggested, including changes in classroom mobilization of bias and changes in the appropriation and application of power and influence resources.

871. Program Design and Development for Gifted and Talented Students. Tuttle, Frederick B., Becker, Laurence A. and Sousa, Joan A. National Education Assn., 1988. 160p. LC: 87-31565. ISBN: 0-8106-0727-1. $11.95. 3rd edition.

A practical, informative guide to designing and developing programs for the gifted. Some minor revisions were made to this third edition but the content remains much the same: rationale for gifted programs, major aspects of program design, curricular models, and program evaluation. Many practical ideas, applications, and workshop activities are provided.

Progress Without Punishment: Effective Approaches for Learners with Behavior Problems *See* **RESOURCES FOR TEACHING (No. 807)**

Psychoeducational Evaluation of Children and Adolescents with Low-Incidence Handicaps *See* **MEASUREMENT (No. 709)**

872. Radical Analysis of Special Education: Focus on Historical Development and Learning Disabilities. Sigmon, Scott B. Taylor & Francis, 1987. 124p. LC: 87-6856. ISBN: 1-85000-230-4; 1-85000-231-2 (pbk.). $36.00; $17.00 (pbk.).

Examines who receives special education and why, through a radical analysis that focuses on the roots or basic elements underlying that education process. The author supports special education but claims it has been "perverted"; this is brought to light by exploring the historical development of special education and current important issues from radical, social, and educational perspectives.

873. Raising Silent Voices: Educating the Linguistic Minorities for the 21st Century. Trueba, Henry T. Newbury House, 1989. 206p. LC: 88-28982. ISBN: 0-06632-612-5. Contact publisher for price information.

Raises the issues and problems facing teachers in the challenge of educating linguistic minorities in American schools. A historical and theoretical framework for analyzing these issues is presented early on; discussed within the framework are identification of linguistic minority students, types of educational programs, legislative and political support for these programs, and execution of the curriculum.

874. Readers and Writers with a Difference: A Holistic Approach to Teaching Learning Disabled and Remedial Students. Rhodes, Lynn K. and Dudley-Marling, Curt. Heinemann, 1988. 329p. LC: 87-23819. ISBN: 0-435-08453-4. $18.00.

Presents reading and writing assessment and intervention strategies to encourage the reading and writing development of learning disabled and remedial readers.

The approach is holistic, taking a developmental view of children's language problems; encouraging reading, writing, and oral language across the curriculum; and integrating all areas of the curriculum.

Reading Instruction for the Gifted *See* **RESOURCES FOR TEACHING (No. 808)**

875. Reading/Learning Disability: An Ecological Approach. Bartoli, Jill and Botel, Morton. Teachers College Press, 1988. 266p. LC: 87-33615. ISBN: 0-8077-2905-1.

Proposes an ecological model for understanding reading failure and for learning to read; this model is holistic, taking into account a student's interrelationships and interactions with the surrounding ecology (environment). From an ecological approach, reading behavior is understood in the larger contexts of family, school, and community; two case studies of students labeled reading disabled are presented through a description of these three major systems in their ecology.

876. Research in Learning Disabilities: Issues and Future Directions. Edited by Vaughn, Sharon and Bos, Candace S. College-Hill Press, 1987. 276p. LC: 87-4233. ISBN: 0-316-10305-5. $26.50.

Based on a research symposium where key professionals were challenged to present position papers on the latest issues and research problems in learning disabilities: models and theories, research, eligibility, assessment, intervention, and public policy. The purpose was to generate a long-range plan for future research in learning disabilities.

A Resource Book for Remediating Common Behavior and Learning Problems *See* **RESOURCES FOR TEACHING (No. 810)**

877. Resource Guide to Special Education; Terms, Laws, Assessment Procedures, Organizations. Davis, William E. Allyn & Bacon, 1986. 317p. LC: 85-18647. ISBN: 0-205-08546-6. $37.95. 2nd edition.

Basic resource guide to special education providing extensive definitions of special education terminology and selected acronyms and abbreviations. Describes selected tests and inventories, provides addresses of agencies and organizations, and reviews pertinent federal legislation.

878. Resources for Educating Artistically Talented Students. Clark, Gilbert A. and Zimmermann, Enid D. Syracuse Univ. Press, 1987. 176p. LC: 86-23183. ISBN: 0-8156-2401-8. $22.00.

A companion volume to the 1984 *Educating Artistically Talented Students*, that provides a wide variety of resources for those responsible for educating artistically talented students. Presents practical information on state policies for the talented, programs available across the country, identification and screening procedures, step-by-step examples of how to initiate a program, and other advice.

879. Risk Makers, Risk Takers, Risk Breakers: Reducing the Risks for Young Literacy Learners. Edited by Allen, JoBeth and Mason, Jana M. Heinemann, 1989. 351p. LC: 88-27400. ISBN: 0-435-08483-6. $18.50.

The focus in this book is not on the at-risk child but on challenging the reader to become a risk-taker, one who reduces factors that increase risks (risk-makers) for young learners in literacy instruction. Stresses successful literacy development programs and projects and describes learning environments where risk reduction has been achieved successfully.

880. School Children At-Risk. Richardson-Koehler, Virginia et al. Falmer, 1989. 283p. LC: 88-26770. ISBN: 1-85000-514-1; 1-85000-515-X (pbk.). $44.00; $20.00 (pbk.).

An extensive study examining the experiences of 12 "at-risk" elementary students; "at-risk" is a recent term generally referring to students in danger of not being educated. Background descriptions of the school, classroom, and homes of the students are provided; formal and informal interviews, observations, and examination of documents were used to collect data. Summarizes information about the nature, experiences, and viewpoints of at-risk students in school and proposes reform in elementary schools to meet the needs of these students.

881. Schools That Work: Educating Disadvantaged Children. (What Works, v.3). United States. Department of Education, 1988. 80p. $3.00.

Provides recommendations for educating disadvantaged children with sections on school involvement, parent and community support, and government involvement. Profiles of specific programs for the disadvantaged are included.

Smart Kids with School Problems: Things to Know and Ways to Help *See* RESOURCES FOR TEACHING (No. 813)

882. Soviet Education: The Gifted and the Handicapped. Edited by Riordian, Jim. Routledge, Kegan & Paul, 1988. 194p. LC: 88-209277. ISBN: 0-415-00574-4. $55.00.

This investigation of Soviet special education is the first to cover the gifted and the handicapped, and what provisions are made for these children. Each essay describes the Soviet system of special education for the gifted, deaf-blind, physically handicapped and learning disabled and what is done differently from the West and why. All the contributors have studied in the Soviet Union.

883. Special Education: A Source Book. Sternlicht, Manny. (Garland Reference Library of Social Science, vol. 375/Source Books on Education, 7). Garland, 1987. 431p. LC: 87-129. ISBN: 0-8240-8524-8. $50.00.

An annotated bibliography of research in ten subgroups of special education: mental retardation; giftedness; visual, hearing, speech, and language impairments; learning disabilities; brain damage; physical, emotional, and behavioral impairments; and mainstreaming. No information is provided on the selection of entries, although most are journal articles.

884. Special Education in Context: An Ethnographic Study of Persons with Developmental Disabilities. Gleason, John J. Cambridge Univ. Press, 1989. 165p. LC: 88-37889. ISBN: 0-521-35187-1. $29.95.

A study over a five-year period of residents of a state school for the mentally retarded and multiply handicapped. Analysis is presented as raw data descriptions of and professional notes on the apartment-type setting and residents; interpretive statements about the residents; theoretical statements proposing reconsideration of our understanding of residents and setting in social and cultural terms. A contrasting picture of life in the apartments unfolds before and after the implementation of federal legislation for the handicapped.

The Special Educator's Handbook *See* RESOURCES FOR TEACHING (No. 814)

885. The Specialware Directory: A Guide to Software for Special Education. Oryx, 1986. 160p. LC: 85-23880. ISBN: 0-89774-192-7. $19.50. 2nd edition.

This second edition identifies some 300 microcomputer software programs for special education students and for those who work with the disabled. Instructional courseware as well as professional and administrative software are represented. Main section is the alphabetical listing of software products with full descriptions. Indexes by curriculum, type of exceptionality, hardware, level, etc. are included.

886. Teaching Aphasic Children: The Instructional Methods of Barry and McGinnis. (PRO-ED Classics Series). Pro-Ed, 1988. 234p. LC: 87-29799. ISBN: 0-89079-171-6. $24.00. Foreword by Patricia I. Myers.

Two classic works on the treatment of aphasic children have been published here together: Hortense Barry's *The Young Aphasic Child* and Mildred A. McGinnis' *Aphasic Children*. Both pioneered early efforts in the 1960s to formalize the language training of young children with severe language disorders; their thoughts on and procedures for language training are still acceptable in the 1980s. The foreword provides a clarification of the terminology used to identify childhood aphasia.

887. Teaching Mainstreamed Students. Stephens, Thomas M., Blackhurst, A. Edward and Magliocca, Larry A. Pergamon, 1988. 396p. LC: 87-32782. ISBN: 0-08-035836-5; 0-08-035835-7 (pbk.). $45.00; $22.50 (pbk.). 2nd edition.

Intended as an introduction to mainstreaming for students in education. The focus is on the need of those students with mild disabilities, those who are most likely to be mainstreamed in regular classrooms for part or all of their school days. Discussion concerns a historical perspective, identifying the mainstreamed population, classroom activities, working with parents, and competencies needed by teachers.

Teaching Students with Behavior Disorders: Techniques and Activities for Classroom Instruction *See* RESOURCES FOR TEACHING (No. 819)

888. Teaching the Moderately and Severely Handicapped Student and Autistic Adolescent: With Particular Attention to Bilingual Special Education. Duran, Elva. C.C. Thomas, 1988. 225p. LC: 88-12309. ISBN: 0-398-05498-3. $37.50.

The teaching ideas presented are intended for teachers, teacher trainees, parents, and other caregivers for students with moderate to severe handicaps. Also addresses the culturally and linguistically different student with these handicaps and the Hispanic issues related to teaching the severely handicapped bilingual student.

Testing Children: A Reference Guide for Effective Clinical and Psychoeducational Assessments *See* MEASUREMENT (No. 719)

Toys for Growing: A Guide to Toys That Develop Skills *See* ELEMENTARY/SECONDARY EDUCATION (No. 414)

889. Transition from School to Work of Persons with Disabilities. Edited by Berkell, Dianne E. and Brown, James M. Longman, 1989. 251p. LC: 88-12757. ISBN: 0-801-30228-5. Contact publisher for price information.

A reference source addressing current issues, trends, and concerns related to the transition from school life to adult and working life for persons with learning disabilities. The focus is not on particular disabilities of youth but on issues related to program development and service delivery: identifying persons needing transition assistance; educator's role in the transition process; collaboration of clients, families, and service providers; and the role of employers.

890. Underachievers in School: Issues and Intervention. Butler-Por, Nava. Wiley, 1987. 181p. LC: 87-8295. ISBN: 0-471-91109-07. $39.95.

An examination of the dynamics and characteristics of the phenomenon of underachievement among children of normal development who can be helped in the regular classroom. Concerns the onset of the problem, characteristics, treatment, and teacher's role. The author proposes an intervention model for dealing with underachievement and reports on the results of experimental testing of the model.

891. Young Exceptional Child: Early Development and Education. Edited by Neisworth, John T. and Bagnato, Stephen J. Macmillan, 1987. 514p. LC: 86-16364. ISBN: 0-02-386300-5. Contact publisher for price information.

An introductory text in early childhood education with emphasis on the young exceptional child. These exceptionalities are described, related to normal development, and dealt with in terms of assessment, treatment, and service delivery systems: communication, neuromotor development, social and emotional development, and vision and hearing. Also discusses exceptionality in infants and toddlers as well as child abuse and neglect.

892. 1988 Special Education Yearbook. Edited by Jordan, June B. The Council for Exceptional Children, 1988. 219p. LC: 88-647534. ISBN: 0-86586-815-4. $26.55. A product of the ERIC Clearinghouse on Handicapped and Gifted Children.

The third volume in an annual series building on the earlier volumes and updating information when possible on federal policy actions, state policy, important reports, and statistical data on exceptional students served and personnel employed. Directories listing key offices and organizations concerned with special education are included. Intended to provide a picture of the state of the art and trends over time.

Journals

893. Academic Therapy. PRO-ED Publishing, 8700 Shoal Creek, Austin, TX 78758-6897. 5/year. $20.00. ISSN: 0001-396X. 1965.

894. American Annals of the Deaf. Convention of American Instructors of the Deaf/Conference of Educational Administrators Serving the Deaf, Keds Pas 6, 800 Florida Ave., NE, Washington, DC 20002. Quarterly. $40.00. ISSN: 0002-726X. 1886.

895. Association for Persons with Severe Handicaps. Journal. Assn. for Persons with Severe Handicaps, 7010 Roosevelt Way, NE, Seattle, WA 98115. Quarterly. $65.00. ISSN: 0274-9483. 1983. Formerly *Association for the Severely Handicapped Journal.*

Association for the Severely Handicapped Journal *See* **Association for Persons with Severe Handicaps SPECIAL EDUCATION (No. 895)**

896. Behavioral Disorders Journal. Council for Children with Behavioral Disorders, A Division of the Council for Exceptional Children, Council for Exceptional Children, 1920 Association Dr., Dept. BD87, Reston, VA 22091. Quarterly. $50.00. ISSN: 0198-7429. 1976.

Career Development for Exceptional Individuals *See* **VOCATIONAL EDUCATION (No. 968)**

897. Education and Training in Mental Retardation. Council for Exceptional Children, Division on Mental Retardation, 1920 Association Dr., Reston, VA 22091. Quarterly. $28.00. ISSN: 0013-1237. 1986. Formerly *Education and Training of the Mentally Retarded* (1966–1986).

Education and Training of the Mentally Retarded *See* **Education and Training in Mental Retardation SPECIAL EDUCATION (No. 897)**

898. Education of the Visually Handicapped: A Magazine for Teachers and Parents of Visually Handicapped Children. Helen Dwight Reid Educational Foundation, Heldref Publications, 4000 Albemarle St., NW, Washington, DC 20016. Quarterly. $33.00. ISSN: 0013-1458. 1969. Formerly *International Journal for the Education of the Blind* (1951–1969).

899. Exceptional Children. Council for Exceptional Children, 1920 Association Dr., Reston, VA 22091. 6/year. $35.00. ISSN: 0014-4029. 1934.

900. Gifted Child Quarterly. National Assn. for Gifted Children, 4175 Lovell Rd., Suite 140, Circle Pines, MN 55014-3501. Quarterly. $45.00. 1957.

International Journal for the Education of the Blind *See* **Education of the Visually Handicapped SPECIAL EDUCATION (No. 898)**

Journal SPECIAL EDUCATION (No. 895)

901. Journal for the Education of the Gifted. Assn. for the Gifted, Univ. of North Carolina Press, Box 2288, Chapel Hill, NC 27515-2288. Quarterly. $40.00. ISSN: 0162-3532. 1977.

Journal for Vocational Special Needs Education *See* **VOCATIONAL EDUCATION (No. 972)**

902. Journal of Learning Disabilities. PRO-ED Publishing, 8700 Shoal Creek Blvd., Austin, TX 78758-6897. Monthly. $60.00. ISSN: 0022-2194. 1968.

903. Journal of Special Education. PRO-ED, 8700 Shoal Creek Blvd., Austin, TX 78758-6897. Quarterly. $55.00. ISSN: 0022-4699. 1966.

904. Language, Speech and Hearing Services in Schools. American Speech-Language-Hearing Assn., 10801 Rockville Pike, Rockville, MD 20852. Quarterly. $30.00. ISSN: 0161-1461. 1970.

905. Learning Disability Quarterly. Council for Learning Disabilities, P.O. Box 40303, Overland Park, KS 66204. Quarterly. $30.00. ISSN: 0731-9487. 1978.

906. RASE: Remedial and Special Education. PRO-ED, 8700 Shoal Creek Blvd., Austin, TX 78758-6897. 6/year. $55.00. ISSN: 0741-9325. 1984.

Teacher Education

Many of the teacher education materials could justifiably have been placed in the **Educational Reform** section. Much of the reform literature addresses the need to begin improving education through better preparation of teachers. Topics covered include teacher evaluation, teacher certification, and teacher preparation. There is a balance between practical handbooks, educational reports, and research materials. Journals have a strong focus on the effective preparation of teachers. Teacher evaluation and certification are strong secondary themes in the journal literature.

Books

The Academic Life: Small Worlds, Different Worlds *See* HIGHER AND CONTINUING EDUCATION (No. 520)

907. Advances in Teacher Education. Edited by Katz, Lilian G. and Raths, James D. Ablex, 1984–. 3 volumes to date (1984, 1986, 1987) ISBN: 0-89391-185-2/0-89391-275-1/0-89391-396-0. $39.40 per volume. ISSN: 0748-0067.

Purpose of this series is to give teacher education a greater visibility by highlighting the current research and scholarship in the field. Each volume addresses a variety of topics in teacher education and promises to provide a regular evaluation of the state of the art in teacher preparation programs.

908. American Education: An Introduction to Social and Political Aspects. Spring, Joel. Longman, 1988. 303p. LC: 88-8083. ISBN: 0-8013-0251-X. $19.25. Fourth edition.

Provides prospective teachers with the major social, economic, and political issues related to education and places them in context in a career in education. Emphasizes the need to understand the structure and functioning of educational systems in order to be an effective educator.

909. Bias Issues in Teacher Certification Testing. Edited by Allan, Richard G., Nassif, Paula M. and Elliott, Scott M. Erlbaum, 1988. 162p. LC: 88-3845. ISBN: 0-8058-0080-8. $24.50.

Of interest to government officials, teacher educators, and education professionals, this book contains several timely articles based on presentations made at the 1987 conference "Eliminating Potential Bias in Teacher Certification Testing" sponsored by National Evaluation Systems, Inc. Legal, administrative, and academic perspectives of bias issues in teacher certification testing programs are provided.

A Call for Change in Teacher Education *See* EDUCATIONAL REFORM (No. 235)

Classroom Encounters: Problems, Case Studies, Solutions *See* RESOURCES FOR TEACHING (No. 784)

910. Colleges of Education: Perspectives on Their Future. Edited by Case, Charles W. and Matthes, William A. (Series on Contemporary Educational Issues). McCutchan, 1985. 206p. LC: 84-61701. ISBN: 0-8211-0230-3. $24.25.

A collection of papers offering different perspectives on the issues currently confronting colleges of education. Historical development, professional status, and pre-service and in-service teacher education are discussed. Subsequent chapters focus on the role of colleges of education in the professional development of human services personnel. Recommends the participation of education professionals in the continuing education of human services practitioners.

911. The Complex Roles of the Teacher: An Ecological Perspective. Heck, Shirley F. and Williams, C. Ray. Teachers College Press, 1984. 212p. LC: 83-17865. ISBN: 0-8077-2748-2. $15.95 (pbk.).

Based on case studies of first-year teachers, this book explores the teaching-learning phenomenon. Treats the many roles of the teacher from a holistic perspective. Roles that are discussed include teacher as person, colleague, facilitator, researcher, administrator, and leader. Emphasis is placed on the many influences affecting the teaching and learning environment. Excerpts from first-year teachers' experiences are used to highlight certain points in the various chapters.

Discipline in the Secondary Classroom: A Problem-by-Problem Survival Guide *See* RESOURCES FOR TEACHING (No. 791)

Ed School: A Brief for Professional Education *See* HIGHER AND CONTINUING EDUCATION (No. 536)

Education's Smoking Gun: How Teachers Colleges Have Destroyed Education in America *See* HIGHER AND CONTINUING EDUCATION (No. 539)

912. Educators' Handbook: A Research Perspective. Edited by Richardson-Koehler, Virginia. Longman, 1987. 676p. LC: 85-23849. ISBN: 0-582-28454-6. $89.95.

Summarizes research on teaching for practitioners and policymakers. Designed to answer specific questions, develop understanding of complex topics, and encourage practitioners to assess their teaching methods, consider alternatives, and implement new teaching strategies. Advocates a functional relationship between research and practice in teaching.

913. Ethical Dilemmas and the Education of Policymakers. Fleishman, Joel L. and Payne, Bruce L. (The Teaching of Ethics, v. 3). The Hastings Center, Institute of Society, Ethics and the Life Sciences, 1980. 76p. LC: 80-10230. ISBN: 0-916558-05-3. $4.00.

Advocates improved teaching in the field of ethics, with a cursory description of currently available courses in the field of ethics and policy. Includes recommendations about curricular change and faculty training. Also describes the range of ethical problems confronting policymakers. Includes a bibliography.

Ethics and the Professor: An Annotated Bibliography, 1970-1985 *See* HIGHER AND CONTINUING EDUCATION (No. 544)

914. The Ethics of Teaching. Strike, Kenneth A. and Soltis, Jonas. (Thinking About Education Series). Teacher's College Press, 1985. 112p. LC: 84-2557. ISBN: 0-8077-2709-1. $8.95.

Textbook for college courses is useful also as an introduction to ethics for in-service workshops and as an overview for practitioners. Provides a series of case studies on topics such as censorship, grading, and professional relationships for discussion. Examines the nature of ethics, the ethical dilemmas confronting teachers, ethical treatment of students, and moral reasoning. The Code of Ethics of the Education Profession is included.

915. Good Teachers: An Unblinking Look at Supply and Preparedness. Hooper, Susan. (Today's Issues in Education, no. 1). National School Boards Assn., 1987. 44p. Contact publisher for price information.

Presents statistical and policy information on teacher supply and preparedness for the benefit of local school boards. Discusses teacher recruitment as well as teacher supply and preparedness and suggests policy actions to be taken at the local level. Very readable material with sound documentation for the local school board member.

A Handbook for Substitute Teachers *See* RESOURCES FOR TEACHING (No. 798)

916. Handbook of Research on Teaching. Edited by Wittrock, Merlin C. Macmillan, 1986. 1009p. LC: 85-4866. ISBN: 0-02-900310-5. $55.00. 3rd edition.

A project of the American Education Research Association that represents the advancing state of knowledge about teaching. Presents research, theories, methodology, and an emphasis on the relationship of these within teaching. This is the premier source of information on research on teaching.

How Teachers Taught: Constancy and Change in American Classrooms, 1890-1980 *See* HISTORY AND PHILOSOPHY OF EDUCATION (No. 643)

917. Improving Teacher Education. Edited by Galambos, Eva C. (New Directions for Teaching and Learning, no. 27, Fall 1986). Jossey-Bass, 1986. 104p. LC: 85-81906. ISBN: 1-55542-994-7. $9.95. ISSN: 0271-0633.

Focuses on the debate on teacher preparation reform. Discusses the current status of teacher education, extending programs, involvement on the part of schools, the need for laboratory schools, a more clinical approach to teacher preparation, a reduction in schools of teacher education, and the need for a liberal arts background in teacher preparation. Concluding chapter recommends better subject matter preparation; more student teaching opportunities; integrating theory; practice and research; and more school involvement.

918. Improving Teaching. Edited by Zumwalt, Karen K. (1986 ASCD Yearbook). Assn. for Supervision and Curriculum Development, 1986. 191p. LC: 85-73379. ISBN: 0-87120-134-8. $13.00. Stock no. 610-86001.

A collection of papers focusing on the value of research on teaching. Each author responds to a hypothetical situation designed to facilitate the professional development of teachers. A diverse number of alternative approaches are presented.

919. The Induction of New Teachers. Ryan, Kevin. (Fastback Series, no. 237). Phi Delta Kappa Educational Foundation, 1986. 38p. LC: 85-63692. ISBN: 0-87367-237-2. $0.90 (pbk.).

Explores the problems confronting new teachers as they begin their professional careers. Addresses the issues from the perspective of the new teacher as well as the school organization. Presents potential solutions to problems that range from improving teacher attitudes to obtaining better support and orientation to the teaching profession from teacher education institutions and school districts.

920. The International Encyclopedia of Teaching and Teacher Education. Edited by Dunkin, Michael J. Pergamon, 1987. 878p. LC: 86-9325. ISBN: 0-08-030852-X. $125.00.

Drawing on articles originally commissioned for *The International Encyclopedia of Education,* this work includes updated bibliographies and revisions. Organized in a conceptual framework so that articles on related topics are grouped together.

921. Knowledge Base for the Beginning Teacher. Edited by Reynolds, Maynard C. Pergamon, 1989. 305p. LC: 88-39939. ISBN: 0-08-036767-4. $85.00. Published for the American Assn. of Colleges for Teacher Education.

Twenty-four chapters by contributors address the need for a reasonable level and range of knowledge for the concerned beginning teacher. Each chapter is supported by footnotes and an annotated bibliography. Discusses the conflict between state-of-the-art standards in education and actual practice, particularly as related to curriculum planning and professional functions and responsibilities. States the standard level of knowledge that should be expected in teacher education today.

922. Methods of Assessing Teacher Education Students: Conference Proceedings. Asburn, Elizabeth A. and Fisher, Robert L. American Assn. of Colleges for Teacher Education, 1984. 80p. ISBN: 0-89333-036-1. $5.00.

Reports the proceedings of a conference co-sponsored by the American Association of Colleges for Teacher Education and Illinois State University. Transcript of the conference contains introductory remarks, discussions of present practices in student assessment, problems in assessment, identification of major issues in assessment, and a summary of the conference. A lengthy annotated bibliography is appended.

923. Models for the Preparation of America's Teachers. Cruickshank, Donald R. Phi Delta Kappa Educational Foundation, 1985. 112p. LC: 84-6216. ISBN: 0-87367-430-8. $3.50 (pbk.).

Focuses on the teacher education curriculum, and instruction in teacher education. Synthesizes research on pre-service curricula, presents an overview of current practice in teacher education, and offers alternative methods to common instructional practice. Discusses the current issues and problems in teacher preparation and in the final chapter presents a summary of recommendations for improvement.

Multicultural Teacher Education *See* **MULTICULTURAL EDUCATION (No. 755)**

924. The NASDTEC Manual: Manual on Certification and Preparation of Educational Personnel in the United States. Edited by Roth, Robert A. and Mastain, Richard. Natl. Assn. of State Directors of Teacher Education and Certification, 1984. 1 vol., looseleaf Contact publisher for price information.

Provides information about certification requirements by state for educational personnel. Offers detailed information about handling disciplinary actions, substandard credentials, misassignments, and out-of-state acceptance of certificates. Presents general and specific data on supply and demand, state standards, support systems for new teachers, and minimum requirements for certification.

A Nation Prepared: Teachers for the 21st Century *See* **EDUCATIONAL REFORM (No. 257)**

925. NTE: National Teacher Examinations. Fox, Daniel J. Arco, 1988. 512p. ISBN: 0-13-625484-5. $10.95.

Provides a description of the National Teacher Examinations (NTE): application procedures, test center locations, studying methods, scoring procedures, and review exams. Answer keys are provided. Useful workbook for NTE preparation. Barron's offers its *How to Prepare for the National Teacher Examinations* by areas, such as elementary education, which is similar in intent.

926. The Preparation of Teachers: An Unstudied Problem in Education. Sarason, Seymour Bernard, Davidson, Kenneth S. and Blatt, Burton. Brookline Books, 1986. 124p. LC: 86-4171. ISBN: 0-914797-26-3. $17.95 (pbk.). Rev. edition.

Provocative critique of the preparation of teachers. Argues that the content and process of teacher education programs often have no demonstrable relevance to the actual task of teaching. After presenting the problem, the current controversy surrounding teacher education is explored. A typical classroom day is described in terms of the instructor's lack of preparation for teaching. Implications of the ongoing lack of instructional ability shown by teachers are discussed and potential remedies suggested.

The Professional Teacher's Handbook: A Guide for Improving Instruction in Today's Middle and Secondary Schools *See* **RESOURCES FOR TEACHING (No. 806)**

927. The Professors of Teaching: An Inquiry. Wisniewski, Richard and Ducharme, Edward R. (SUNY Series in Teacher Preparation and Development). State Univ. of New York Press, 1989. 172p. LC: 88-12655. ISBN: 0-88706-901-0. $39.50.

Contributors address the issues confronting professors of education, particularly the demands for direct involvement in school reform and for scholarly research. Provides descriptive and analytical views of the education professoriate and advocates reform in schools, colleges, and departments of education.

928. Profiles of Preservice Teacher Education: Inquiry into the Nature of Programs. Howey, Kenneth R. and Zimper, Nancy L. (SUNY Series in Teacher Preparation and Development). State Univ. of New York Press, 1989. 273p. LC: 88-19995. ISBN: 0-88706-973-8. $54.50.

Provides descriptive and in-depth personal accounts of elementary teacher education institutions. Includes a small liberal arts college and major research universities. Also summarizes the findings, compares programs, and offers recommendations for improving teacher education.

Reforming Teacher Education: The Impact of the Holmes Group Report *See* **EDUCATIONAL REFORM (No. 270)**

929. Requirements for Certification of Teachers, Counselors, Librarians, Administrators for Elementary and Secondary Schools. Univ. of Chicago Press, 1989. 259p. LC: A43-1905. ISBN: 0-226-10394-3. $31.00. 54th edition.

Published annually since 1935, this publication serves as an excellent source of information about certification requirements on a state-by-state basis. Covers certification requirements for school personnel, including counselors, librarians, and teachers. Recommendations regarding certification from regional and national associations are included as are the addresses of state certification offices.

930. Research Perspectives on the Graduate Preparation of Teachers. Edited by Woolfolk, Anita E. (Rutgers Symposium on Education). Prentice-Hall, 1989. 219p. LC: 88-20962. ISBN: 0-13-774357-2. Contact publisher for price information.

Papers presented at the first Rutgers Invitational Symposium on Education were edited to form this research-based collection of essays. Provides an overview of the debate on quality of teacher preparation, presents case studies, discusses the benefits of classroom research, covers student teacher supervision and teacher evaluation, and relates graduate teacher preparation and professionalism as keys to quality teacher education. Much of the content is equally applicable to undergraduate teacher preparation.

931. Rethinking Teacher Education. Edited by Hopkins, David and Reid, Ken. Croom Helm, 1985. 262p. LC: 84-28555. ISBN: 0-7099-3705-9. Contact publisher for price information.

Research-based analysis of teacher education. Explores four major themes: the contemporary context of teacher education programs, the organization of teacher education endeavors, the purpose and function of teacher training, and a review of the issues currently facing teacher education programs. International in scope with a strong emphasis on the United Kingdom and Canada. Contributors explore the history and practice of teacher education and project some of its future trends.

932. Studies in Teacher Appraisal. Turner, Glenn and Clift, Philip. Falmer Press, 1988. 223p. ISBN: 1-85000-267-3. $44.00.

An overview of British practices of teacher appraisal, this publication focuses on a research project at the Open University into "the nature, impact and effectiveness of school or college based schemes for teacher appraisal." Informative comparison to U.S. procedures for appraisal and certification, particularly as British practice reflects commercial or industrial certification procedures.

Successful Student Teaching: A Handbook for Elementary and Secondary Student Teachers *See* RESOURCES FOR TEACHING (No. 817)

Supervision in Education: Problems and Practices *See* EDUCATIONAL ADMINISTRATION AND LAW (No. 167)

933. Teacher Evaluation and Merit Pay: An Annotated Bibliography. Karnes, Elizabeth Lueder and Black, Donald D. (Bibliographies and Indexes in Education, no. 2). Greenwood, 1986. 400p. LC: 85-27226. ISBN: 0-313-24557-6. $46.95.

Annotated bibliography on teacher evaluation and merit pay that encompasses books, papers, journal articles, and dissertations. Covers 1980 through 1984 with inclusion of significant earlier works. Teacher evaluation materials from school districts are included in a separate chapter. Addressed to teachers, administrators, school boards, teacher educators, and teacher organizations.

934. The Teacher's Voice: A Sense of Who We Are. Raphael, Ray. Heinemann, 1985. 137p. LC: 85-5471. ISBN: 0-435-08221-3. $12.50.

Personal accounts from practicing teachers offer an inside view of their work lives, concerns, and commitment. Written for the benefit of the general public, other teachers, and administrators. Teachers are represented across several grade levels, types of schools, and years of service.

935. Teaching As a Moral Craft. Tom, Alan R. Longman, 1984. 236p. LC: 83-17520. ISBN: 0-582-28307-8. $15.95 (pbk.).

Argues against the commonly held belief that teaching should be viewed as an applied science. Author views teaching as involving a subtle moral relationship between teacher and student in the attempt to bring important content, concepts, and critical thinking skills to the student's attention. Addressed to practitioners, administrators, and teacher educators. Author's philosophy of teaching is extensively documented with research as indicated in the lengthy bibliography.

936. Tomorrow's Teachers: A Report of the Holmes Group. Holmes Group. 1986. 97p. $6.50.

Comprised of education deans from the nation's research universities, the Holmes Group outlines its goals for the reform of teacher education in this report. Goals and recommendations to achieve goals are presented in an effort to reform both teacher education and the teaching profession.

937. Toward High and Rigorous Standards for the Teaching Profession: Initial Policies and Perspectives of the National Board for Professional Teaching Standards. Natl. Board for Professional Teaching Standards, 1989. 88p. $7.00.

Defines the basic policies and plans of the National Board for Professional Teaching Standards in its efforts to set new standards for the teaching profession. The Board's goal is "to establish high and rigorous standards for what teachers should know and be able to do and to certify teachers who meet those standards." Discusses the rationale for the establishment of the Board, the certification process, and reform priorities.

938. An Urgent Imperative: Proceedings of the Wingspread Conference on Teacher Preparation. American Assn. of State Colleges and Universities (AASCU), 1986. 24p. LC: 86-14071. ISBN: 0-88044-075-9. Contact publisher for price information. Wingspread Conference on Teacher Preparation, Racine, Wisconsin, 1984.

Identifies critical areas requiring immediate attention in teacher education institutions. Teacher education programs confront the "urgent imperative" to revitalize and reevaluate their efforts. Focus is on the AASCU. Explores efforts to interest top students in teaching, provide excellent programs, offer support to inservice teachers, assist disadvantaged students, and challenge teaching faculties to improve their efforts.

939. Visions of Reform: Implications for the Education Profession. Association of Teacher Educators. ATE Blue Ribbon Task Force. Assn. of Teacher Educators, 1986. 66p. ISBN: 0-317-60474-0. $8.00.

Report from the ATE Blue Ribbon Task Force presents an analysis and implications of three current and major education reform reports. These three reports, NCATE redesign, the Holmes Group, and the Carnegie Forum were considered to be the most critical to teacher education. A matrix comparing the issues addressed by the three reports provides an intriguing overview of the recommendations. The implications of these findings for specific agencies and higher education institutions are explored in detail.

What Next? More Leverage for Teachers *See* EDUCATIONAL REFORM (No. 278)

940. What's Happening in Teacher Testing: An Analysis of State Teacher Testing Practices. Rudner, Lawrence M. et al. Office of Educational Research and Improvement, U.S. Dept. of Education, 1987. 145p. ISBN: 0-318-23535-8. $7.50 (pbk.).

As the subtitle suggests, this report provides data on teacher testing programs in the U.S. on a state-by-state basis. The data are analyzed and interpreted for the benefit of the teacher. Additional information is supplied on the history of teacher testing, legal issues, equity, supply and demand, and related teacher evaluation issues. Excellent source of descriptive information about teacher testing practices in the U.S.A.

Journals

941. Action in Teacher Education. Assn. of Teacher Educators, 1900 Association Dr., Reston, VA 22091. 4/year. Membership fee. ISSN: 0162-6620. 1978.

942. American Educator. American Federation of Teachers, 555 New Jersey Ave., NW, Washington, DC 20001. Quarterly. $8.00. ISSN: 0148-432X. 1977.

943. American Teacher. American Federation of Teachers, 555 New Jersey Ave., NW, Washington, DC 20001. 9/year. $7.00. ISSN: 0003-1380.

California Journal of Teacher Education *See* Teacher Education Quarterly TEACHER EDUCATION (No. 946)

944. Contemporary Education. Indiana State Univ., 1005 School of Education, Terre Haute, IN 47809. Quarterly. $16.00. ISSN: 0010-7476. 1968. Former title: *Teachers College Journal.*

Journal of Industrial Teacher Education *See* VOCATIONAL EDUCATION (No. 975)

945. Journal of Teacher Education. American Assn. of Colleges for Teacher Education, One Dupont Circle, Suite 610, Washington, DC 20036. Bi-monthly. $35.00. ISSN: 0022-4871. 1950.

Supervisors Quarterly *See* **Teacher Educator TEACHER EDUCATION (No. 947)**

946. Teacher Education Quarterly. California Council on the Education of Teachers, 416 Longshore Dr., Ann Arbor, MI 48107. Quarterly. $30.00. ISSN: 0737-5328. 1973. Former title: *California Journal of Teacher Education.*

947. Teacher Educator. Ball State Univ. Teachers College, Ofc. of Professional Lab Experiences, Muncie, IN 47306. 4 per year. Free. 1965. Former title: *Supervisors Quarterly.*

Teachers College Journal *See* **Contemporary Education TEACHER EDUCATION (No. 944)**

948. Teachers College Record. Teachers College, Columbia Univ., 525 W. 120th St., New York, NY 10025. Quarterly. $40.00. ISSN: 0161-4681. 1900.

949. Teaching and Teacher Education: An International Journal of Research and Studies. Pergamon, Journals Division, Maxwell House, Fairview Park, Elmsford, NY 10523. Quarterly. $120.00. ISSN: 0742-051X. 1984.

Vocational Education

This section is fairly evenly divided between career counseling and career education, and the issues surrounding vocational education. Many materials have a British perspective on the vocationalism movement in education. Essentially this trend to educate for a job or career, rather than a liberal arts background, is viewed by the authors included as a negative direction for education. A collection that balances the materials in this section with the **Educational Reform** materials will offer readers the opportunity for some thoughtful reflection. Some overlap with **Educational Psychology/Guidance/Counseling** occurs because of the dual focus of counseling and guidance within vocational programs and the counselors' related activities.

Books

950. Career and Vocational Education for Mildly Learning Handicapped and Disadvantaged Youth. Gardner, David C., Beatty, Grace Joely and Gardner, Paula L. C.C. Thomas, 1984. 210p. LC: 83-640. ISBN: 0-398-04818-5. $23.00.

Book of readings that addresses the barriers to employment and education confronting mildly learning handicapped and disadvantaged students. Addressed to parents, teachers, and counselors, this book discusses curriculum, mainstreaming, career assessment, and individual vocational programs. Concludes with recommendations for improving vocational and career education for the disadvantaged.

951. Career Planning Materials: A Guide to Sources and Their Use. Egelston, Roberta Riethmiller. American Library Assn., 1981. 177p. LC: 81-12801. ISBN: 0-8389-0343-6. $20.00.

Useful to both librarians and counselors, this volume presents information about career planning materials and how to locate additional resources. Covers training, careers, occupations, availability of jobs, job searching, and maintaining a collection of career resources and aids. Materials of interest to particular populations such as the handicapped or minorities are highlighted.

952. Chronicle Career Index. Chronicle Guidance Publications, 1989/90. 159p. LC: 79-640396. ISBN: 1-55631-035-8. $14.25 (pbk.). Revised edition.

Listing of vocational and guidance materials for counselors and students. Lists sources alphabetically and is cross-referenced by occupational, professional, or educational subjects. Valuable aid to developing a resource collection of career education literature.

A Counselor's Guide to Vocational Guidance Instruments See EDUCATIONAL PSYCHOLOGY/GUIDANCE/COUNSELING (No. 189)

953. Current Career and Occupational Literature. Goodman, Leonard H. H.W. Wilson, 1984. 198p. LC: 80-646591. ISBN: 0-8242-0703-3. $35.00.

Published since 1973 and regularly updated, the 1984 volume includes material published between 1981 and 1983. Includes books and pamphlets listed under specific job titles with an indication of appropriate attention level, such as elementary, middle school, or adult. Additional components include resources on educational institutions, financial aid, career planning, reference sources for counselors, and equal opportunity trends. A directory of publishers and distributors rounds out this useful compendium.

954. A Directory of Public Vocational-Technical Schools and Institutes in the U.S.A. Edited by Johnston, Marliss. Minnesota Scholarly Press, 1988. 400p. ISBN: 0-933479-46-6. $65.00. 4th edition.

Describes public schools and institutions offering non-degree postsecondary occupational education. Geographic listings by state include names and addresses of schools, directors' names and telephone numbers, and complete course listings. Valuable indexes provide access by title of the school program and by specific occupations, such as accounting or legal transcriptionist. Regular updating of this volume enhances its usefulness.

955. Education, Training and the New Vocationalism: Experience and Policy. Edited by Pollard, Andrew, Purvis, June and Walford, Geoffrey. Open Univ. Press, 1988. 206p. LC: 88-1687. ISBN: 0-335-15845-5. $65.00.

Collection of papers documenting and analyzing the new vocationalism in Great Britain as perceived by students and teachers. Contains empirical research with differing perspectives of the British vocationalism effort. A final chapter focuses on the relationship between ethnography and policy, particularly as it affects vocational research. The discrepancy between the policy of vocationalism and the perceived results by the recipients is explored in this volume.

956. Encyclopedia of Careers and Vocational Guidance. Edited by Hopke, William E. J.G. Ferguson, 1984. 3 vols. LC: 84-4176. ISBN: 0-385-19345-9. Contact publisher for price information. 6th edition.

Provides introductory information about career planning, aptitude tests, finding a job, future prospects, and additional resources. Extensive information about different occupational fields is provided by experts from those fields. Each chapter provides an overview of the industry or occupation, a glossary of terms, and the future outlook for the field. Additional information about each occupation is summarized in a separate section.

The Experiences of Work: A Compendium and Review of 249 Measures and Their Use *See* MEASUREMENT (No. 699)

Improving Guidance Programs *See* EDUCATIONAL PSYCHOLOGY/GUIDANCE/COUNSELING (No. 201)

957. Materials for Occupational Education: An Annotated Source Guide. Edited by Schuman, Patricia Glass, Rodriquez, Sue A. and Jacobs, Denise M. (Neal-Schuman Sourcebook Series). Neal-Schuman, 1983. 384p. LC: 83-8195. ISBN: 0-918212-17-0. $39.95. 2nd edition.

Lists sources of information in a variety of occupational areas including agriculture, business, child care, engineering, fashion, food processing, health, hotel management, mortuary science, police science, and urban technology. Resources include publishers, agencies, and organizations that provide services, publications, and training materials. Useful compendium of vocational and occupational resources.

958. Microcomputers in Vocational Education: Programs and Practices. Rodenstein, Judith. Prentice-Hall, 1986. 205p. LC: 85-5675. ISBN: 0-13-580507-4. $25.00 (pbk.).

Discusses the role of the microcomputer in administrative and instructional activities in vocational education. Introduces the history and jargon of computers, provides guidance in evaluating hardware and software, presents educational and administrative applications, and explores specific applications in areas such as agriculture, business, distributive education, health, and industrial education. Glossary and evaluation checklists are appended.

959. Perspectives on Vocational Education: Purposes and Perspectives. Edited by Lewis, Morgan V. and Pratzner, Frank C. (Research and Development Series, no. 247). Natl. Center for Research in Vocational Education, 1984. 73p. ISBN: 0-318-17788-9. $7.95.

Examines what vocational education should be accomplishing and its current status. Based on a variety of research reports, most of the major contemporary view of the roles and purpose of vocational education are reflected. Public acceptance of vocational education, outcomes, functions, and policy implications are discussed in the four separately authored chapters.

960. The Politics of Vocational Education. (Yearbook of the American Vocational Assn., 1983). American Vocational Assn., 1982. 290p. ISBN: 0-89514-041-1. Contact publisher for price information.

Discusses the utilization of politics to gain support for vocational education. Presents a theoretical base for understanding political action, individual political tactics, case studies, and statements from politicians and legisla-

tors about effective political action. Practical strategies to gain political support are discussed. A glossary of legislative terms and an overview of how political/legislative change occurs are also provided.

961. Principles and a Philosophy for Vocational Education. Miller, Melvin D. (Special Publication Series, no. 48). Natl. Ctr. for Research in Vocational Education, Ohio State Univ., 1985. 250p. ISBN: 0-318-17790-0. $17.00.

Defines a practical philosophy of vocational education to assist practitioners and policymakers in their mission. Provides a historical overview for the context of vocational education and presents individual principles for various aspects of vocational education. Each principle is followed by a discussion and pertinent references. Combines theory and practice in the statement of vocational philosophy and principles.

962. Skills and Vocationalism: The Easy Answer. Edited by Holt, Maurice. Open Univ. Press, 1987. 179p. LC: 87-11252. ISBN: 0-355-10290-5. $65.00.

The easy answer to the problems of unemployment and the economy is to blame the schools. Argues that vocationalism may appeal to the public but that it is unsound. Specifically addresses the British system of schooling. Criticizes the emphasis on vocational skills and career preparation to the detriment of a liberal education. Contributed chapters address specific features of the educational system in Great Britain while making comparisons to other countries including West Germany, Japan, and the U.S.

963. Vocational Counseling: A Guide for the Practitioner. Raskin, Patricia M. (Guidance and Counseling Series). Teachers College Press, 1987. 160p. LC: 87-1972. ISBN: 0-8077-2860-8. $5.95 (pbk.).

Argues that vocational counseling requires the ability to help an individual integrate personal needs with a real and limited opportunity structure. Intended for beginning counselors with limited experiences, this text integrates vocational development theory, counseling theory and technique, psychology of adjustment, and developmental psychology for their benefit. Discusses the profound effect that career choice has on overall quality of life for an individual.

964. Vocationalizing Education: An International Perspective. Edited by Lauglo, Jon and Lillis, Kevin. (Comparative and International Education Series, vol. 6). Pergamon, 1988. 339p. LC: 87-7220. ISBN: 0-08-035855-1. $43.95.

Selected papers from a conference on the vocationalization of education address the trend toward education for practical skills rather than a liberal arts background. The prevalence of vocationalism in affluent as well as Third World countries is a disturbing trend explored by the contributors. Countries include Great Britain, France, West Germany, Sierra Leone, Argentina, and Zimbabwe. Goals, justifications, policy, context, and empirical evaluation of vocationalism are addressed.

965. What Color Is Your Parachute? A Practical Manual for Job-Hunters & Career Changers. Bolles, Richard Nelson. Ten Speed Press, 1989. 397p. LC: 84-649334. ISBN: 0-89815-272-0. $16.95. Rev. edition.

Published regularly since 1970, this eminently readable book focuses on career planning in relation to self-assessment. Tips on job hunting, career changes, and life planning are provided. Resources such as agencies, books, and counseling services are described. A variety of activities to aid in self-assessment are incorporated in the text.

966. Where to Start: An Annotated Career Planning Bibliography, 1983–1985. Rockcastle, Madeline T. Cornell Univ. Career Center, 1983. 206p. Contact publisher for price information. 4th edition.

Presents new and selected career information in books, pamphlets, audio-visual, and computerized resources. Covers 20 broad career fields with detailed resources about specific occupations. Also provides information about career planning, job hunting, study abroad, financial aid, and related resources. Additional resources are listed in the appendixes.

Journals

967. Agricultural Education Magazine. Agricultural Education Magazine, 1803 Rural Point Rd., Mechanicsville, VA 23111. Monthly. $7.00. ISSN: 0732-4677. 1929.

American Vocational Journal *See* **Vocational Education Journal VOCATIONAL EDUCATION (No. 979)**

968. Career Development for Exceptional Individuals. Council for Exceptional Children, Division on Career Development, 1920 Association Dr., Reston, VA 22091. 2/year. $16.00. ISSN: 0885-7288. 1978.

Career Development Quarterly *See* **EDUCATIONAL PSYCHOLOGY/GUIDANCE/COUNSELING (No. 213)**

Home Economics Education Association Newsletter *See* **Home Economics Educator VOCATIONAL EDUCATION (No. 969)**

969. Home Economics Educator. Home Economics Education Assn., 1201 16th St., NW, Washington, DC 20036. Quarterly. Membership. 1981. Former title: *Home Economics Education Association Newsletter.*

970. Home Economics Research Journal. American Home Economics Assn., 2010 Massachusetts Ave., NW, Washington, DC 20036. Quarterly. $35.00. ISSN: 0046-7774. 1972.

Industrial Arts and Vocational Education *See* **Industrial Education VOCATIONAL EDUCATION (No. 971)**

Industrial Arts Magazine *See* **Industrial Education VOCATIONAL EDUCATION (No. 971)**

971. Industrial Education. James A. Cummins, 26011 Evergreen Rd., No. 204, Southfield, MI 48076-4446. 9/year. $20.00. ISSN: 0091-8601. 1914. Former titles: *Industrial Arts Magazine; Industrial Arts and Vocational Education.*

972. Journal for Vocational Special Needs Education. National Assn. of Vocational Education Special Needs Personnel, Box 13857, North Texas State Univ., Denton, TX 76203. 3/year. $18.00. ISSN: 0195-7597. 1978.

973. Journal of Career Development. Univ. of Missouri, 72 Fifth Ave., New York, NY 10011. Quarterly. $75.00. ISSN: 0894-8453. 1972. Former title: *Journal of Career Education.*

Journal of Career Education *See* **Journal of Career Development VOCATIONAL EDUCATION (No. 973)**

974. Journal of Home Economics. American Home Economics Assn., 2010 Massachusetts Ave., NW, Washington, DC 20036. Quarterly. $20.00. ISSN: 0022-1570. 1909.

975. Journal of Industrial Teacher Education. National Assn. of Industrial and Technical Teacher Educators, 108 Center for Vocational and Adult Education, Thach and Donahue, Auburn Univ., Auburn, AL 36849-5526. 4/year. $10.00. ISSN: 0022-1864. 1963.

976. Journal of Studies in Technical Careers. Southern Illinois Univ., School of Technical Careers, Carbondale, IL 62901. Quarterly. $15.00. ISSN: 0163-3252. 1978.

977. Journal of Vocational Behavior. Academic Press, 1250 Sixth Ave., San Diego, CA 92101. Bi-monthly. $180.00. ISSN: 0001-8791. 1971.

978. Journal of Vocational Education Research. American Vocational Education Research Assn., National Center for Research in Vocational Education, Ohio State Univ., 1960 Kenny Rd., Columbus, OH 43210. Quarterly. $50.00. ISSN: 0739-3369. 1976.

979. Vocational Education Journal. American Vocational Assn., 1410 King, Alexandria, VA 22314. 10/year. $20.00. ISSN: 0884-8009. 1926. Former titles: *VocED; American Vocational Journal.*

VocED *See* **Vocational Education Journal VOCATIONAL EDUCATION (No. 979)**

Author/Editor Index

Title Index

Subject Index

NANCY P. O'BRIEN is the Education Subject Specialist at the University of Illinois at Urbana-Champaign. She currently serves on the National Advisory Board for ACCESS ERIC, a project of the U.S. Office of Educational Research and Improvement. Professor O'Brien compiled *Test Construction: A Bibliography of Selected Resources* (New York: Greenwood, 1988).

EMILY FABIANO is an Information Services Librarian specializing in education at Rutgers University. She has many years of experience as an educator and public services librarian. Her most recent publication is *Index to Tests in Educational Dissertations* (Phoenix: Oryx, 1989).

Both authors have worked together on other educational or measurement-related publications such as *Guide to the Development and Management of Test Collections* (Chicago: American Library Association, Association for College and Research Libraries, Ad hoc Committee on Test Collections, 1985) and *Testing Information Sources for Educators* (Princeton: ERIC Clearinghouse on Tests, Measurement and Evaluation, Educational Testing Service, 1987).